FLEETWOOD MAC
The First 30 Years
BOB BRUNNING

OMNIBUS PRESS
LONDON · NEW YORK · SYDNEY

First published in the UK by New English Library,
a hardcover imprint of Hodder & Stoughton.

Cover designed by Chloe Alexander
Picture research by Nikki Russell

ISBN: 0.7119.6907.8
Order No: OP 48069

Exclusive Distributors
Book Sales Limited,
8/9 Frith Street,
London W1V 5TZ, UK.

Music Sales Corporation,
257 Park Avenue South,
New York, NY 10010, USA.

Music Sales Pty Limited,
120 Rothschild Avenue, Rosebery,
NSW 2018, Australia.

To the Music Trade only:
Music Sales Limited,
8/9 Frith Street,
London W1V 5TZ, UK.

Every effort has been made to trace the copyright
holders of the photographs in this book but one or
two were unreachable. We would be grateful if the
photographers concerned would contact us.

Printed and bound in Great Britain by
MPG Books Ltd, Bodmin, Cornwall.

A catalogue record for this book is available from
the British Library.

Visit Omnibus Press at
http://www.musicsales.co.uk

For Peter Green

Contents

Acknowledgements

I could not have written this book without the help of a large number of people. My special thanks to Clifford Adams (a.k.a. Davis), Sheila Creegan, Trevor Dann, Peter Dogett, Deborah Gardiner, Klaus Greisbeck, Anne Morgan, Dave Peabody, Edward Schwab, David Simmons, Phil Sutcliffe, David Tedstone, Mike Vernon, Dave Walker, Rebecca Wall, Warner Brothers' UK Staff, Bob Welch, Bob Weston, Snowy White, Dave Wilkinson and Su Assinen.

Thanks also to my family.

Bob Brunning

Prologue

Sunday, August 13th, 1967, 11 a.m. The pale blue Ford Transit van quietly crunched to a halt in front of East Putney railway station in south-west London. The usual rendezvous. Two people were already aboard. The three waiting figures quickly got inside the van, and sat themselves carefully on the various amplifiers and boxes in the back. The driver gently shifted the gears of the new van, and swung out on to the Upper Richmond Road.

There was an uncharacteristic silence on board. Usually the van was full of laughter and ribald jokes as the band members travelled to rehearsals together. But today was different. The four musicians looked pale and nervous. Jokes fell flat and conversation died. The guitarist drove steadily towards the band's destination: Balloon Meadow, part of the Royal Windsor Racecourse on the Maidenhead Road. The journey did not take long. London's roads were quiet at this time on a Sunday morning. But it seemed like a lifetime.

The driver swung the van off the A308 into a special area reserved for artistes, showing the pass sent to him the previous week. Security was tight. With musicians like Eric Clapton, Ginger Baker, Jack Bruce, Donovan, Jeff Beck, John Mayall around, it had to be. This was, after all, the third and final day of the United Kingdom's biggest and most prestigious annual open air rock festival. The Windsor Jazz and Blues Festival, no less.

No wonder the band was so anxious. Their appearance at the festival would be unlike that of any other performer on the long and impressive bill. Nothing to do with the style of music they would play. Or the way they looked. Slightly scruffy, long haired, be-jeaned. The way blues musicians were supposed to look. No.

Quite simply, it would be the very first time the band had performed together in public. Anywhere.

Out of the van clambered Peter Green, Mick Fleetwood, Jeremy Spencer and Bob Brunning.

Fleetwood Mac had arrived.

1 Beginnings

London, England, April 1967. John Mayall, talented organist and vocalist leader of the long-established UK blues band, the Bluesbreakers, was faced with a familiar problem. The departure of one of his musicians. No stranger to this situation, Mayall had successfully weathered the storm following the departure of his renowned guitarist Eric Clapton to form Cream the previous year. This time the problem lay in the drum seat. Aynsley Dunbar had left the Bluesbreakers a few days previously to join the new Jeff Beck/Rod Stewart band. His replacement, UK r'n'b scene stalwart Mickey Waller, was to last only a few days as the new drummer.

John wasn't too worried. After all, against all odds Eric Clapton's replacement was proving to be a worthy successor, highly talented and increasingly popular in the clubs. John's long-serving bass player was also still providing a solid and reliable service on his battered Fender. Additionally Mayall's new guitarist knew a promising drummer who was temporarily working as an interior decorator, with whom he'd previously worked in an excellent band. Peter Bardens' Looners, soon to become known as 'Peter Bees', were a reliable and talented band, well known around the London circuit. The drummer was briefly auditioned, and immediately hired.

John Mayall wasn't to know it, but the presence of these three musicians in his band was to prove highly significant. For the first time Peter Green, John McVie and Mick Fleetwood were to play together, and to form an alliance which would lead to the formation of a new band: Fleetwood Mac.

There is no doubt that of the three Peter Green was to be the creative, driving force of the yet unformed band. His talent was prodigious. Anyone who has seen him play is unlikely ever to forget it.

Peter Greenbaum was born in October 1946. He had started his career in a little known band called Bobby Denim and the Dominoes, which performed a mixture of chart favourites and rock 'n' roll standards. His real love, however, was blues music, as performed by the legendary American, largely black, artistes like Muddy Waters, Howling Wolf, Freddie King, John Lee Hooker and his acknowledged mentor, B. B. King.

His next musical move was to the Muskrats, a much more r'n'b orientated band, with Dave Bidwell on drums, who was later to join Chicken Shack, Fleetwood Mac's Blue Horizon record label stablemates in 1967.

Then followed a move to the Tridents, a band in which Peter played bass, followed by a significant period in Peter Bardens' Looners, where he met Mick Fleetwood. Peter Green's spell with Peter Bardens also saw his recording debut with a single: 'If you wanna stay Happy' b/w 'Jodrell Blues'. Excellent though the Peter Bees were, they weren't doing too well financially. It was decided to expand the band into a kind of rhythm and blues/soul revue, and thus was born Shotgun Express. The basic line up of the Bees was extended by the addition of one Rod Stewart, fresh from Steampacket, featuring Long John Baldry and Beryl Marsden. Shotgun Express was not to prove successful, though Mick Fleetwood manfully soldiered on with them round the United Kingdom's so-called Northern Soul circuit. He recorded a couple of singles with them along the way, his first glimpse of the inside of a recording studio.

Peter in the meantime had made a *very* important and prestigious move. In August 1965 Eric Clapton, John Mayall's guitarist, had suddenly taken off on a crazy trip to Greece with musicians Jake Milton, Ben Palmer, Bernie Greenwood, John Bailey and Bob Ray. Hughie Flint, the Bluesbreakers' drummer, remembers the incident well.

'Eric talked to me about it. The plan was to leave John's highly organised set up, buy an old bus and then travel the world via India, Australia and America. I was ostensibly going to be the drummer for this mad escapade. Eventually the grandiose aims were whittled down to a more modest suggested destination: Greece. When it came to the crunch, I had a wife and child, and it just seemed a reckless thing to do. I couldn't afford it.'

Eric's abrupt departure from the Bluesbreakers caused more than a few headaches for John Mayall. Replacing Eric Clapton, a revered guitarist on the UK scene, rapidly becoming described as 'God' by his ever-increasing number of fans, was hardly the easiest thing to do. John used quite a few players during the two months that Eric was away. Guitarist Mick Taylor, later to join John Mayall permanently – and hence to join the Rolling Stones – was one. And so was the youthful Peter Green.

In spite of John Mayall's anger, Eric Clapton nevertheless walked straight back into the Bluesbreakers' guitar seat on his return, due to his immense popularity. However John did not forget Peter Green's contribution and talent. In July 1966 Eric Clapton finally quit the Bluesbreakers for good to form Cream. John immediately contacted Peter. Mike Vernon, a Decca Records producer at the time, clearly recalls Peter's debut.

'The day of the recording session for our second album with John Mayall and Eric Clapton came along. Gus Dudgeon, my engineer, and I were really excited about it. We were there really early in the morning, 9.30 or so, and everything was set up. John Mayall arrived and the equipment started coming through the door. In came this guitar amplifier that we *certainly* didn't recognise, followed by this musician dressed in jeans and lumber jacket who we *certainly* didn't recognise either! Gus looked at me, and I looked at Gus, as if to say, "That's *not* Eric Clapton!" I walked gingerly up to John and said, "Where's Eric?" and he said, "Oh, he's not with us any more, he left us a few weeks ago." '

Mike remonstrated with John Mayall for not keeping him better informed about the situation, but then John really set him back on his heels.

Mike: 'Well, I was in a shocked state, but John said, "Don't worry, we've got someone better!" I said, "Wait a minute, hang on a second, this is ridiculous. You've got someone *better*? than *Eric Clapton*? I find that hard to believe!" Then John said, "He might not be better *now*, but you wait, in a couple of years he's going to be the *best*." Then he introduced me to Peter Green.'

John Mayall was wrong in only one respect. It took no time at all for Peter to prove himself to be an accomplished, fluid, soulful and exciting player within the Bluesbreakers. 'A Hard Road', the album Peter recorded with the Bluesbreakers, shows his consummate skills; and one track in particular, 'The Supernatural', was an eerie precursor of work to come later with Fleetwood Mac. The Bluesbreakers personnel at this time comprised Mayall, Green, Anysley Dunbar and John McVie. John had already been in the band for over three years, surviving two 'sackings' due to his drinking habits. In addition to the 'Hard Road' album, the band recorded a single, 'Sitting in the Rain' b/w 'Out of Reach', and an extended-play single with American harp player Paul Butterfield.

Eight weeks after 'Hard Road' was released Aynsley left, and for a short while, following Mick Fleetwood's debut, three-quarters of the embryonic Fleetwood Mac existed within the Bluesbreakers. The line up was not to last. Within a month Mick Fleetwood was sacked for the same reason as John McVie before him, although John's forced departures were never to last long. However the quartet recorded two excellent singles produced by Mike Vernon for Decca UK during this short period: 'Double Trouble' b/w 'It hurts me too' and 'Curly' b/w 'Rubber Duck'. The Bluesbreakers also recorded another track during the same period; using some studio time given to Peter by John Mayall as a birthday present, the band recorded a prophetically titled instrumental, 'Fleetwood Mac'.

Peter Green also recorded another album for Mike Vernon with American bluesman Eddie Boyd. Eddie regarded Green's work very highly, saying, 'He's the *only* one playing the real thing.' Peter's stint with John Mayall and Decca was rapidly coming to an end. Mick Fleetwood had already left the band, and a dispute with John Mayall led to Peter's departure in May 1967.

Peter had no plans at that stage to form a new band. He was very keen to visit the United States with John McVie, and told English journalist Chris Welch, 'When I left John Mayall, I didn't *want* to form a group. I wanted to go to Chicago, but it was difficult to be sure of being safe; so I ended up dropping the idea. I was happy doing nothing, but Mike Vernon said, "Why not?" He talked me into it.'

Peter then started to consider the possible line up of a new band. He immediately thought of the tall, lanky drummer with whom he'd enjoyed working with Peter Bees and John Mayall. Mick Fleetwood.

Mick Fleetwood's background was very different from Peter Green's. Peter had been a trainee butcher before joining Bobby Denim's band, and came from a working-class East End Cockney background. Mick had been brought up in the Home Counties by his mother and Royal Air Force Wing Commander father. He attended a fashionable public school; and was an interior decorator in Liberty's, the up-market London store, before meeting Peter Bardens through his accomplished actress sister Susan.

Mick Fleetwood had briefly worked in another band, the Bo Street Runners, whose main claim to fame was winning a competition for bands, organised by the producers of the then hugely popular live TV programme *Ready Steady Go*. Gary Thomas, band member and currently a London head teacher, remembers Mick's debut well.

'We were playing at a club in Nottingham which was unlicensed, so we nipped out to the local pub during the interval. We were walking back doing some head rehearsals, singing "Mojo" or something like that, when we were suddenly set upon by a bunch of local gorillas, much to Mick's consternation because he wasn't enthusiastic about that sort of brutality at all. We kept shouting, "We're the band, we're the band," and these guys suddenly realised that we *weren't* members of the local gang of mods from whom they were seeking violent retribution after a recent feud. So they picked us up and dusted us down, and escorted us back to the club, full of apologies. The club owner was really upset by it, and said, "Here's your money, lads – you needn't play the second set," so that was a slight compensation for us. But Mick Fleetwood was really horrified because he thought that was the usual pattern for a Bo Street Runner gig. You got beaten up in the interval!'

Mick made his recording debut with the Bo Street Runners on a single featuring a song written by Tommy Moeller, the talented writer of Unit Four Plus Two's 'Concrete and Clay'.

Gary Thomas: 'It was an *atrocious* record. We'd gone back to a very r'n'b orientated style with Mick Fleetwood, so we ruined what was actually a very melodic and interestingly constructed song.'

Mick had continued his friendship with Peter Bardens, with whom he'd played in the Cheynes before he joined the Bo Street Runners. In September 1965 Peter asked Mick to join his new band, the Looners, with Dave Ambrose on bass and Mick Parker on guitar. Mick didn't hesitate. Mick Parker was soon replaced by Peter Green, and the friendship between Mick Fleetwood and Peter Green was born. Peter admired Mick's solid, unpretentious, reliable drumming style, which drove the band like a machine. The respect was mutual.

Mick: 'He was wonderful! I roomed with Peter on the road for most of the time. He had a great sense of humour, and he knew exactly what he wanted to do and how he was going to do it.'

Peter Green's choice of bass player was obvious. John McVie had been working as a professional musician since the early sixties, having abandoned a brief career as a trainee tax officer. He had played in a Shadows type band (Cliff Richard's legendary group) until John Mayall abandoned his Manchester group the Syndicate, taking Alexis Korner's advice to travel to London in order to consolidate his career. John thus formed the Bluesbreakers with Ricky Brown on bass and Davey Graham on guitar. By April 1963 Ricky was out and John McVie was starting his lengthy sojourn as the Bluesbreakers' bass player, eventually to become the longest serving Mayall sideman. John McVie worked with a large number of excellent musicians within the Bluesbreakers including Bernie Watson, Roger Dean, Eric Clapton, Peter Green, Mick Taylor, Dick Heckstall–Smith, Hughie Flint and many more. He was a driving, solid, if occasionally unadventurous player. His road experience aptly qualified him for the job.

The nominee for the fourth piece of the musical jigsaw puzzle that was to become Fleetwood Mac came not from Peter, however, but from Mike Vernon.

Mike was not only a house producer for the Decca UK record label, but also an enthusiastic and knowledgeable blues fan. He and his friend Neil Slavin had been running a modestly successful blues magazine *R'n'B Monthly*. Mike decided to extend his involvement with blues music by starting not one but *three* tiny, independent record labels: Purdah, Outasite and Blue Horizon. Operating from his front room with the help of his brother Richard, the energetic pair released singles by Eric Clapton, John Mayall, Champion Jack Dupree, the early Savoy Brown Blues Band, Lowell Fulson and several more artistes.

Mike: 'I also put out an awful thing by Jimmy McCracklin called "Christmas Time Parts One and Two". We released about twelve or fourteen singles before we finally concluded a deal. The giant CBS record company would release and distribute material on our Blue Horizon label.'

However his role as Decca's talent scout and producer had taken Mike to Birmingham to hear a local blues group.

'I heard from this little band in Lichfield near Birmingham called the Levi Set Blues Band, who were not all that good. The drummer couldn't play in time, the bass player couldn't play with the drummer. But they had this little guitarist who sounded *uncannily* like Elmore James. I brought them down to London to do an audition, which, apart from the guitarist's performance, turned out to be terrible. If I could have erased everybody apart from him it would have been fantastic, because he was great, but the tapes were so bad I didn't even bother to play them to the Artiste and Repertoire people at Decca. Apparently the guitar player had once talked to Peter Green at a John Mayall gig, but Peter hadn't heard him play.'

By this time Green was closely involved with discussions with Mike about the new band. He had already agreed to record the new line up with Mike's Blue Horizon label. The name for the new band had evolved from the instrumental 'Fleetwood Mac' that Mick, John and Peter had recorded during their Bluesbreakers stint. With typical modesty, Peter wanted the band's name to feature the names of the rhythm section rather than his own. In fact the band became known as 'Peter Green's Fleetwood Mac' for the first few months of its life.

Mike: 'I told Peter about these audition tapes, warned him about the incompetence of the band and played them to him. He literally went white, said "My God", jumped in the band's newly purchased van, and drove straight to Lichfield. I think he must have grabbed the guitar player by the scruff of his neck and said, "Right, you're in my band!" Two days later the guy was in Fleetwood Mac.'

The name of the diminutive guitarist was Jeremy Spencer. Jeremy was born in West Hartlepool on July 4th, 1948. His early musical influences were not gleaned from bluesmen but rock 'n' roll artistes.

Jeremy: 'My earliest influences came from Buddy Holly, Elvis, the Everly Brothers, Fabian and Cliff Richard! Primarily I'm a rocker rather than a bluesman. But I heard a record in 1964, a blues LP with a track on it called "The Sun is Shining". That was the first time I heard Elmore James. I was never a blues fan, but that particular sound and the vocal as well started it all. Before then I was just playing rock 'n' roll.'

Jeremy started training as a bank clerk after leaving school, and learned piano in his teens, turning to guitar later. In 1964 he formed his own band, the Levi Set, with two local brothers, John and Ian Charles, and then wrote to Mike Vernon. Mike was interested, and arranged the abortive recording audition with Decca. It is rumoured that the poor quality audition tapes *did* finally surface on an Immediate Blues compilation album, with overdubs by Bob Hall playing piano and John Dummer on drums. The songs concerned are 'Look Down at My Woman' and 'Who's Knocking?'.

Having discovered the work of Elmore James, Jeremy decided to change his guitar style accordingly. Then followed a frustrating period of trial and error while he attempted to master Elmore's bottleneck style of playing.

'I read somewhere you could use a piece of metal, so I fixed a piece of metal to my finger, but that didn't work. Then I used a glass, but I couldn't use my fingers!'

Jeremy soon discovered that the guitar needed to be tuned to a chord, Hawaiian style. He eventually found that a piece of brass or copper tubing on the little finger of the left hand allowed use of the other fingers, as well as producing the authentic slide guitar sound he yearned for.

'I also found that the action (the distance from the strings to the fretboard) had to be high, and that thick, heavy gauge strings were best.'

Jeremy may have had to teach himself painfully to play guitar like his mentor James, but his astonishingly authentic singing style came naturally. However he never abandoned his rock 'n' roll roots. His Cliff Richard, Elvis Presley and Fabian parodies were to become firm crowd favourites at Fleetwood Mac concerts.

At last the new band was complete, and Peter Green began eagerly to arrange rehearsals to prepare for the dates already booked by the Gunnel Brothers Agency. But he immediately hit upon a truly daunting setback. John McVie would *not* leave Mayall's Blues-breakers until he was absolutely sure that the new band was going to be commercially viable. John Mayall provided regular work and a good steady income. Why risk losing all that for the sake of a risky new venture?

John: 'No, I wasn't the band's original bass player, because I wouldn't leave John Mayall. Peter had asked me, when he left John Mayall, to join the band but I didn't want to leave John, for I guess security reasons. The Bluesbreakers was a very popular band, "steady wage", as it were. So I held off for a couple of months.'

Peter Green and Mick Fleetwood put their heads together. They decided to advertise for a bass player in the then best-known British music weekly the *Melody Maker*. The appointment would hopefully be temporary as Peter *definitely* intended the 'Mac' in Fleetwood Mac to be John McVie. The advertisement appeared in July 1967.

In the same month I had just finished my college career at St Mark and St John's College of Education in Kings Road, Chelsea, London. I had been the bass player in our college band, Five's Company, which had been moderately successful within the London college circuit, recording three singles for Pye Records. The band folded as its component members left college to go their separate ways, though all its members have continued to play: Ian Pearson, drummer, with a variety of bands; Colin Jordan, guitarist, with various line ups (he was later to contribute to Brunning Sunflower Blues Band albums); Eddie Broadbridge, vocalist, to Denmark to his own band plus a

career as teacher, writer and broadcaster; and Steve Jones, keyboards
and vocalist, with Lonnie Donegan. Steve subsequently found fame
and fortune as a radio and television presenter of games and variety
shows (in 1990 he was voted Variety Club's Independent Radio
Broadcaster of the Year).

I was determined to prove to myself that I *could* become a fully
professional musician. I'd always liked r'n'b, and rock 'n' roll music,
so I started to scan the *Melody Maker* small ads for something
suitable. I soon spotted Peter's advertisement. It simply read 'Bass
player wanted for Chicago-type blues band' followed by a phone
number, which I called. It proved to be a wrong number owing to a
misprint, but a hunch told me to pursue it and I called the paper to
get the correct one. I got through and arranged to audition.

I turned up at a council flat in Putney. I was greeted by a guy
who introduced himself as Peter Green. Although I hadn't seen the
Bluesbreakers, I'd heard about Peter Green the brilliant successor to
Eric Clapton in the John Mayall band, so I said to him, 'You've
certainly got the right name for a blues guitarist – do you know
about your namesake, who plays with John Mayall?'

'You bloody idiot,' he said, 'I *am* Peter Green!'

Mightily abashed I nevertheless managed to fumble through the
audition, at the end of which Peter announced that I was in the band.
I then asked him when and where the first band gig was going to be,
expecting to hear the name of a small blues club.

'Windsor Jazz and Blues Festival, in a month's time,' Peter replied.

This was terrifying news. The festival was one of the biggest in
the country, which regularly attracted about a hundred thousand
people. What a debut!

We started rehearsing in the Black Bull, a pub in Fulham Road
opposite my old college; and in Peter's girlfriend Sandra Elsdon's
beautiful house near Windsor. The rehearsals went well. We started
putting an act together for our important debut performance at the
festival, for the staggering fee of £40. The festival was later to move
to a more permanent home and become known as the Reading (Rock)
Festival.

We also started recording copiously. Three tracks on which I
played were eventually released: 'Long Grey Mare', 'Ramblin' Pony'
and 'I Believe My Time Ain't Long'. We certainly recorded a great
deal of material. Most of it quite illegally in the middle of the night
at Decca's West Hampstead studio.

Mike Vernon: 'Yes, extremely late at night, in the big studio at
Decca, again we shouldn't have been there, when nobody at Decca

knew that we were doing it! And it was with those tapes that we managed to clinch the Blue Horizon distribution deal with CBS.'

Clifford Davis, soon to become the band's manager, claims that he owns both the original Decca tapes and rights to release them, having paid the Vernon brothers £5,000 for them in 1968. Mike Vernon has no recollection of the deal. It would certainly be interesting to hear them.

The next logical step for Fleetwood Mac was to record the first official Blue Horizon album at the CBS studios, but before that could happen we had the terrifying hurdle of playing the festival. The list of performers for the weekend was impressive. There we were, tucked away at the bottom of the bill – along with Pentangle and Denny Laine – on Sunday, August 13th, 1967.

We stepped out in front of a huge audience, there to see Cream, Jeff Beck, John Mayall and the like. Stepping up to the microphone to announce the band and the first number, I got as far as saying, 'We'd like to play . . .' and completely forgot the title of the song. We survived the ordeal and were extremely well received; and much enjoyed our later set in a kind of 'fringe festival' tent on the site, where we could play for an hour and really let our hair down.

Jeremy was already playing an important musical role within the band, milking his astonishingly authentic-sounding Elmore James riffs and vocals to the full.

But Peter's sparse, emotive, liquid guitar-playing was moving to hear, and his voice too was already rich and full of feeling and power. He was being tremendously helpful to me at this time, lending me piles of blues albums so that I could absorb different blues styles, and teaching me riffs and runs: he was a first-class bass player himself. But I learned something else about Peter's personality – which I was to realise was a sad precursor of more bizarre behaviour to come. It didn't do to admire anything he owned, or he was likely to give it to you. I once commented favourably on a new record deck he'd bought himself, and he absolutely insisted on my taking it! I never made the same mistake again, but I fear other people took advantage of this kind of obsessionally generous behaviour.

We also started hitting the road, providing me with my first experience of intensive touring. I still have a gig list for October and November 1967, scribbled on the back of one of my college theses. It reads:

October
4 London
7 Sheffield University
13 Bradford College
14 Chelsea College
16 Cook's Ferry Inn
19 Southampton University
23 100 Club, Oxford Street
27 White Hart, Acton
28 Wolverhampton
29 Manchester

November
2 North Wales

3 Leicester
4 Birmingham
10 Rugby
11 Enfield Technical College
12 Guildford
19 Grimsby
24 Marquee Club, London
25 Brighton
26 Nottingham Boat Club
28 Hanley

December
8 Basildon
10 Turnstall

However the next gig after the Windsor Jazz and Blues Festival was at London's well known Marquee Club on September 15th. In 1987, to my astonishment, I received a good quality tape from a German collector containing a recording of the entire one and a half hour performance, taped illegally from the front row of the club – surely Fleetwood Mac's first bootleg. Rumour has it, however, that both the Windsor Jazz and Blues Festival performances were taped, and are circulating somewhere.

We set off to fulfil the dates booked by the Gunnel Brothers, our agents.

We hardly travelled in luxury: the whole band plus sound equipment in a small Ford Transit van (Mick Fleetwood always insisted that I travelled in the 'death seat', as he darkly called the front passenger seat), and we often shared one dormitory-style room in cheap bed and breakfast guest houses. I used to like staying at 'George's' in Newcastle. We would invariably be joined at breakfast by amusing and often extremely shapely strippers and dancers working the northern Working Men's Club circuit. Their jokes and stories certainly helped to wake us up, along with mounds of toast and gallons of tea!

By December John McVie had finally made up his mind to join the band, and I retired, having thoroughly enjoyed my spell with Fleetwood Mac.

I immediately joined the Savoy Brown Blues Band. But I left to begin my enjoyable career as a teacher, spanning twenty-two years to date. However I have never stopped playing blues and r'n'b music. With my current band, the De Luxe Blues Band, I recently recorded my thirtieth album.

Meanwhile Green, Fleetwood, Spencer and McVie got down to the next job in hand, recording their first album for Blue Horizon and CBS. I stayed very friendly with the guys in the band, and went along to the session. It stretched from an early evening start until late at night, when John McVie fell asleep after a couple of glasses of wine. And so I played bass for a couple more tracks, unreleased for very good reasons, I'm sure.

Outside the recording studio, out there in the clubs, the word was going round: a hot new blues band was on the scene.

Mike Vernon endorses the huge interest in the band which was reflected by the attendance at their gigs: 'The band became the biggest draw around; the queues went round the block. People were fighting to get in.'

Fleetwood Mac were on their way.

2 The Band Expands

On the face of it, the success of the early Fleetwood Mac was quite extraordinary. Not a single member of the band was known outside a rather restricted club and pub circuit, and the band's debut album was an unadulterated and undiluted tribute to their blues influences.

John: 'Oh yes, we were a blues band, and fairly rigid about it too. Like there was *very* little outside blues. If it wasn't blues, then we didn't want to know about it.'

Mick: 'Blues was very important to John and Peter, and then I really became versed into listening to that stuff through them. It was just what we were doing, and was certainly what was natural to Peter, who basically identified with that stuff.'

There is no doubt, however, that the album 'Peter Green's Fleetwood Mac', recorded in two days on a tiny budget, nevertheless amply demonstrated the talents of all the members of the Mac. It was full of strong songs, and was released at a time when blues music was enjoying a resurgence of popularity, following the heady early 1960s which had seen the emergence of many fine r'n'b bands. The Rolling Stones, Blues Incorporated, featuring Alexis Korner and Cyril Davies, the mighty Graham Bond Organisation, the early Clapton-dominated Bluesbreakers, the Pretty Things and Animals were all making huge waves in the UK club and festival scene at the time.

Peter Green in particular was consolidating his burgeoning reputation as one of the United Kingdom's finest guitar players. John McVie, asked about what was so special about Peter's playing said, 'His amazing feel. There was no one like him, it just stood out, his incredible soul.'

Snowy White, guitarist with Pink Floyd and Thin Lizzy, who was also to work with Peter in his post-Fleetwood Mac career: 'When I first heard Peter play, what it did for me, what it did for a lot of people was incredible.'

Cliff Adams, soon to be a major influence on Fleetwood Mac's career, also remembers the early Peter: 'I arranged to go and see the band. They were playing a charity gig in Guildford. I was absolutely stunned. I'd been around a lot of big bands in my time, but I just could not *believe* the talent of Peter Green.'

The album and the live concerts also revealed the talent of the other members of the band. The empathy between John McVie and Mick Fleetwood was already obvious. Many years later they were asked to comment on the reasons for their success as a rhythm section.

John: 'Mick just keeps it simple. That's basically it. Simple and just solid. He's very easy to play with.'   .

Mick: 'Oh, the same reason. It's hard to define. I mean, after twenty-two years with John, it's just one of those chemistries. We've talked about it, because a lot of people have been kind enough to say we're a decent rhythm section. I tend to play behind the beat, John plays slightly in front, and we meet somewhere in the middle. And we've discovered that's what it is!'

Jeremy Spencer, fresh to the recording studio, unlike the other members of the band, was making the most of the opportunity to recreate his beloved Elmore James slide guitar riffs. Grunting, growling and moaning his way through classics like 'My Heart Beat Like a Hammer' and 'Shake Your Moneymaker', his work was already beginning to hint at his black humour and self-deprecating style.

Around the same period Fleetwood Mac went into the studio with producer Mike Vernon to cut an album with American bluesman Eddie Boyd. Released on Blue Horizon titled '7936 Rhodes', the album featured Messrs Fleetwood, Green and John McVie supplying a sympathetic and tasteful supporting band to the talented pianist. Fleetwood Mac virtually became the 'house band' for Blue Horizon at this time, additionally recording with Peter Green/Mike Vernon discoveries like Duster Bennett and Gordon Smith.

November 1967 saw the release of Fleetwood Mac's first single in the UK, 'I Believe My Time Ain't Long', b/w 'Rambling Pony'. The two tracks were an odd choice for this important release. The 'A' side featured Jeremy Spencer playing and singing an old Elmore James song, rather than Peter Green singing his own original material. Peter Green *was* featured on the 'B' side (oddly enough with your author on bass rather than John McVie). The record was not a hit, but the album, released in February 1968, certainly was. Much to the astonishment of all concerned, it shot into the UK record charts, propelled by a great deal of interest from the music press. 'Peter Green's Fleetwood Mac' on Blue Horizon went into the top five, stayed in the top ten for fifteen weeks, and remained for a scarcely credible *year* in the top twenty. The feat was all the more astonishing considering that, in that period of popular music history, *nobody* managed to release hit albums before they achieved hit singles.

The band were consolidating their success with a great deal of work round the clubs. The Gunnel Brothers arranged touring schedules taking Fleetwood Mac all over the United Kingdom. On January 16th and 17th the boys made their BBC Radio One debut on *Top Gear* for the grand sum of £30, the first of many radio shows they would record.

However the next important job for Fleetwood Mac was to organise the recording and release of the second Blue Horizon single.

Wisely Mike Vernon and Peter chose an original Green composition for the 'A' side which would amply illustrate Peter's rapidly developing songwriting talents: the classic 'Black Magic Woman'. A modest hit for the Mac in England, the song much later went on to be a huge success for Santana in the United States. The 'B' side featured the young Jeremy singing an Elmore James classic, 'The Sun is Shining'. (In the USA the 'B' side of 'Black Magic Woman' was 'Long Grey Mare'. Once again it curiously featured your author on bass, rather than John McVie.)

During the spring Fleetwood Mac enjoyed a European trip to Copenhagen, Norway and Sweden, appearing on television for the first time. The band also returned to the studios to record material for the second album. Mike Vernon made an odd decision regarding the recording techniques to be used in the studio. At the insistence of the band, still anxious to maintain their credibility as out and out bluesmen, he set up the studios as crudely as possible.

Mike: 'It must have been one of the strangest, weirdest recording sessions of the 60s. To give the album an authentic, Chess-Studios-in-the-40s feel, Mike Ross, the recording engineer, and I spent a lot of time manoeuvring amplifiers and speakers around the studio to get a murky, muddy sound.'

They even went as far as to put all the vocals through an old Vox amplifier, and overdrove all the guitar amplifiers. Mike and the band certainly achieved what they wanted: the recording sound was crude, mostly in mono, and *distinctly* distorted at times. However, apart from the saxophone section, which played noticeably out of tune, the talents of Messrs Green, Spencer, McVie and Fleetwood shone through the murk. The album, after much discussion, was titled 'Mr Wonderful'. It featured the disconcerting sight of a flower beridden, semi-nude Mick Fleetwood on the sleeve. I suggested the title myself to Peter while we were fooling around in a restaurant one evening.

We were mimicking and satirising television talk-show hosts' tendencies to eulogise their guests by announcing them as 'the truly wonderful' etc. He liked the title and it stuck. The title was to have been 'A Good Length', but CBS firmly vetoed that one!

The album, released in August 1969, featured a guest artiste – who could hardly have imagined what a significant portent for the future her invitation to record with the band was to be – Christine Perfect. Christine was John McVie's girlfriend, but it was not nepotism which brought her into the band for the recording. Christine was a highly talented piano player and singer in her own right with Fleetwood Mac's friendly Blue Horizon rivals, Chicken Shack.

Another important change had occurred within the band's organisational structure. In August 1967 Peter Green had gone to visit the Gunnel Brothers Agency, which was handling all the group's work. He wasn't very happy about the way the agency was doing its job, and decided to express his dissatisfaction to the 'new boy' in the office. Cliff Adams had been working for Brian Epstein, the Beatles' manager, before being brought in to run the Gunnel agency. He listened sympathetically.

Clifford: 'Peter Green came into the office and said, "You're the new boy here aren't you? Well, I've just formed this band called Fleetwood Mac and your mate's naff." I said, "What do you mean, 'naff'?" He said, "You know, a lazy bastard. He's not getting us enough work!" '

Like Peter, Clifford was a tough, East End Cockney boy. He liked and respected Peter Green straight away. He immediately obtained more work for the band, which he thought was 'stunning'.

A little later Peter visited Clifford with another complaint.

Peter: 'I went to see Clifford and said to him, "I've got a record deal with my friend Mike Vernon. We've got a record out called 'Black Magic Woman' which isn't doing much. Not only that, your governor Rick Gunnel is bending my ear, pressuring me to sign an exclusive management deal or he says he'll throw me out of the agency!" '

Clifford's response was swift. He assured Peter that it wouldn't happen, and supported the band through the pressure. He also instantly agreed to take on the management of Fleetwood Mac when Peter offered him the job a few days later.

Clifford: 'I went and confronted Gunnel, had a big row with his brother down at a club that night and knocked him out!'

Not a man to mess with, Clifford was a qualified martial arts instructor.

Work continued, and the pace quickened. Peter Green, good and kind friend that he was, nevertheless managed to find the time to come and play guitar on 'Trackside Blues', the second album to be released by my own band, the Brunning Sunflower Blues. He made an impressive contribution, unsurprisingly. It included a moving solo version of 'If You Let Me Love You'. The song was a firm favourite in the Mac's live set, but he never recorded it with them. An alternative take of his instrumental on 'Trackside Blues', 'Ah Soul', reappeared on my third Brunning Sunflower Blues album, gleefully retitled by Peter Green, 'Uranus'.

Fleetwood Mac's next hurdle to overcome was the band's first American tour. Oddly, with the exception of John McVie, the band wasn't very keen to go.

Peter: 'I'm not at all that keen on going. It's too violent there. You can't walk about on your own. It really frightens me. Life's not worth a light over there. Mick Fleetwood feels the same, although John McVie is really looking forward to it. Jeremy Spencer doesn't want to go for various reasons, either.'

Notwithstanding this lack of enthusiasm, off Fleetwood Mac went. Peter's gloomy prophecy was to prove accurate, though not quite for the reasons he had feared. From the end of June and for most of July the band toured. Their first album and single were released on Epic, but some felt that the record company did absolutely nothing to promote the records or the band. The American management was ineffective, the tour conditions atrocious, and the few gigs they did were mostly as an opening act for major British or American bands. All this for a band whose album had just been voted the *second* most popular in the UK, beating the Rolling Stones and Beatles! However Fleetwood Mac did visit New York, San Francisco and Chicago, eagerly seeking out the blues clubs, and seeing some of the artistes they had idolised from afar for so long.

Peter Green: 'I *really* enjoyed seeing Howlin' Wolf, Buddy Guy, Freddie King and White bluesman John Hammond. He came as a *big* surprise to me – I never liked him on record, but he was very good. We also heard Big Brother and the Holding Company, and the Grateful Dead. Also Janis Joplin with the Holding Company. She's incredible. I've never seen anything like that.'

They returned home to some good news. Fleetwood Mac's third single, released in July 1968, was showing signs of being a minor hit. Peter Green and Clifford had chosen 'I Need Your Love So Bad', a song written by Little Willy John which had been tastefully recorded by Peter's hero, B. B. King. The recording featured Christine Perfect (soon to become Mrs McVie) and strings arranged by Mickey Baker. Peter was very impressed that Mickey was prepared to come from Paris to work on the session. Green was featured on both sides this time. The 'B' side consisted of a driving track from the 'Mr Wonderful' album: 'Stop Messin' Around'.

The record was being played on the more popular radio shows, and actually became a top thirty hit. 'Mr Wonderful' was released in August and, like 'Peter Green's Fleetwood Mac' before it, made the album charts, eventually achieving a creditable number four position in the UK.

With two best-selling albums under their belt, plus a top thirty single, Fleetwood Mac were certainly gathering momentum. Peter Green was continuing to expand his own musical parameters by listening to a wide range of musicians. He attended the entire season of the Henry Wood Promenade Concerts at the Albert Hall that year in order to widen his knowledge of music generally. He also guested on one track of his old boss's new album, John Mayall's 'Laurel Canyon'. In addition to all this he enjoyed searching out and encouraging new talent with his friend Mike Vernon. Green was looking for a way to expand the band, and perhaps change its direction. He didn't want to lose his beloved blues but felt he wanted to open out Fleetwood Mac's approach to musical styles in general, so that more original material could be brought into the show.

His two goals were dramatically combined when he saw a young blues band in Southend called Boilerhouse. Like Jeremy's Levi Set, the guitarist's talent far outstripped those of his two musical colleagues, Trevor Stevens (bass) and David Terry (drums), neither of whom wanted to make a living as musicians anyway. Peter arranged auditions to replace the pair but couldn't find any suitable musicians, in spite of receiving over three hundred replies to his *Melody Maker* advertisement. He then had a brainwave. Here was the solution to his dilemma about the future musical direction of Fleetwood Mac.

Danny Kirwan was invited to join Fleetwood Mac, much to his astonishment and delight. A fresh-faced, rather insecure eighteen-year-old, born in Brixton on May 13th, 1950, he was already an accomplished guitarist who had been heavily influenced by Hank Marvin of the Shadows, and, more importantly, by Django Reinhart, the renowned French gypsy guitarist. He became particularly interested in blues music after seeing Eric Clapton with the Bluesbreakers.

Boilerhouse had supported Fleetwood Mac a few times, and both Cliff Adams and Mike had tried to further the band's career.

Clifford remembers Danny well: 'A very bright boy. I felt a little sorry for him. His mother had split from his father, and Danny was always trying to find him, and he had a lot of problems with self-confidence and security. He found it hard to handle being in Fleetwood Mac. He had very high musical standards. When we were on the road he would constantly come to my room, saying, "Come on, Clifford, we must rehearse, we must rehearse, *don't you understand*, we've got to rehearse." But he was the originator of all the ideas regarding harmonies and the lovely melodies that Fleetwood Mac would eventually encompass.'

Danny was the ideal musical foil for Peter's new direction. He spoke to Bob Dawbarn of the *Melody Maker* soon after joining Fleetwood Mac.

Danny: 'I'm not too keen on blues purists who close their ears to all other forms of music. To put down one sort of music just because it isn't something else is obviously wrong. The blues in England now is being interpreted wrongly. It's all getting very narrow. Personally I like any good music, particularly the old big-band type things. Django Reinhart is probably my favourite guitarist – but I like any music that is good. Whether it is blues, popular or classical.'

Danny was largely welcomed into the band, although Jeremy Spencer understandably wasn't too keen on the presence of a third front man. He played gentle, supportive rhythm guitar to Peter and Jeremy's fiery solo work and introduced vocal harmonies to some of the songs. He also played on stage his own, clearly Django-influenced 'Jigsaw Puzzle Blues', a slow blues along the style of 'Something Inside of Me', and his own fast and furious instrumental 'Like it This Way'. His 'Jigsaw Puzzle Blues' was to be the eventual 'B' side of the new single, the recording of which was the next task for the boys before they set off on the second tour of the United States, from December 1968 to mid-February 1969.

The choice of material for the 'A' side seemed quite extraordinarily out of context with the band's musical style. Peter, Danny, Mick and John recorded Peter Green's slow, atmospheric, gentle instrumental composition. It featured harmonic, echoey guitar parts over a laid-back, simple bass and drum part. The piece sounded far more like Santo-and-Johnny-meet-Hank-Marvin than the tough, energetic, bluesy Fleetwood Mac sound the fans were used to. However it was an inspired choice, and on November 25th, 1968 the single was released, the last one to appear on Mike and Richard's Blue Horizon label.

'Albatross' was born, and the bird was to help Fleetwood Mac fly to the very top of the hit parade. Nobody was in the least bit worried about the albatross's mythical association with death and disaster. What could possibly go wrong? Fleetwood Mac were soaring high!

3 Albatross: The Pious Bird of Good Omen?

Ironically, when 'Albatross' hit the top of the UK record charts in December 1968, giving Fleetwood Mac the number one hit they had only dreamed about, they weren't around to enjoy their success. Peter sent me a wry postcard from Detroit.

It said, 'Hallo folks, thanks for buying all those copies of "Albatross"! Christmas Eve here and snowing outside. My hotel room is very hot though. Everywhere except New York a huge success so far. (New York was our first gig and we had problems with it.) Wish I was there, honest! In Detroit right now, not the kind of place to spend Christmas at all. Happy New Year! I love you all. Peter Greenbaum.'

The second tour was certainly more successful than the first, and included a highly productive visit to the legendary Chess Recording Studios in Chicago. Marshall Chess, Mike Vernon, Willie Dixon and Neil Slavin organised a recording session for Fleetwood Mac which would see the band combining forces with some very well-known black blues musicians. In addition to Mac members Danny, Jeremy, Peter, John and Mick, the Chicago element included Walter 'Shaky' Horton, Buddy Guy, Honey Boy Edwards, J. T. Brown, Willie Dixon, Otis Spann and S. P. Leary. Such projects sometimes fall flat on their musical faces, but this one didn't, in spite of some early 'white boys can't play the blues' resistance from the Chicago contingent. Fleetwood Mac's combination of genuine enthusiasm and more than adequate musical ability aptly qualified them for the session and made it a great success. In particular the Elmore James numbers, featuring the youthful Jeremy Spencer sliding furiously away on guitar accompanied by J. T. Brown, Elmore James' one-time sax player, remain a fine monument to the notion of musical 'fathers and sons'. The whole session, released nearly a year later by Mike on a Blue Horizon double album entitled 'Blues Jam at Chess' is a great delight to listen to, including as it does false starts, alternate takes, engineer's instructions, chat from musicians and lots of laughter.

The Chess session was not to be the only recording the members of Fleetwood Mac were to undertake in the United States. Busy and energetic producer Mike arranged a further session in New York in January 1969 at which the Mac (minus Mick Fleetwood and Jeremy Spencer) recorded a very fine album with pianist/singer Otis Spann, and S. P. Leary on drums. Peter in particular made some stunning contributions on guitar, and John and Danny additionally provided some very creditable support. The album, titled 'The Biggest Thing Since Colossus' was released on Blue Horizon the same year, in September 1969.

Fresh from the triumphs of the US, Fleetwood Mac were welcomed back to Britain with the news of the enormous success of the single 'Albatross'. Sales had been boosted by its use as background music for a television documentary and the single went on to sell over a million copies. Unsurprisingly, some of the die-hard blues purist fans of the Mac didn't like it, but the band defended themselves vigorously.

Peter Green: ' "Sold out" – that's just a stock phrase! We're still playing the same stuff on stage. Whenever we play "Albatross" it just brings the place down every time. These are just narrow-minded people. I'm going to play what I like when I like. We've always been commercial; blues is commercial. Before we made "Albatross" we drew crowds and crowds. "Albatross" will never date. It's like one of those great old instrumentals like "Apache". It might even become a standard.'

Prophetic words indeed when one considers that 'Albatross' is still regularly heard on television and radio, twenty-one years later!

Jeremy Spencer was also irritated by the die-hards: 'There are some places where we play, where if we don't play blues, we get shouted down. But good audiences will listen to *anything* you do, if you do it well. There are too many labels in music! "Albatross" hasn't made any real difference to where we play, just in the number of people who come to hear us. Which has done us some good obviously.'

Mick Fleetwood had more positive feelings about the benefits 'Albatross' had brought to the band: 'We found that when we first came back from America with "Albatross" being a big hit and us not here playing, we tended to get hurt by some of the criticism. But it seems to have been only from a small minority. The fact was that we were out of the country and it was a record completely foreign to what we'd been playing on stage.'

Mick emphasised that the hit had not changed the kind of places the Mac were choosing to play.

'We're still playing places like the Fishmonger's Arms and the Toby Jug, Tolworth, which I'm happy about. More people are coming along because they've heard the record, and didn't know about us before.'

However the record was helping to expand the band's horizons.

'We're finding that we are getting more and more offers of work abroad. The records are like an advert for us. We've got more time and more security. I hope we can now say "Let's stop work for a month" without worrying about whether we'll lose everything we've gained up to now.'

However Fleetwood Mac certainly didn't stop work.

The band had already recorded the follow-up single to 'Albatross' during their trip to New York. Another Peter Green composition, 'Man of the World' was to prove highly significant as an indicator of Peter's state of mind at the time. The sensitive, introspective lyrics of the song were deeply sad. Peter was beginning to become disillusioned by fame and increasing fortune and 'Man of the World' represented a real cry from the heart. A beautiful song, nevertheless, it was the second smash hit for the band, climbing to number two on the nation's pop chart.

Peter spoke about the song before its release in March 1969: 'Our new single will be "Man of the World". It's in the same vein as "Albatross", but it's a song. It's a sad song, so it's a blues, but people will say it's not, because it hasn't got twelve bar format. It's got a really great melody, and I've got some good ideas to make it more complete. It's very sad, it was the way I felt at the time. It's me at my saddest.'

The single was virtually a solo Peter Green effort. The 'B' side consisted of a novelty number. Credited to Earl Vince and the Valiants, 'Someone's Gonna Get Their Head Kicked in Tonight' was an amusing pastiche of early rock 'n' roll. The band had been featuring Jeremy's rock 'n' roll medley in their stage show for some time, and here was a chance to record an example of that aspect of their act. Plans were made to release an extended-play four-track single featuring Earl Vince along with Fleetwood Mac's next album, but the idea was eventually shelved.

Another highly significant turn of events with regard to the release of 'Man of the World' was the record label on which it appeared:

Andrew Loog Oldham's Immediate label rather than Mike's Blue
Horizon. Why on earth should Mike and Richard Vernon have al-
lowed such potentially profitable recording artistes as Fleetwood
Mac to move to a new record company? Occasionally small independent record companies *do* 'sell' their artistes to major ones if the
price is right. The classic example had been when Sam Phillips of
the tiny Memphis-based Sun Records sold his new recording star
Elvis Presley to the giant RCA Recording Company of New York.
Did Andrew Loog Oldham and his partner Tony Calder make the
Vernon Brothers an offer they simply couldn't refuse? Sadly, no. The
loss of Fleetwood Mac from Blue Horizon was the result of a simple
but devastating mistake on the part of Richard Vernon. He simply
didn't watch the calendar, an error eagerly exploited by Fleetwood
Mac manager Clifford Davis. (Cliff Adams changed his name to
Davis to avoid confusion with the British group of vocalists, the
Clifford Adams Singers.)

Clifford: 'I think the biggest coup I ever pulled off for Fleetwood
Mac was getting them out of their Blue Horizon recording contract.
At the time people were saying there was a lot of financial bribery
going on, but the truth of it was a lot more simple. Mike Vernon
very successfully ran the artistic side, and his brother Richard ran
the business side. Now, no disrespect to Richard, but he made a
terrible mistake. The deal Peter Green had struck with Mike Vernon
prior to me coming on the scene as the band's manager was simple.
One year's recording contract, followed by two one-year options on
Blue Horizon's side, to be taken up only if they still wanted the
band. I just sat praying that Richard wouldn't notice the renewal
date for the contract coming up. And he didn't! I notified Blue
Horizon the following day that they had failed to take up the option,
and therefore Fleetwood Mac were free of any further contractual
obligations to Mike and Richard Vernon.'

The band was number one in the charts at the time.

Sharp practice, perhaps, but perfectly legal.

Mike Vernon: 'Yes we were young and green, still running the
company virtually double-handed. In big record companies you have
people whose *sole* job is to watch renewal dates, but we didn't have
anybody like that, and we simply missed the date.'

However Mike did not think the situation was irreversible. He
felt the spirit of the agreement ought to be honoured, particularly as
he had already negotiated a new signing advance for Fleetwood Mac
of £250,000 from CBS.

'We certainly had a gentleman's agreement with Clifford Davis for the Mac to sign with CBS, but he welched on it. The single was *always* supposed to be released on Blue Horizon.'

Clifford Davis's reasons for not going along with the CBS deal were complex. Peter Green had signed away his copyrights in a bad deal with Malcolm Forrester, part of the old John Mayall Blues-breakers team. Malcolm Forrester had subsequently thrown his hat in with Immediate Records. In order to extricate the valuable Fleetwood Mac songs and copyrights from Forrester, Clifford claims that he had to agree to allocate the band's single 'Man of the World' to Immediate. They promised to match the CBS offer.

Mike Vernon: 'The band didn't see a penny of the supposed quarter of a million pounds.'

Clifford agrees: 'No, the money was not forthcoming. We had no signed agreement with Immediate. I was negotiating a deal with Warner Brothers, and I *needed* that single out as a follow up to "Albatross", so in good faith I gave them the tapes. They just done us! But it served its purpose, it was a big hit. I made sure of that. I spent a *lot* of money getting it to the right people, making sure it was played on the right programmes. And you can read into that whatever you like!'

Clifford also sorted out the various band members' songwriting publishing contracts, clearing the ground to form a new Fleetwood Mac publishing company.

'I said to the boys, "If you give me £50 each we can form our own publishing company and you can own your own copyrights." But they weren't interested! Peter said to me, "I'm not interested about publishing or the business side of it all." I said, "Look, I'm your *manager*, I'm not a publisher." Peter took a hat that was lying on my desk and put it on my head and said, "Right, now you're a publisher." The others didn't want to put up the money, they were a bit tight in those days, to be honest. So that's how Clifford Davis became a publisher.'

Then all the band signed individual songwriting agreements; and Clifford set up contracts whereby the band 'owned' their own pro-ductions.

While all the legal wrangles were going on behind the scenes, another, more important issue dominated the members of Fleetwood Mac. The need for a new, third album. The band trooped back to the studio to work on what was to become their first album for Warner Brothers/Reprise. Clifford had secured them a healthy advance plus a good royalty rate. However cracks were beginning to show in the Fleetwood Mac set up. First 'Then Play On', as the album was to be titled, was the first one on which Jeremy Spencer simply did *not* 'play on'. It was becoming obvious, at least in the recording studio, that his strength was also his limitation: he was completely obsessed with his adept imitations of Elmore James, and could certainly turn in amusing and entertaining Elvis Presley and Cliff Richard parodies. But he had already exhausted his repertoire of such numbers on the band's previous releases. However a minor consolation for Jeremy came in the shape of his first solo single release: 'Linda' b/w 'Teenage Darling', backed by Fleetwood Mac minus Peter Green. It was a fun re-working of Tommy Roe's rock 'n' roll hit, but commercially it was a total flop.

The situation with Peter Green was becoming more serious, however. He also virtually took a back seat during the recording sessions for 'Then Play On' and, apart from the mildly obscene and effervescent 'Rattlesnake Shake', contributed gloomy and pessimistic songs, leaving the bulk of the work to Danny. Much of the album featured obviously unrehearsed jams, which might have illustrated the two guitarists' impressive techniques but nevertheless would hardly merit repeated listening.

While in the United States Peter had renounced his Jewish faith, and had embraced both Buddhism and Christianity among other theological interests. He had taken to wearing red and white robes to complete the image. And he was increasingly concerned about his wealth.

Mick Fleetwood remembers the time well.

'I had conversations with Peter Green around that time and he was obsessive about us *not* making money, wanting us to give it all away. And I'd say, "Well you can do it, I don't want to do that, and that doesn't make me a *bad* person." '

Notwithstanding the rumblings of discontent, 1969 proved to be yet another busy year in the recording studio for Fleetwood Mac members. The pressure to produce the next single was paramount, but as always the talented Peter Green came up with the goods. However the musical direction it would take surely illustrated that Peter was becoming more and more estranged from the rest of the band and the music business in general. The song could not have been more removed from the band's blues style. Virtually a double-sided instrumental, apart from two enigmatic verses, 'Oh Well, Parts One and Two' seemed to suggest that Peter Green's musical path was becoming an increasingly solo one. The lyrics hinted strongly towards religious fervour and his desire to eschew the trappings and images of a rock musician. Peter played every instrument on the record apart from one. His lovely girlfriend Sandra contributed a pretty recorder solo. The rest of the Mac made a large bet with Peter that the record would be a flop, but, as always, his talent for writing commercial material did not fail him. The single went to number two in the UK and became the band's first USA chart entry at fifty-five. Whether he collected his winnings is unknown.

During the same year Fleetwood Mac backed their manager Clifford on his version of 'Man of the World' and 'Before the Beginning', released as a single on Warner/Reprise. Mick Fleetwood and Danny Kirwan, notwithstanding their status as chart-toppers, were kind enough to come along to the DeLane Lea recording studios in London's Soho to record an album with my new band Tramp with fellow band members Bob Hall, Dave Kelly and sister Jo Anne Kelly. The album featured an explosive guitar solo from Danny Kirwan, titled 'Hard Work', and Mick's wonderful, solid, driving drumming. My old friends in the Mac had always been supportive. When my bass amplifier was stolen from the BBC that year Danny immediately gave me a vintage Marshall amplifier, which I use to this day, and John McVie arranged for me to collect, free of charge, a Marshall 4 × 12 bass speaker from the music shop which supplied the Mac with their equipment. Kind lads!

Peter Green was becoming increasingly uncomfortable with his status within the band, and yet remained musically ambitious. He was now a fully-fledged rock star, known as a highly accomplished guitarist performer and composer. But as always this clashed with his natural modesty and humility. He'd started out with a 'can-a-poor-East-End-Jewish-boy-make-good' syndrome, and had found it all too easy. His burgeoning wealth, and susceptibility to the freely offered sexual pleasures of his many girl fans, was beginning to make him very uncomfortable. He sought musical refuge in jamming with musicians outside the Fleetwood Mac set up, and started experimenting with special effects, like the newly developed 'wah-wah' pedal. He played with anyone who interested him, and recorded an album at this time late at night with Peter Bardens and his band featuring Bruce Thomas, Reggie Isadore and Andy Gee, a somewhat drunken session organised by his old mate Bardens.

Peter entered a period of intense self-examination during this time. He questioned his own beliefs, his spirituality and the attitudes of all those around him. Green's occasional bitterness and unhappiness at what he felt were the trivialities of the music business certainly spilt over into his work.

However the work continued, and saw the band, minus Peter,

producing Jeremy Spencer's solo album. It comprised a very witty collection of Spencer's various parodies and imitations, showing his real skill at satirising his heroes with humour and affection. Accomplished and amusing, the album, released on Reprise in February 1970, nevertheless died a death in the record racks. Fleetwood Mac also backed manager Clifford on his second single 'Come On Down' and 'Follow Me' b/w 'Homework', which suffered the same fate as Jeremy's solo work.

December 1969 had brought a heartening accolade for Fleetwood Mac. To crown an astonishing year they were judged by the music press the most successful band of 1969 in the UK, beating both the Beatles and the Rolling Stones in the readers' polls. John's wife, Christine, had been voted the UK's 'best female vocalist'.

In early 1970 the band toured extensively in Europe. Fleetwood Mac were playing a lot of material from the 'Then Play On' album and were continuing to feature Jeremy's rock 'n' roll parodies. Spencer was beginning to emphasise this side of his musical personality in preference to his obsessional Elmore James imitations.

However Peter Green's personal problems were coming to a head. He was becoming more confused, taking less interest in the band and surrounding himself with a lot of eccentric people who were certainly having a bad influence on him. His religious feelings were developing dangerously towards paranoia, and his state of mind was not helped by copious doses of LSD.

Clifford Davis remembers the period: 'The truth about Peter Green and how he ended up how he did is very, very simple. We were touring Europe in late 1969. When we were in Germany, Peter came to me and told me he had been invited to a party. I knew there were going to be a lot of drugs around, and I suggested that he didn't go. But he went anyway, and I understand from him that he and Danny Kirwan took what turned out to be very bad, impure LSD, and so did plenty of people. He was *never* the same again. The changes were slow to come about, but they did come. Later I talked to Peter about his addiction. He told me he had taken the drug again in this country. Peter told me once that he thought he was Jesus, that he thought everyone was greedy, and that's why he gave all his money away to charity. I've read a lot of articles saying that Peter Green was a religious maniac. I'm afraid that the truth of the matter is different. Sadly, he was suffering from drug induced delusions.'

Mick also remembers the incident in Germany: 'I think there is certainly some credence given to the idea that Peter's condition could be in some way blamed on the bad acid trip he had in Germany.

We called the group who held the party the "Munich Jet Set". They were basically a bunch of very rich brats who were living in a commune, and they sort of whisked him away, and I don't think it did him too much good.'

Peter himself, in an interview with Trevor Dann in 1988, had no illusions: 'I'm at present recuperating from treatment for taking drugs. I was a sucker for taking drugs. It was drugs that influenced me a lot. I took more than I intended to. I took LSD eight or nine times. The effect of that stuff lasts *so* long, twelve or twenty-four hours. Yet it's only on a tiny piece of blotting paper or something. I once slept out all night in the snow; it *snowed* on me!'

He also clearly recognised the confusion he was experiencing in his attempt to reconcile his religious feelings with his drug-taking.

'I wanted to give away my money, if we ever earned any big money. I went kind of holy; no, not holy, *religious*. I was kind of religious. So I thought I could do it, I thought I was *all right* on drugs. My failing!'

In spite of all these problems, Peter once again turned his attention to Fleetwood Mac's current need: a follow up single to 'Oh Well'. His skills as a writer had certainly not diminished. He wrote the powerful, angst-ridden 'Green Manalashi', apparently inspired by an appalling nightmare. The lyrics were full of disturbing images relating to Satan, the Bible and his own unhappiness. A little less accessible and commercial than the previous three singles, it didn't do quite as well as them, reaching number ten in the UK pop charts. Nevertheless it was an impressive piece of work. The single would be released in April 1970.

1970 would prove to be a traumatic year for the music industry. The Beatles broke up, Diana Ross and the Supremes split and Simon and Garfunkel parted their ways. Brian Wilson withdrew from public exposure, and two sixties iconoclastic figures tragically died: Jimi Hendrix and Janis Joplin.

Before then, however, the crunch would come for Fleetwood Mac. Matters came to a head when Peter told the other members of the band that *all* profits made by the band after the expenses were covered would go to charity. He received little support for this idea from the rest of the band, though Jeremy, who was himself becoming quite a religious zealot, reading and quoting the Bible liberally, liked the idea. The band and Clifford Davis completely rejected the notion. Peter accepted their view but felt his position in the band was becoming intolerable. There were other factors that were causing him concern as well.

Clifford Davis: 'I've read many stories about why Peter left the band. None of them accurate. There were several reasons. Firstly, he no longer wanted to be tied down to a particular musical format. He wanted to be free to play with whoever he wanted to and not to be constrained by the rhythm section of Fleetwood Mac. He also had other differences with members of the band. They were quite strong differences both musically and personally. Although he and Mick had been together in a variety of bands over the years, he constantly complained that Mick was "slowing up rhythmically all the time". His main complaint about John McVie, like John Mayall before him, was John's drinking.'

There were also personality clashes with Danny Kirwan.

'Peter had a problem with Danny who was going through this big thing about "I'm the glamour boy in the band, and I'm really as good as you and yet you're getting all the attention". That really made Peter fed up. The only person he had no problems wih was Jeremy. He liked him very much.'

Peter Green finally made the decision to leave the band to which he had contributed so much in May 1970. On the tour bus during the band's European trip he poured out his heart.

Clifford: 'We were sitting in the bus in Sweden. He came up to the back of the bus to sit with me and said, "I'm leaving the band!" I said, "Why?" He said, "Apart from anything else I've just had enough of these shits, Clifford. But it's actually a bit deeper than that." He talked to me for about twenty minutes about all his reasons. Then he went up to the front of the bus and said, "All right, you lot, I've got something to tell you," and he announced he was leaving!'

He certainly did not let the band down in terms of honouring his existing commitments.

Clifford: 'There were absolutely no arguments; I asked him to stay to honour the contracted gigs we had. He did just that.'

Mick Fleetwood also recalls Peter's responsible attitude: 'Yes, he was drifting away from the band, and then it happened. He left! But he left Fleetwood Mac in a very responsible fashion. He said, "I will be leaving, but I will be doing all the gigs we're contracted for," and that's exactly what he did. So it was not an irrational move, it was a very deliberate move on his part. He had obviously come to the end of the line as to what he could do creatively with the band. If there were other things involved I was not aware of it. We were always the best of friends, as he was with John McVie.'

John McVie was devastated by Peter's decision: 'Ah, it was, I'm not kidding you, it was trauma city! We were in the middle of a European tour. We just didn't know what to do. That whole period was beyond belief!'

John had no illusions about the importance of Peter's role within the band.

'It was *very* hard to find yourself out on a limb without Peter who had become the band's writer, guitar hero, lead singer and the main focal point of the band. And for *that* to go, I mean, it was very traumatic!'

Traumatic though it was, Peter finally left Fleetwood Mac on the 31st May, 1970. The single 'Green Manalishi' was climbing the UK charts, his final contribution to the band he had created, nurtured and brought to the pinnacle of the UK music industry. It is perhaps an apt testament to his talent that the single would be the last chart hit for Fleetwood Mac for a full six years.

Peter Green would go on to record several more singles and albums with various different line ups, and perform with his new band Kolors. But sadly, his creative fire seemed to become ever duller as his illness took over. Peter became aggressive and dismissive about music, eventually giving away his guitars, vowing never to play again. Paranoid about receiving money due to him, he threatened his accountant David Simmons with a shotgun. Menial jobs followed. Happily, manager Clifford Davis ensured that he would always have a secure income from his royalties. A long spell in the Priory, a private London hospital, helped but full recovery seemed always to be tantalisingly out of reach. Offers of help from old Mac colleague Mick Fleetwood would be spurned, as was a massive advance Mick negotiated with Warner Brothers for a recording deal in the 1980s.

4 Californian Crises

Fleetwood Mac, however, played on. Lesser bands might have folded under the pressure of losing someone with the extraordinary talent, drive and creativity of Peter Green, but Mick and John in particular were beginning to reveal the kind of resilience which would take them through some very turbulent times to come. Without Peter's front-line strengths, the band naturally turned to their two other guitarists/singers, Kirwan and Spencer. The mantle of joint leadership fell uneasily on the pair of them. Jeremy Spencer in particular became unhappy about his own role within the band. He had always been an odd character. When he stayed in my flat after coming to London to join the Mac in 1967, if he forgot his key Jeremy several times gained entrance by breaking the windows. He would be genuinely surprised at my anger about this irritating habit. When his first child was born I expressed great interest, and offered sincere congratulations to him and his wife Fiona. I was amazed when he simply could not remember the name of his brand-new baby! His bizarre decision in 1968 to go on stage at London's Marquee Club with a large wooden dildo protruding from his trousers, resulting in the band's banishment from the prestigious club, also attested to his eccentricity.

Danny too was beginning to display some disturbing behaviour, mainly due to his excessive drinking. However the pair manfully took on the next major task, the production of a new single and album. The album unsurprisingly heralded a change of direction. Gone were Peter's powerful, emotional and heartfelt contributions. Jeremy and Danny were obliged to fall back on their old strengths. Spencer turned out several Buddy Holly and Elvis Presley-influenced rockers; and Kirwan interspersed some tortured laments alongside some very melodic Beatle-inspired material. The album was critically well received, however, though the single 'Dragonfly', a plaintive Kirwan song, was not at all commercially successful.

'Kiln House' also featured old Mac friend Christine McVie, John's wife. She was uncredited on the album for contractual reasons.

Clifford: 'She was still with Blue Horizon, and they were still pissed off because they had lost Fleetwood Mac. I just gave her the session money. She was quite happy to do that. It came about quite naturally. She had said she was going to "retire" early. Her solo career had not really taken off.'

Christine was enjoying simply being Mrs McVie.

The links between Fleetwood Mac and Christine had been further forged early in 1970 when John McVie and Danny Kirwan had joined Chicken Shack plus Top Topham and Rick Heyward of Savoy Brown to produce Christine's solo album 'Christine Perfect'. It included Christine's beautifully performed 'I'd Rather Go Blind'. Her performance almost certainly resulted in Christine winning the prestigious *Melody Maker* award for the best UK female singer for two years running. Christine had additionally fronted her own band from November 1968 to April 1970, consisting of Martin Dunsford, bass, Chris Harding, drums, Rick Heward, guitar and Top Topham, guitar. It was not a commercial success.

Finally, however, the decision was made. Christine was invited to join Fleetwood Mac on a permanent footing in August 1970. She had already made plenty of contributions to their recordings, dating right back to the second album, 'Mr Wonderful'. Her inception was dramatic: 'One minute I was a housewife; next minute I was on stage with the Mac in New Orleans!'

In 1971 the band, now in its fifth configuration, set off on another tour. This one was to promote 'Kiln House', and the band members at last began to claw back some of their self-confidence and self-esteem. Two weeks into the tour, however, disaster struck. Clifford remembers it all too well.

'We'd arrived in Los Angeles, and had checked into the Hollywood Hawaiian Hotel. Unbeknown to me, Jeremy had gone out shopping during the afternoon. When roll-call came, the time to leave for the gig at the prestigious Whiskey a Go Go, Dennis, who was looking after the band, knocked on my door and said, "I can't find Jeremy anywhere, and we're leaving in half an hour." Mick Fleetwood told me that he thought Jeremy wanted to look for a bookstore. I sent a couple of lads out to scout around, but they couldn't find him.'

Then came the bombshell!

'The next thing I heard was that he'd been "stolen" by a clan, a religious cult or commune. The police told me he'd been seen talking to a member of the Children of God in the street, and Jeremy had then disappeared.'

Consternation followed. The gig was cancelled, and Clifford pulled all the strings he possibly could to find out where Jeremy was being held, if indeed that *was* the case. The police were helpful, and so was the local radio station, who put out Clifford's appeal for help and information. The radio appeal worked. At three in the morning a Fleetwood Mac fan came to Clifford's hotel room, and told him he knew exactly where Jeremy was. With the fervent religious cult, the Children of God! And his advice was to get him out. Fast.

Clifford immediately phoned them and asked if Jeremy was there. They refused to confirm or deny it and forbade Clifford to go near the headquarters. Ignoring this warning, Clifford and Dennis jumped into the car and drove straight over to the cult's centre.

'I was surrounded by about four hundred people, pushing and shoving me. It was a bit scary, but I was determined to find him if he was there. Eventually they let me in. I spoke to the leader and asked him if Jeremy was there. He said he was, but that he wasn't known as Jeremy Spencer any more. They'd given him a new name. I can't remember what it was! I said I'd like to see him and the guy said that I couldn't. At this point Dennis started freaking out.'

Clifford asked Dennis to go and wait outside in the car, realising that threats of brute force would get them nowhere.

'I said to the guy, "I'd just like to see Jeremy for some time on my own. I promise I *won't* put any pressure on him to leave the Children of God, I *won't* take him away if he tells me *of his own free will* that he wants to stay." '

After about half an hour Clifford was granted his wish. To his shock, however, Jeremy had already had his hair cut really short. His long, wild, curly hair had always been a Spencer characteristic, and the sudden transformation worried Clifford.

'I said to Jeremy, "Are you *sure* you know what you are doing?" He simply said, "I've been waiting for this for a long time. Today and here was the right time and right place. This is where I want to be." I said, "Fair enough," and I kissed him goodbye, and that was it.'

Time would prove that it was no mere whim on Jeremy's part. More than twenty years later Jeremy, his wife Fiona and their eight children are still with the organisation, though rumours abound of 'pressure' on him to stay. His membership of the Children of God has taken him from LA to Brazil, Hong Kong, and many other countries including one or two rare visits to the UK. He keeps in regular touch with his mother and father – a retired RSPCA officer – who still live in Lichfield. According to his mother he is still very happy with the organisation. Surprisingly, his recording career was by no means over. In September 1973 an album 'Jeremy Spencer and the Children of God' was released on the CBS label. In August 1979 a single, appropriately called 'Travelling', was released, followed in October by another album, 'Flee'. Both were released by Atlantic Records. The material was mostly religious in its inspiration, however, and the records were largely released to 'spread the message' and raise funds for the organisation.

Back in the Fleetwood Mac camp in LA in 1971, pure panic ensued as Clifford had visions of cancelling the rest of the tour, with all the disastrous financial implications that would ensue. He then had a brainwave. He picked up the phone and dialled a number. Peter Green's.

'I said to Peter, "Can you do me a favour. Can you come over?" He said, "You're fucking joking aren't you?" I said, "I'm not asking you for the *band*, I'm asking you for *me*." Peter then said, "You don't think I want to play with that bunch any more, do you?" I said, "It's really important, for me, I'm going to lose a *lot* of money if I get sued." Peter said, "Would you do the same for me?" I said, "Do you really need me to answer that . . . !"'

Peter immediately agreed. But on the condition that his friend Nigel, Clifford's brother-in-law, came too to keep him company on the road. Twelve hours later Clifford picked them up from the airport and drove immediately to the Swing Stadium in San Bernardino. Peter went straight on stage, unannounced. (He was to insist on being referred to as 'Peter Blue' for the entire tour.) He saved the show. Fleetwood Mac did not miss another gig, and Clifford breathed a huge sigh of relief. The tour was a great success. One of the high notes was at Bill Graham's famous Fillmore East in New York.

Clifford: 'Peter had been very laid back on the tour, but suddenly, for some reason, he grabbed the microphone, and he started playing "Black Magic Woman", something he hadn't done on the whole tour up until then. He was letting people know, "Hey, this is *me*, I'm back, Peter Green." The whole place erupted, *they* knew who he was!'

Bill Graham went to Clifford and told him to get the band off stage or there would be a riot.

'I said, "If you take them off, you're going to have a riot anyway. Leave them on." This was at five minutes past midnight. At *four o'clock* in the morning Peter finished. He was fantastic, electric. He had the crowd eating out of his hand.'

Clifford is in no doubt that Peter's helping him out on the US tour certainly constituted the biggest favour Green had ever granted. But there was no question of Peter's rejoining the band permanently. Something had to be done about Fleetwood Mac's front line following Jeremy's abrupt departure.

Christine McVie was undoubtedly providing a valuable contribution to the band's sound and image, but it wasn't quite enough.

Back in the UK the band started to think about hiring a new front man. Judy Wong, an old friend of the band, remembered a guitarist/singer she had first met in San Francisco when he was playing with his hot soul band, the Seven Souls. Wong had subsequently married Glenn Cornick, the bass player in the successful UK band Jethro Tull. When Jethro Tull played in Paris, Judy and Glenn met her old friend there. He was playing with a less than successful band called Headwest, which was touring Europe. The band folded shortly afterwards following a humiliating incident during which all their equipment was confiscated, due to the huge debts previously incurred by the Seven Souls. The guitarist had been reduced to living off the immoral earnings of a friend's wife, who was turning some pretty expensive tricks, happily supporting the pair of them.

The guitarist was Bob Welch.

Bob: 'I didn't know what to do! I didn't know whether to go back to Los Angeles. I had no money, so I couldn't afford the air ticket. The whole thing had turned out to be a nightmare, and I was getting very depressed, and wondering what to do. Then Judy Wong rang and asked me if I'd heard that Jeremy Spencer had quit Fleetwood Mac. I had. I asked her whether the band was actively seeking a replacement. She said, "Well, no, but why don't you come over. I think you guys would *really* get along." '

By this time Clifford Davis had bought jointly with Fleetwood Mac a large house in Hampshire, called Benifold. He paid £23,000 for it in 1970. The entire band lived in it. The mansion changed hands in 1989 for over a million pounds, and enjoys the reputation of being one of the finest houses in Hampshire.

Bob didn't hesitate. He got the next plane to England, and stayed with Judy and Glenn for a couple of days in London before catching the train to Guildford, the nearest mainline station to the Mac's mansion. He was met by Mick Fleetwood in his yellow Volkswagen Beetle. Bob was clutching his only possessions. A cheap, nylon-strung acoustic guitar, and a bag containing a couple of shirts and a few pairs of underpants.

'I didn't even *own* an electric guitar: I'd ended up selling my really nice Gibson to pay for a ticket from Paris to Madrid.'

Bob was impressed with the house.

'Oh yes, but it was quite intimidating. It was an English house stemming from the traditions whereby you would find one mansion every fifty miles; *very* Lords and Ladies!'

The occupants before Fleetwood Mac had been the members of some kind of monastic order.

'So you had Mick and Jenny Boyd (Mick's wife) living in one part. John and Christine McVie lived in another wing, with their own little kitchen and living-room. Danny Kirwan and his girlfriend Clare lived in the attic quarters. They weren't married at that point.'

Bob wryly remembers their subsequent marriage.

'Yeah, the whole band went along to the wedding. We took Mick's dog with us in the car, which proceeded to throw up all over my nice white suit. We cleaned it up as best we could, but the wedding photos show a *very* nasty brown stain indeed!'

Then followed a two-week period during which, in a very indirect and convoluted way, the band 'sounded out' Bob Welch as to his suitability as a Mac member.

'We spent a lot of time socialising, which really meant a lot of sitting around smoking, and drinking a lot of brandy. The band let it be known that they were *not* looking for a Peter Green clone, which suited me, because I was basically more influenced by Steve Cropper than Peter's hero B. B. King. I didn't think *anybody* could be as good as Peter Green anyway. He had the body of a twenty-three-year-old Cockney, but the soul of a fifty-year-old black bluesman.'

Christine McVie also hinted that they were looking not only for front-line singing and playing skills for Fleetwood Mac, but also for a third songwriter. Danny and Chris were contributing songs at the time, but the band wasn't quite sure of the musical direction to take. They certainly needed some fresh creative input.

'I did have some songs I'd put on tape over the years. Fleetwood Mac said, "Well, let's hear them," and Danny and Christine seemed to like my songs, so I kinda got the message that they were looking to change their style. They hadn't specifically thought *how* their style was going to change. They had done no conscious planning. They were simply looking for something they hadn't done before.'

The band eventually decided that Bob Welch had passed his curious, long-winded audition. He was hired as Fleetwood Mac's new front man in April 1971. Clifford Davis, however, was not so sure about Bob Welch.

'I thought he was quite a weak singer. I didn't think he added anything up front. I simply didn't think he filled the enormous vacancy left by the departure of Peter Green and Jeremy Spencer.'

With the benefit of hindsight, it's hard to imagine that any single musician would be able to do that. However, Clifford thought Bob was a very likeable guy who wrote 'very pretty songs'.

As always, the next job for the band was to record a new album. Clifford hauled the Stones' mobile recording studio down to Benifold, and work commenced on the album 'Future Games'.

Clifford: 'I think it was an OK album, not brilliant. We had to rely heavily on studio techniques to get Bob Welch's voice over.'

Bob Welch: 'We made the "Future Games" album at Benifold. I wrote two songs on that album. I was just trying to go with the flow of the band, I was very happy to have just two songs on it. I mostly did the rhythm guitar parts. Danny and I worked together pretty well.'

The old pattern continued, and the band once again set off for the United States to promote 'Future Games'.

Clifford: 'Every time we had a piece of product out in the States, I arranged a tour to promote it. Or perhaps a couple of short tours of eight or nine weeks' duration, with six to eight weeks off for the band between them.'

Bob Welch was particularly delighted: 'I was just thrilled to be coming back to the USA in glory compared to everything else which had fallen through, it was great!'

Clifford wasn't so sure: 'We toured with Bob Welch. It was very "iffy". One day it was OK, another day it was dire.'

The relationships within the band were once again deteriorating. Bob Welch felt bemused about Clifford's role as manager of the band.

'He had a real East End Cockney boy, cocksure attitude. Not much depth, but a lot of balls. I think the person who related best to Clifford Davis was Peter Green. That was because they were like two peas in a pod. Once Peter left, the rest of the band were completely ill-equipped to deal with this guy. After we made "Future Games" I said to Mick Fleetwood, "Jesus, what's the deal with Clifford?" Mick said, "Yeah, I know he's difficult, and *nobody* likes him, but he's been there since the beginning." The band always had that loyalty to anybody who had been there from the "good old", Peter Green days. It was a lot to do with tradition. Same with Danny Kirwan, when he became really impossible to work with. They would go through seven bells out of hell to sack *anyone*! I'd say, "Mick, he's become such a pain in the arse, the guy doesn't show up to rehearsals, he's embarrassing, he's paranoid, we've spent five hours dealing with him," but Mick, John and Christine remained loyal to him! Why? Simply because he was Peter's protégé.'

Although the cracks in the Fleetwood Mac organisation were growing, the band returned to the UK and got on with the job of recording the next album, Fleetwood Mac's seventh. 'Bare Trees', released by Reprise records in 1972, was an underrated but rather rewarding album. It would be unleashed during what was a curiously confused year as far as the music business was concerned. T Rex retained their title as top group of the year, but the raucous Slade were also popular, enjoying four top ten hits in the UK. Australian folkies the New Seekers were very successful, and Elton John, Don MacLean and Gilbert O'Sullivan underlined the success of a newly emerging breed of singer/songwriters. Teenyboppers Donny Osmond and David Cassidy signalled a slide which culminated in Donny's younger brother Jimmy's finding himself at the top of the Christmas hit parade. However, hope was at hand. Elvis and Chuck Berry also made the charts. Sadly, Berry's 'My Ding-a-Ling' hardly represented his best work.

'Bare Trees' featured some first-class work from both Danny Kirwan and Christine McVie and the album also included a fine Bob Welch song, 'Sentimental Lady', which was chosen by Warner Brothers Reprise to be the band's next single.

Bob: 'They released "Sentimental Lady" as the single. Unfortunately what happened was that Arlo Guthrie had *his* new single released at the same time by Reprise, and the record company quietly put "Sentimental Lady" on the back burner. Record companies never admit that they do that, but they *do!*'

Nevertheless the band once again flew off to the United States to promote 'Bare Trees' and the new single. Fleetwood Mac were not headlining all the shows on this tour, but opening up for big acts like Deep Purple, Savoy Brown and the like in the larger stadiums.

Another problem was developing.

Danny's behaviour had been bothering Bob since the very first time he'd met him at Benifold: 'I thought he was a nice kid, but a little bit paranoid, a little bit disturbed. I would go up to his room and really try to work with him, to be open with him, but he would always take things that I said wrongly. For a while I thought it was just me, but as I got to know the rest of the band, they'd say, "Oh yes, Danny, a little . . . strange!" He'd play something, and I'd say, "That's kinda nice," and he'd say, "KIND OF NICE? YOU MEAN YOU DON'T LIKE IT?" He would take offence at things for *no* reason.'

Matters came to an abrupt head during the 1972 tour. Bob remembers the gruesome details: 'We had a university gig somewhere. Danny started to throw this *major* fit in the dressing-room. He had a beautiful Gibson Les Paul guitar. First he starts banging the walls with his fists, then he threw his guitar at the mirror, which shattered, raining glass everywhere. He was pissed out of his brain, which he was for much of the time. We couldn't reason with him. Next thing, he goes out to the mixing desks out in the audience and would not come on stage to play!'

There followed a highly embarrassing gig for Fleetwood Mac. Danny flatly refused to play with the band, but instead drunkenly heckled and 'advised' them from the mixing desk. The farce continued. Back at the hotel he insisted on conducting a ghastly post-mortem, saying things like, 'Well, it was a pretty good set, but I think you could have been a bit tighter at such and such a point.'

Danny was summarily sacked. Then and there.

Clifford wasn't on the road with the band at that point, but he entirely agreed with the band's decision that Danny *had* to go, although his sacking caused Davis some major problems.

'I quite supported what they did. I thought it wise. I'd had problems with Danny when I'd been on the road, and was quite sympathetic when they told me. What it *did* mean however was that this was the first of several tours that had to be cancelled. Promoters lost money, and that's BAD news for the acts concerned.'

Danny's problems had been complex. Hurtled into the Fleetwood Mac circus in his teens, performing with a band enjoying a number one hit single within months of his arrival, he found the fame hard to cope with. Alcoholism developed fast, and Danny Kirwan had compounded his problems by joining Peter's trip to the party organised by the notorious Munich Jet Set, the 'rich brats' referred to by Mick Fleetwood. Danny, too, had taken bad acid at the party. The organisers of that party can take the dubious credit for ruining the careers of *two* highly talented and innovatory musicians.

Like Jeremy and Peter before him, however, Danny's recording career did not entirely cease with his departure from Fleetwood Mac. Clifford continued to look after his interests, but it wasn't easy.

'I produced two albums for Danny after he left Fleetwood Mac, for DJM Records. The second one was *so* bad! He had to finish it for contractual reasons, but I had to put down the acoustic guitar part, and the vocals, and everything else! I even picked the songs. The funny thing was that the album actually made the charts in the States!'

Danny managed to record four singles and three albums for DJM Records. None of the releases was commercially successful.

Interestingly, guitarist Bob Weston was recruited to help Danny out on the album 'Hello There Big Boy'. Guitarist Kirby also featured on the same album. Both were to play a large and controversial part in future Fleetwood Mac plans.

In 1974 Danny Kirwan kindly returned to the Southern Music Studio in Denmark Street with old Fleetwood Mac colleague Mick Fleetwood to record the second album recorded by your author's band Tramp, with myself on bass, Dave and Jo Anne Kelly on guitar and vocals, ex-Savoy Brown pianist Bob Hall on piano and Dave Brooks on saxes. Danny also joined us for a BBC Radio One live broadcast to promote the album, this time with Keef Hartley on drums.

Much sadder was my last encounter with Danny. Wanting to interview him for this book in 1989, I tracked him down to the St Mungo Community Hostel for the homeless in London's Soho. I wrote to him in advance, and checked with the warden that my visit would not be uncomfortable for him, or embarrass him. He shuffled out of his room, still slim, but puffy-cheeked and highly agitated. He couldn't talk to me coherently. He simply patted his stomach, continually repeating, 'Can't help you, Bob, too much stress, you know, too much stress.' Our encounter lasted about a minute.

There is no doubt that Danny's sad departure represented the end of an era for Fleetwood Mac. His was the last link with the blues and r'n'b phase of the band. He had been a talented and soulful protégé of his mentor Peter, and had contributed much fine work to the band's repertoire. The band would now enter a new phase of their chequered career. But it would be somewhat fraught.

Bob Weston and Dave Walker were about to join.

5 Weston and Walker

In 1972 Fleetwood Mac was by no means the only British band which had found American audiences sympathetic and receptive to its sound. Several UK groups whose musical roots were embedded in the blues were also enjoying success on quite a large scale. Eric Clapton, Ten Years After, The Animals, Long John Baldry and many other performers were making waves in the US. Re-exporting their beloved r'n'b music.

One member of the UK exodus was the Savoy Brown Blues Band, later to become known simply as Savoy Brown. The band had experienced a bewildering number of personnel changes since its humble inception in 1966. Your author joined one shortlived Savoy Brown line up immediately after leaving Fleetwood Mac in 1967. The personnel then comprised myself on bass, Lonesome Dave Peverett, vocal/guitar, Chris Youlden, arguably the finest *ever* Savoy Brown singer, Hughie Flint on drums (straight from the Blues-breakers) and the indefatigable Kim Simmons on guitar. I didn't last long in Savoy Brown. I was sacked along with drummer Hughie when we began to complain about our very low wages. Harry Simmons, Kim's brother, was a larger than life character who managed the band for many years before finally falling out with the diminutive but impressive Kim.

In January 1971, following the departure of Dave Peverett, Tone Stevens, bass, and Roger Earle, drums, to form the highly successful US band Foghat, Kim and Harry quickly needed replacements. They hired Paul Raymond on keyboards and one Dave Walker as their new vocalist. Other personnel changes occurred in the band in the next year or so, but Walker persevered with Savoy Brown until September 1972, when he received an offer he felt he simply couldn't turn down.

Dave: 'Things had *always* been a bit shaky with the personnel in Savoy Brown. I heard from somebody who was *very* much in the know in New York that I was going to be replaced. I wasn't making a lot of money with Savoy Brown, and I had had an argument with

Harry Simmons about that! The next thing I knew, I got a call from John McVie in New York saying that Danny Kirwan was leaving the band and Fleetwood Mac needed a different kind of front man. Was I interested in joining Fleetwood Mac? I was!'

Then came a hiccup in the form of an urgent phone call from Jenny Boyd, Mick Fleetwood's wife. She told Walker that the offer should be disregarded, as the band was acting a 'little prematurely'. However, whatever had been going on behind the scenes in Fleetwood Mac was finally resolved and Dave joined the band in the autumn of 1972. He was shortly to be joined by another musician who had been working with Long John Baldry.

Baldry was a UK blues veteran with a distinguished history. He had played with one of the UK's best-known blues bands of the fifties, Alexis Korner's seminal Blues Incorporated. He had then joined the astonishing Cyril Davies in his original Rhythm and Blues All Stars. He also played in Steampacket, Mick Fleetwood's old band, then with Bluesology, which featured the young, green but promising pianist Elton John. Seduced by the promise of commercial success, Long John Baldry then made a series of successful, but bland singles for the UK's Pye label. However, John never abandoned his blues roots and regularly toured the United States and Canada with his successful blues-orientated band.

The Long John Baldry Band often opened shows for Fleetwood Mac during their 1971 tour, and Mick Fleetwood could occasionally be seen hovering in the wings, watching the band. His attention was particularly drawn to Long John's young guitarist who had recently replaced Sam Mitchell, the talented but wayward Liverpudlian National Steel guitar player.

Bob Weston: 'My big moment came when I was asked to join Long John Baldry's band. Sammy was going through some personal problems, and he had been sacked. We trotted off to America. It was wonderful! But the money was terrible. £60 per week. We often opened for Fleetwood Mac, however. Mick Fleetwood was being particularly friendly at the time. I thought, "Nice people, very charming".'

The Long John Baldry band finished their tour and returned to England. Meanwhile Fleetwood Mac continued their own gruelling schedule of dates.

Bob Weston: 'I caught my breath and counted all my money. That didn't take long, however, as it amounted to pretty well zero, because I'd been robbed in my hotel the very night before we left New York! I arrived home with a fiver.'

Three weeks later Bob received a phone call. At first he treated it as a joke, which he attributed to one of his friends who loved to tease him.

'The voice said, "This is Fleetwood Mac calling from Chicago, do you want to join the band?" So I said, "Clive, piss off, I've had a bad day," and slammed the phone down.'

Mick Fleetwood luckily did not give up, and the next phone call convinced Bob that this was no joke.

'Of course I said yes. It was an ideal musical situation for me. I was well tweaked up, already playing every night of the week, and with my blues influences, it was a natural progression for me to join Fleetwood Mac.'

Dave Walker, the other new boy, having by then joined, off they all went to Fleetwood Mac's grand country mansion to rehearse for the new album and inevitable follow up promotional tour. Bob Weston remembers some tensions.

'Oh yes, Fleetwood Mac were a bit tense. After all, they had lost a *lot* of wind out of their sails. They were at a dangerous point in their careers. Fleetwood Mac had a bit of a history, but the *really* potent performers/songwriters in the band had long gone, that is, Peter Green and Danny Kirwan. They had young Bob (Welch). He was an energetic young fella. He was writing songs all the time. But Christine McVie wasn't wholly confident at that time about her ability as a writer/performer.'

Fleetwood Mac rehearsed conscientiously at Benifold, and prepared for a warm-up tour in Scandinavia, a region which had always supplied a sympathetic and enthusiastic audience for the band.

'Off we went to Norway and Sweden. We could make plenty of mistakes up there and no one would notice! The tour dispelled the lack of confidence within Fleetwood Mac which, oddly enough, seemed to be mainly emanating from the *original* members of the band, and not from the new boys.'

The two new members, Dave and Bob, clearly remember feeling like two new boys at boarding school.

Bob Weston: 'Mick was always paternalistic, and *slightly* condescending.'

Nevertheless Fleetwood Mac fired up, took a deep breath, and psychologically prepared themselves for the new album and tour. John McVie's enduring interest and concern for ecological matters had resulted in the band adopting the beleaguered Arctic survivor, the penguin, as their symbol. The band decided to dedicate their new album to this shy and awkward creature.

The album 'Penguin', however, was certainly not a wholly successful venture for the band. Bearing in mind the doom-ridden events
that had followed the release of 'Albatross', perhaps Fleetwood Mac
should have been a little more wary of identifying the image of the
band so wholeheartedly with another seabird! Christine's songs were
sweet but rather lightweight, and Walker's 'Roadrunner' sounded
laboured and plodding. Welch's contribution also sounded lack-
lustre, featuring his uncharacteristic twelve-string guitar work. The
album received bad reviews. It must be considered to be one of the
band's poorest pieces of work to date. Dave Walker hardly featured
on the album except for the one song.

Dave: 'It still mystifies me to this day why I wasn't used more in
Fleetwood Mac. Initially I was led to understand that Bob Welch was
leaving when I joined the band. Bob had a very distinctive style, and
still does. I thought at the time, "Well, if Bob's leaving, that leaves
the field open for the singer, which is *me*." I had the feeling that
Fleetwood Mac might be wanting to get a bit more rock 'n' rollish
than they were at that time.'

But he was wrong on all counts.

It wasn't a happy time for Dave. He was drinking excessively. He
felt burnt out after his lengthy and gruelling Savoy Brown tour
experience, and was additionally very worried about his recent marriage. He felt frustrated.

'Yeah, I felt angry and aggressive. I was afraid my marriage would
break up, you know, "rock 'n' roll singer marries model" stuff. It
did. I didn't do enough in Fleetwood Mac to warrant being in the
band. It was very, very strange, because they were *really* nice people.'

His involvement in the recording of 'Penguin' symbolised the
precarious nature of his role within the band. His performance of
'Roadrunner' was almost an afterthought.

'Yeah, I was down the pub! I got a call from the band saying, "We
just had an idea, come up and record "Roadrunner" for us." '

Bob Welch was also puzzled about Dave's low-key role within
Fleetwood Mac, but sensed some deep conservatism and perhaps
even jealousy from John, Christine and Mick.

'I saw Dave as a real potential star front man. Although I had large
ambitions, I didn't think of myself as the lead singer at that point. I
wanted to be *part* of something that was big. Bob Weston was a *hell*
of a nice guy and a real good guitarist, and I thought to myself, "This
is it." Mick, John and Christine liked Dave, but he was a little too
flash for them, you know, the Indian jewellery, the snakeskin boots.'

Clifford Davis thinks there were more complicated and diverse reasons which would lead to yet another personnel change for the Mac.

'Dave Walker was a real "Mr Personality". A front man with a lot of balls. I liked him and Bob Weston. We did the album "Penguin", then out we went to the States to promote it. It was a very successful tour! Walker was known from his Savoy Brown days and Bob Weston was also up front on stage a lot of the time. Then suddenly there seemed to be a lot of resentment. Because Dave was hogging the spotlight and picking up a lot of girls, stealing the show, you know!'

Matters rapidly came to a head. Mick, John and Christine decided that Dave simply wasn't right for Fleetwood Mac. They summoned Clifford to a conference.

'They said, "You're the manager, you've got to tell him that he's fired." So I said, "OK, I'm your manager. But if I do sack him I'm going to do it in *front* of you. I don't think what you are doing is very nice. Dave gave up the Savoy Brown thing to be with the band. He's done one tour, one album and now you want to get rid of him because he goes down a storm on stage!" '

Clifford and the band gloomily trooped off to Dave's house, and Clifford announced to Dave that he had something to tell him.

'He said, "What's that?" and I said, "You're fired." I told him why and he turned to the band and said, "You bunch of shits! Why did you have to get Clifford to do that? Why didn't you tell me yourselves?" '

In 1989 Dave looked back philosophically: 'I liked them a lot as individuals. I really liked them, and I still *do* like them. I found Clifford Davis to be a *very* fair and astute man. He really cared about the people he represented. He might have come across at times as being abrasive, but he'd been a performer himself, and I think a lot of his abrasiveness was a kind of defence mechanism against what he'd had to put up with himself as a performer.'

However, the experience of being sacked certainly upset Dave a great deal.

'It undermined my confidence immensely. I'd never been fired from a band before! I couldn't even *sing* for six months, and I didn't do anything musically for about four years. It was a little ugly at the time. I had a really nasty scene with the band's then road manager, John Courage. But I think it was just so difficult for *anyone* to come into a band like Fleetwood Mac, which had been established for some considerable time in a certain form, and start throwing their weight around. I'm not that kind of person!'

Let Bob Weston, the other new boy in the band, have the last word with regard to Dave's short sojourn in Fleetwood Mac.

'Dave was suffering badly. He was like a fish out of water. He'd done a couple of songs on the album that didn't really work. His parts on stage were getting smaller and smaller. I think it was just bad judgement on the part of Fleetwood Mac to have invited him to be the singer in the band in the first place. He was totally misplaced musically. He just didn't fit in.'

In June 1973 the seventh configuration of Fleetwood Mac was finished. The year had seen the charts dominated by music which was somewhat removed from Fleetwood Mac's style. Glitter, Glam and Teenybop music dominated. Slade, Sweet and Wizzard achieved considerable chart success, and Paul McCartney's Wings also sold large amounts of records. Gary Glitter and Mud had seven hits between them, and David Bowie found himself in the top ten five times. But Perry Como was the most unlikely chart star: sixty-two weeks in the UK top ten with two singles!

Bob Weston was to survive as a Fleetwood Mac member for just a few months more. His eventual departure would herald the biggest problem the band had yet faced in its already stormy and dramatic career.

6 Disarray

Way back in 1969 when Christine Perfect was singer and keyboard player with Chicken Shack she had become very fond of John McVie.

Christine: 'John was engaged when I first met him. And then the engagement was broken off!'

Christine loved John's bizarre sense of humour, and found him very endearing. Their relationship developed, and eventually John asked her to marry him. Christine didn't hesitate.

'I loved him. He loved me. Good reason enough to marry!'

Shortly afterwards Christine became a Fleetwood Mac member. Initially the marriage was very successful.

Christine, looking back in 1989: 'We had no problems prior to me joining the band. I think that we were actually *really* happy. But I think it's the kiss of death to be in the same band as your husband, it really is difficult for a relationship. You're in each other's pockets just too much. To have to travel everywhere together, think about the same things, have the same business interests, socialise with the same people. We felt as if we were Siamese twins, without an individual personality of our own.'

Mick Fleetwood's marriage to the pretty Jenny Boyd had taken him into a kind of rock 'dynasty'. Jenny's sister Pattie was married to George Harrison of the Beatles; but she was to be ardently pursued by a lovesick Eric Clapton, who wrote 'Layla' in her honour and eventually won her from Harrison. Quite an inspirational girl. Harrison had also composed the beautiful 'Something' in her honour.

However in the early 1970s cracks were beginning to show within the two relationships. Bob Welch remembers some tensions at Benifold.

'Yeah, I had got married to a nice girl, my first wife. We were commuting backwards and forwards from California to Benifold and it was obvious that things weren't going all that well for either couple.'

Things were soon to come to a dramatic head.

Work nevertheless continued. As always, the next job for the band was to produce a new album, Fleetwood Mac's ninth. The new, post-Walker, Fleetwood Mac was now a quintet. It comprised John, Mick, Christine, Bob Welch and Bob Weston and it would be the eighth line up of the band in its six-year history. Once again the Rolling Stones' mobile was hauled down to Benifold, and recording commenced. Significantly, the recording engineer on the session was Martin Birch, who had been a member of the Fleetwood Mac crew for some time. He would become *very* close to one member of the band.

'Mystery to Me' was released on October 10th, 1973 to very mixed reviews indeed. One reviewer would say of Christine's contributions: 'Christine's vocalised efforts are all good solid, undangerous yet classy pieces of super-amplified folk-rock. They're all very well produced, well executed and highly melodic.' Another would comment: 'The only drawbacks of this album are rockers penned by Christine McVie, who insists on maintaining her identity as a rocking mama.' Bob Welch came in for the same kind of treatment. His songs were variously described as 'silly at best, and forced at worst', in one review, and 'strong examples of the soft, textured rock the group excels in' in another.

Nevertheless, following the usual Fleetwood Mac policy, Messrs Weston, Fleetwood, Welch and the McVies set off across the Atlantic to promote it. By now a very familiar trip for the band. However trouble was brewing fast within Fleetwood Mac. There were two main causes. First the McVie marriage was in real trouble. Christine was having a barely concealed affair with Martin Birch the sound engineer, while John was enjoying the opportunities this gave him to indulge himself.

'Oh, yes,' he was to recall wryly during an interview in 1988, 'I had my moments!'

John and Christine's marriage was nevertheless to soldier on until 1976, when Christine finally made the break, and the McVies divorced.

A far and away more serious situation was currently developing in the camp. New guitarist Bob Weston was having a much more damaging affair. With Jenny Boyd, Mick's wife. The reasons were not particularly unusual.

Dave Walker: 'I don't think Mick was able to pay as much attention to Jenny as maybe he should. Jenny Boyd was a very sweet, nice and friendly girl and Bob Weston is a *very* charismatic guy. I wouldn't trust him with any woman!'

Bob Welch recalls the period: 'When I first joined the band in 1971

Jenny was as big as a house, just about to have their first child. John and Christine were going through one of their periodic "don't speak to each other" things. However in 1973 things got much more tense within the band.'

Bob feels that Jenny and Bob Weston were left to their own devices for far too long during the recording of 'Mystery to Me'.

'Christine had fallen out with John and was being all cosy in the Rolling Stones' mobile studio with Martin Birch. Bob Weston didn't get to be part of the inner Fleetwood Mac "club" that did the final mixes. So there was me, Martin, Chris and Mick totally involved in all that. Mick Fleetwood is like me: once he's mixing or recording or even performing he tends to neglect everything in favour of that. So Jenny became a kinda football widow at that point. Bob Weston also had a lot of time on his hands, so I guess he went to have a cup of tea or something with Jenny, and got *real* thick!'

A video film of the band during the following US tour starkly contrasts the image of Mick Fleetwood sitting on one side of a hotel swimming pool looking lonely and morose, with Jenny and Bob chatting animatedly and affectionately on the other side, looking very much like a 'couple'.

Bob Weston: 'It's really rather embarrassing to recall, especially as she is such a charming woman. Jenny and myself had a good empathy, we were best mates. She was a very nice, sensitive woman. We had a very good communication between us. Could be because we were born within the same hour of one another.'

Bob claims that the Fleetwoods' marriage at that time was virtually finished, and that Jenny and Mick were remaining together simply because of Amy, their first daughter, who was born shortly after Bob Welch joined the band. Weston also claims that theirs was not an affair in the generally accepted sense of the word.

'We got on, but certainly not in a lustful way. We were just very good soul mates. We were just emitting these incredible love vibrations. There was never anything sexual. Strange but true.'

However his account stretches credibility.

Other people around Fleetwood Mac at the time have a different recollection.

Clifford: 'We had a whole *series* of marital problems within the band. Bob Weston was having an affair with Jenny. At the same time Christine was having an affair with Martin Birch. It was a real sad situation!'

Bob's personal feelings about Jenny took him by surprise: 'I was the happy bachelor in the band; quite self-contained, enjoying having a good laugh and looking forward to the prospect of going home with some money. Then straight out of the blue came a very subtle change in my feelings for Jenny. From good friendship to *love*! I was pretty naïve. I didn't coldly weigh up the pros and cons of my career versus my inner feelings. What do you do? You take a deep breath and take a step in one of two directions. I thought the band was on its last legs anyhow. John and Christine were saying, "You leave the band and I'll stay; no *you* leave and I'll stay." And they were the kingpins of Fleetwood Mac! Bob Welch was saying,"Fuck this, I'm going to have to go and pursue a solo career." Christine's affair with Martin was rattling on. It was all in tatters!'

Weston decided that if it came to the crunch he would rather spend his time with Jenny than continue with Fleetwood Mac. The crunch came sooner than he expected.

'I remember sitting at a beach where we were staying for a stopover. Christine was sitting at the bar with Jenny. The girls were talking. You know,"girls' talk"! My affair with Jenny was becoming more and more public, and Christine was saying, "I'd *much* rather give up the band and be with Martin." The next week, the shit hit the fan! They were all up at that end of the hotel, and I was at the other end. I was like Judas or a leper. An early AIDS model!'

Bob told Jenny he felt that he ought to be the one to tell Mick about their affair. Weston saw himself, oddly, as a good friend of Mick, plus a fellow musician. However Jenny insisted on doing so herself. Then followed a lengthy, fraught and difficult late night discussion about the future of the group with the other members of the band. It was decided that the situation was intolerable.

Weston had to go.

Dave Walker had a lot of sympathy for Mick.

'I can only say from what I briefly saw it must have been extremely difficult for Mick. Extremely hurtful and extremely painful. I've been through similar situations, but not where I had to *work* with the guy in the same band!'

Dave was realistic about apportioning blame: 'You can't altogether blame Bob. It takes two to tango!'

Bob Welch also recalls the events of the time.

'We went on the American tour to promote "Mystery to Me". Clifford was extremely annoyed because Dave Walker was not going to be on the tour, but we had some pretty big dates booked. At this point the romance between Bob Weston and Jenny was in full bloom, we were *all* aware of it. Nevertheless we were on the road again backing up the album, doing headlining dates. The band was sounding really good, even without Dave. But then the thing between Bob Weston, Jenny Boyd and Mick Fleetwood started to cause difficulties. Eventually it came out into the open, you know, phone calls going back and forth, "He's sleeping with your wife." '

Whatever the rights and wrongs of the whole issue, the net result of the discovery and admission of Jenny Boyd and Bob Weston's affair was to prove chaotic for the entire band.

Bob Welch: 'Mick became an emotional basket case. He said to me, "I just can't do the rest of this tour. Jenny and I need to be away from this Weston guy." I pretty much had to go along with it because Mick is an extremely emotional guy. He can be extremely analytical and calculating, but he can also kick that emotional thing straight into gear.'

Welch was delegated to phone Clifford at 2 a.m. London time.

'I had to call him and tell him that we were not going to continue with the tour. He made a big show of understanding, but I'm sure something snapped inside Clifford. He said, "Can you do anything? Can you get another guy? I'll let you take two weeks off to find a replacement!" In retrospect it was probably a good idea, but it didn't seem so at the time.'

Replaced he wasn't but sacked Weston certainly was.

'I got a phone call early one morning after a gig, about eight. I hadn't even had a cup of tea! Next thing, there's a knock at the door, and the entire road crew was standing there. They were all looking daggers at me, very menacing, all broken noses and scars. I was unceremoniously handed a plane ticket, bundled off to the airport, and flown home. That was it! It was horrible seeing all those lads with whom I'd worked so happily emanating such a lot of hostility towards me. I think I was a scapegoat. There were all these other affairs going on within the band, but I wasn't good at boxing. I didn't duck at the right time!'

Bob felt relieved to get back to England and have some time off, after what had seemed to be years of touring. He claims that Jenny Boyd came over and joined him for a few months in his London flat.

'I felt I'd been on the edge of an abyss! Jenny came back and we spent some time together. It was really very brief, however.'

Clifford Davis was absolutely horrified about the State-side dramas. The tour was only two weeks old, and the band were already doing 'make up' dates at greatly reduced rates because of earlier missed concerts dating from previous internal conflicts and problems.

'Two weeks into the tour Phil McDonnel, the band's roadie, or

Bob Welch, I can't remember which, phoned me in England with a bombshell! Mick had announced that he couldn't continue with the tour because he'd just found out about Jenny's affair with Bob. Weston had been sacked, and was on his way home. Christine and John were at each other's throats, and so the band just decided to split up!'

Clifford still feels bitter at what he considered to be irresponsibility on the part of Mick Fleetwood.

'OK, these things do happen in your personal life, and they are traumatic and upsetting, but Mick was part of a multi-million pound industry, and he had a *job* to do! You don't just throw your responsibility away like that!'

Clifford spoke to Mick on the telephone. He expressed his sympathy, and tried to persuade Fleetwood to complete the tour dates none the less. Mick simply said, 'I'll do tonight's gig, and that is IT.'

The band seemed to be in absolute disarray. Clifford faced a multi-million pound lawsuit as a result of all the cancelled concerts. The members of Fleetwood Mac fled their different ways. John McVie went straight to Tahiti, Christine flew back to England, Mick flew to Africa and Bob Welch returned to Los Angeles to lick his wounds and consider his next move.

Clifford Davis, his back to the wall, made a momentous decision. It would be followed by some awesome repercussions.

Facing financial ruin, he decided to put the notorious 'fake' Fleetwood Mac on the road.

7 Fakes and Frauds

The series of events which followed Fleetwood Mac's sad, final concert of the aborted US tour in Lincoln, Nebraska on October 20th, 1973 were both bizarre and dramatic. The band would be virtually brought to its knees by this, the biggest crisis yet experienced in what had already been a chequered career for the band members. Clifford Davis would face financial and personal ruin. The story is a complex one. It would take lawyers many months to resolve the issue whether or not the band Clifford put on the road in the United States could possibly be the 'real' Fleetwood Mac. Contradictions and anomalies abound within the tale. People involved with the band at the time have very different perceptions as to where the truth really lay.

Manager Clifford Davis, usually labelled villain of the piece, remains convinced to this day that he was justified in doing what he did. Constrained for many years not to tell his side of the story, he feels that enough time has now elapsed to reveal a crucial element of the sorry saga, which, if true, certainly puts a different light on his apparently dubious actions back in 1974.

First, Clifford was apparently absolutely convinced that the Fleetwood Mac line up, comprising the McVies, Welch and Mick himself, was finished for good. Bob Weston's affair with Jenny Fleetwood seemed to be the straw that broke the camel's back. Clifford was by no means alone in this view.

Audio engineer Robert Simon was in the band's crew at the time: 'Mick Fleetwood told me that he hadn't eaten for five days, and was on the verge of a physical and mental breakdown. Bob Weston was having an affair with his wife, and he told me that the October 20th date in Lincoln would be the last show of the tour and we would have to cancel the remaining twenty-six dates.'

To add to the difficulties, Mick wasn't the only band member having personal problems. John McVie told Robert that because of the marital problems he and Christine were having he had finally decided to leave the band. He also felt he had become a 'stagnant' member of Fleetwood Mac. Simon recalls the trouble-filled night of the 20th.

'I got a phone call requesting my presence at a late night meeting. Present were Mick Fleetwood, John and Christine McVie, Bob Welch, Phil McDonnel the road manager and Jenny Levin. The band members told us the tour was over and Fleetwood Mac was breaking up, with its members going their different ways. Mick was to return to England before going to Kenya, John was to travel to Tahiti and then LA and Christine was going to return to England to work as a solo artiste for Clifford Davis. Bob Welch seemed highly disgruntled with all that was taking place.'

Long-time Fleetwood Mac associate Phil McDonnel was also sure that the band was through as far as the 1973 line up was concerned.

Clifford Davis was absolutely horrified at the news he received via the transatlantic phone call during that long night. He faced enormous financial problems as a result of the cancellation of nearly thirty concerts, many of them already 'make up' dates booked at a cheap price to compensate for previously cancelled gigs. He started to think fast. Very fast.

Clifford: 'Mick Fleetwood came round to my house with Christine on November 10th, 1973 to discuss the huge problem we had. I told him that we could just about get away with saying that he had had a nervous breakdown, but we simply *had* to do the new set of "make up" dates within three months, or we would be heavily sued and Fleetwood Mac would undoubtedly be finished for *good*.'

Mick asked Clifford if he had any ideas. Christine had already told Clifford during the course of the same meeting that she and Martin Birch were in love, and that she wanted to start work on a solo project with him.

'She asked if I would finance it, and I said I would, providing I approved of the songs. So I was quite sure *she* wouldn't be in any future Fleetwood Mac line up. I said to Mick, "I do have some ideas. I've got a couple of lads I'm recording at present. Elmer Gantry is the singer, and the guitar player is called Kirby." I played him the tapes I'd recorded with them, which he liked a lot. So I arranged for Mick to meet the two guys.'

Then came Clifford's audacious idea. The plan was quite simple. A 'new' Fleetwood Mac would be born. However, at the heart of the new band *had* to be the imposing, lanky drummer whose name provided half the original band's title. Mick Fleetwood.

At this point in the story accounts begin to differ. The differences hinge mainly on the claims and counter-claims that Fleetwood Mac had *really* broken up, or were merely 'taking a break' as various band members would later assert. The other issue at stake was whether or not Mick Fleetwood really had agreed to give the 'new band' some kind of credence and credibility with his presence in the drum seat. After all, as Clifford wryly claimed, his presence was *vital*. He was the *only* original member of the Mac left. This claim, though technically true, rests upon the flimsy premise that your author was the 'original' bass player in the band. Perhaps even the most die-hard fans would feel that would be stretching the point just a *little* too far!

These issues would be the subject of a long and bitter legal dispute between Clifford and the Fleetwood Mac members, which was eventually settled out of court on confidential terms. There was never, therefore, a solution as to who was 'right' or 'wrong' and so no blame can fairly be attributed to either party. As we will see, the essence of the dispute seems to be two sides disagreeing fundamentally with the other's version of events.

Clifford had no such doubts: 'Mick told me that he was off to Africa to stay with some friends of his brother-in-law, ex-Beatle George Harrison. He told me to go ahead and organise auditions with the help of Kirby and Elmer. We were to hire a bass player, a keyboard player and a *temporary* drummer. He said that we should "rehearse the band up" and that he would come back a week before the departure date, rehearse with the band, and then go on tour.'

Davis went ahead and put together a band consisting of Australian drummer Craig Collinge, Paul Martinez on bass, Dave Wilkinson on keyboards, plus Elmer Gantry and Kirby.

However, rumblings regarding the 'new' Fleetwood Mac were beginning to reach the ears of the old band.

Phil McDonnel: 'I was making practical arrangements for auditions and rehearsals for the "new" group in the middle of December 1973. I met John McVie in a pub in Chelsea. John asked me whether or not Cliff would "get away with" what he was doing. I asked him what he meant, and he said, "Putting completely different faces on a stage and calling them Fleetwood Mac." I said I did not think he would be wasting his time doing so if he thought it would not succeed.'

By this time Mick Fleetwood had joined them in the pub. When Mick was in the toilet, John McVie asked Phil a question.

'He asked me whether I thought Mick fully intended to carry on with the new line up, to which I replied that I thought he had every intention of returning to Fleetwood Mac as soon as he had sorted out his personal affairs.'

Later on during the day, Phil McDonnel claims he had the chance to speak to Mick while the two of them were on their own.

'I asked him the same question which John had asked earlier. He told me that John McVie had been trying to persuade him not to carry on with the new line up, but that it was in fact his intention to do so, irrespective of John's views.'

Phil next met Mick Fleetwood in a discothèque in January. Mick asked him how the auditions were going, and Phil told him that a bass player and keyboard player had been chosen.

'Mick made a point of asking me whether it had been made clear to Craig Collinge, the drummer, that his position was only a temporary one. I told him that Clifford had made that *quite* clear to him.'

On January 11th Phil spoke to Christine McVie on the phone.

'I rang her to say goodbye before leaving for America. She enquired about the group, who I told her were "very good". During our conversation the name Fleetwood Mac was used in relation to the group. She wished me well, and invited me to be her guest for a few days after I returned from America.'

John McVie had already sent Clifford a postcard from Tahiti wishing him 'good luck with the new band'.

Bob Welch's recollection is different. 'I went back to my little rented apartment in Los Angeles with my wife. We told Clifford Davis that the band was *not* breaking up. The band just needed some breathing space, some time off because Mick had this difficult situation. It was mainly Mick's situation. John and Christine might well have been going through another struggle, but they could still stand to look at each other. It was specifically Mick who could not deal with the whole thing.'

Confusion abounded. Sol Saffian, who worked for American Talent International Ltd in Beverly Hills, recalls a meeting with John McVie.

'In October 1973, when the Fleetwood Mac tour was aborted due to the personal problems of Mick Fleetwood, John McVie came into my Beverly Hills office and informed me that he was "retiring from the road" and was in fact going to live on the island of Maui in the Hawaiian Islands. I asked him what the situation was going to be with Fleetwood Mac, and he told me that he did not know, and "did not care" since he was "retiring".'

Sol asked John about Christine's plans.

'He stated that he did not know what her plans were, but that she would be living in London, and he was going to live in Maui. He also seemed to think that the group that had existed would no longer be performing together.'

Dave Simmons, Fleetwood Mac's accountant at the time, recalls: 'Clifford Davis telephoned me and told me that the 1973 tour had been called off because of personal reasons within the band. He told me that because of this the group had found it impossible to continue to play together and that they each wanted to go their separate ways.'

Dave Simmons' recollection of whether or not Mick was to be part of the new band is curiously self-contradictory, however. In an affidavit he signed on April 2nd, 1974 he states: 'I also gathered from him (Clifford Davis) that Mick Fleetwood was going to be a member of a new band and this as far as I was aware was the first mention of any new band. He explained that he was going to get together an entirely new band but that Mick Fleetwood *would not be taking part in the tour of the United States that had been planned for January 1974 because he needed a rest'* (author's italics). However later in the affidavit (a legal document carrying the same weight as evidence given in a court of law) Simmons said, 'I understood the new group was to be centred round and largely influenced by Mick Fleetwood.'

Looking back in 1989 David Simmons allows himself the luxury of hindsight.

'I would say that if the band had been given time, they would have got back together fairly soon in some form of the band "that was". Clifford actually put them under a lot of pressure at that time to make a decision and jumped in very quickly. I don't think Clifford did it with bad intentions, but I think that if they'd gone away for six months, they'd have sorted it out. That's not an unreal situation from a musician's point of view!'

Simmons felt that Clifford himself was under a lot of pressure, for obvious reasons.

'He said to the band, "Right, you're cracking up, but *I'm* going to carry on. Who wants to be *with* me?" and I think Mick said, "Yes" . . . !'

Whatever may have been going on in the minds of the band members, Clifford nevertheless forged ahead with rehearsals and preparations for the 1974 tour. In the meantime he had written to Christine, John, Bob and Mick requesting the return of the share certificates they held in the Fleetwood Mac company name. Only Christine formally responded to this request and returned her certificate.

According to Clifford, sinister problems rapidly began to develop just before the tour.

'About a week before we were due to leave for the States, I got a call from Mick. He said, "I can't bear to do the rehearsals, I haven't sorted out the schooling for the kids yet and Jenny has just pissed off and left me." Mick then asked me to ask Craig Collinge to do the first two gigs on the tour, and said he would meet us all in Baltimore.'

Clifford alleges that he shared his concern with Fleetwood about sending over a band billed as Fleetwood Mac that contained not *one* original member of the band.

'But I said, "All right." I'd managed the guy for seven years, and he'd *never* broken his word to me, ever.'

Craig agreed to do the first two gigs, but not without some modest blackmail.

'He said, if you *give* me the drum kit, I'll do it. I gave him the drum kit!'

Dave Walker, though recently sacked from Fleetwood Mac, was still very much in touch with the band. His understanding of what was going on largely concurs with Clifford's.

'Mick knew all about this "bogus" band. He was going to join them when he felt better. The band Clifford put together was very good. Clifford is absolutely accurate there when he says that Mick was present when he was telling us all about the new band.'

Whatever was going on behind the scenes did not stop the 'new' Fleetwood Mac, well prepared and rehearsed, taking a deep breath and boarding the plane for the United States, though, as they were very conscious, with not a single original Fleetwood Mac member aboard, their claim to 'be' Fleetwood Mac was tenuous in the extreme. Still, Mick Fleetwood would be with them on the third gig, wouldn't he? But Baltimore came . . . and went, surprisingly with no negative audience reaction.

Phil McDonnel, the band's road manager, anxiously phoned Mick when he didn't show.

'On January 23rd, 1974 I phoned Mick from Baltimore asking whether he was ready to come over yet. He replied that he was not, and still had a lot of personal matters to clear up before he could. He sounded a little strange – as if he was trying to say something but could not do so. When I pressed him about his plans he said that he did not think he would be able to come on the tour at all!'

Phil slammed the phone down and immediately called Clifford.

'Phil told me that Mick had not turned up in Baltimore, and that he was sounding very strange on the phone. I immediately rang Mick to ask him which flight he was going to be on, and he said, "John's with me and I can't talk right now." I said, "What do you mean?" But he just sounded weird.'

Bob Welch recalls the fraught atmosphere.

'I was in LA when I got a phone call from Bruce Payne, Fleetwood Mac's booking agent. He said, "Sorry to hear you had to cancel all those dates, but it's good to see that we are gonna see you back into gear here on the new tour. I look forward to seeing you at the first gig." I said, "Whaaaat are you talking about?" Then I suddenly realised.'

And the shit hit the fan.

Ten minutes after talking to Mick Fleetwood on the day (according to Davis) he was due to join Collinge, Gantry, Wilkinson, Kirby and Martinez in Baltimore, Clifford's phone rang in London.

'It was my lawyer. He said, "John McVie, Christine McVie, Bob Welch and Mick Fleetwood just sued you." I was dumbstruck. I said, "I don't believe this." He said, "I don't believe it either, but that's what they are doing. They're suing you for passing this band off as Fleetwood Mac." '

Clifford claims that although all the contracts signed with the American promoters had listed the band members' names in full (including Mick Fleetwood's), he had nevertheless notified them that Mick's presence on the tour would be 'delayed'.

Clifford: 'They were quite happy.'

But not everybody was happy. Clifford began to receive some hostile phone calls from the press.

Unsurprisingly. All was far from well on the American tour.

8 'I *am* Fleetwood Mac'

What was life like on the road with the 'fake' Fleetwood Mac? Dave Wilkinson, their keyboard player, has vivid memories of what was surely to be the most peculiar phase of his musical life.

Dave started his career in Manchester, backing people like Dave Berry, Wayne Fontana and Joe Brown. However in 1971 a friend called him from London, suggesting that he came and auditioned for the new line up of Chicken Shack. Dave jumped on a train, went to the Kensington pub and competed with Dave Rowberry for the job.

'I played three numbers, Dave played three numbers. Afterwards there was all this tension for half an hour or so, you know, little conversations in corners. The first time I'd ever been through anything like that!'

Dave was offered the job, and lasted the course with the irrepressible Stan Webb for over a year. The band finally fell apart in Munich. Wilkinson was then offered a job in Stan's new band, the Boogie Brothers, but as rehearsals took shape it became obvious that with a front line of no less than three guitarists, Stan Webb, Kim Simmons from Savoy Brown and Miller Anderson, a keyboard player was hardly necessary.

Dave then joined Mungo Jerry, a band which had enjoyed a huge hit with 'In the Summertime'.

'I thought, "Oh, God." But I didn't have anything else to do. I liked Ray Dorset, however, and it turned out to be not too bad. It was OK. But I didn't see a future in it.'

Shortly after joining Mungo Jerry, Dave got a mysterious telegram, telling him to call a number *urgently*. He did so and spoke to guitarist Kirby. He told him it was in connection with a 'highly secret project', the details of which he couldn't reveal, but would he come for an audition? Curious and with some trepidation, Dave turned up at the rehearsal rooms, and played three or four numbers with the band.

'They went into a huddle in the corner and talked, and then they came back and said, "Well, you've got it!" So I said, "I've got *what*?" They said, "We'll tell you all about it in a minute." '

Dave was hauled off to the pub next door where he met Clifford Davis, who informed him that he'd just been recruited into an exciting new venture.

'He said, "Well, basically it's Fleetwood Mac!" I said, "Where's the *old* Fleetwood Mac?" '

Clifford explained that the band was going to be called the New Fleetwood Mac, and told Dave that Mick Fleetwood was going to be the 'fulcrum' of the new band, but that he was currently in a state of personal confusion and 'would be coming along later'.

Dave: 'So I thought, "Well, I'll go along with it, see what happens!" '

Rehearsals commenced. In the repertoire were a few Fleetwood Mac songs, including Peter Green's classic composition 'Green Manalishi'. In a throwback to the old Jeremy Spencer style, the band also put in some ancient rock 'n' roll hits like 'Move It' and 'Endless Sleep'. Dave remained highly dubious and sceptical whether the promised US tour would materialise, but sure enough visas and work permits turned up and plane tickets were booked. In January 1974 Messrs Martinez, Kirby, Gantry, Collinge and Wilkinson flew off to New York.

The boys had been told that Mick Fleetwood would join them in New York, about four or five gigs into the tour. For Dave Wilkinson he couldn't come soon enough.

'I thought *right* from the word go that Craig just did not cut the mustard. I said to myself, "I know how Mick Fleetwood plays. What's *he* doing here!" '

The first gig was in Pittsburgh.

'The first concert went down a storm. We thought everything was going to be all right, although there were a few questions asked.'

The band then flew straight to New Orleans. It had been freezing in Pittsburgh.

'We all got on the plane in Afghan coats and really warm clothing. Coming into land at about 8.45 a.m. the pilot said, "The weather in New Orleans is very humid, with a temperature of 82°." We thought, "We couldn't have heard that right." Next minute we're standing at the top of the steps with all these photographers at the bottom taking pictures of a band dressed up for the Arctic!'

The New Fleetwood Mac duly turned up in New York.

'It was my first time in New York. We got picked up in these enormous stretch limos, one *each*! The ridiculous thing was that you had to sit right back in your seat and then you couldn't see a thing! All the way in the guy is pointing out the sights but I couldn't see them!'

The band might have appeared in New York but Mick Fleetwood certainly didn't. The gigs rolled on. Dave remembers that in the early part of the tour there were few problems with regard to the validity of the band. 'Just the occasional call: "Where's Mick?" and "Where's John?"'

Internal problems were brewing within the band however. According to Wilkinson, drummer Craig was proving to be very unpopular with the rest of the boys.

'Craig was in the process of being ostracised. I don't think he was playing well. His character didn't fit in with the rest of the band. He'd never buy a meal! You know that in America you can have as many little packets of biscuits as you like with coffee: you just pay for the coffee. He'd just eat loads of those.'

Dave Wilkinson also remembers making a fool of himself at a prestigious gig at the Warehouse.

'I was walking on stage. You have to walk along a little wooden parapet where the entire audience can see you, you can't help but wave to them. I was first out, you know, leading the team on stage. The next minute I was flat on my back on the stage! I didn't realise that at the end of the walkway there were about five stairs. I was so busy waving to the audience and being a big star. Then, "crunch". It really hurt. But it was more painful to have ten thousand people laughing at you!'

However, worse 'crunches' were to come. The word was beginning to spread that the New Fleetwood Mac had nothing to do with the old band. The shouts of protest were getting louder. Dave resigned himself to what he thought would be the inevitable.

'We were in New York, supposed to play at an important venue, the Academy of Music. I'd heard conversations and saw the long faces, and it was finally confirmed that there was *no* way that Mick Fleetwood was going to come out. The news was beginning to spread that this wasn't the "real" Fleetwood Mac. It was a surrogate band put together by the manager.'

Clifford, now aware of the rising tide of disapproval, had flown out to see if he could sort out the mess. Dave wryly recalls Clifford's actions.

'Everyone's getting worried. Clifford Davis was limbering up in the bandroom, you know, karate chops and stuff, busily fighting *imaginary* people! Outside twelve thousand *real* people are baying for his blood!'

Never short of bottle, tough East Ender Clifford went out and bravely faced them. He stood on stage, took the microphone and called for silence.

'He said, "Don't worry, I *am* Fleetwood Mac!" He then delivered a little speech claiming that he was the one who put the band together, he *owned* the name and basically if he wanted to call this band Fleetwood Mac then it *was* Fleetwood Mac.'

But the audience didn't accept his view. And they wouldn't calm down. The clamour grew, and things grew from bad to worse.

The band flew to Denver where they were supposed to play with Uriah Heep and Manfred Mann's Earth Band. But they didn't.

Dave: 'We got banned! We were told we weren't really welcome because we weren't the real Fleetwood Mac.'

Clifford had returned to London by this time, leaving the diplomacy to be handled by the faithful Phil McDonnel, though it couldn't have been very easy for him. The next five or six gigs were completely blown out by promoters. The band next flew to LA where promoter Bill Graham had booked some West Coast dates.

Dave: 'I just accepted the whole thing philosophically. I thought, "Fuck it, I'm in America for the first time, I've always wanted to see it. I'm getting paid, I'm enjoying myself!" '

When they arrived in LA Bill Graham was very angry. The band got shunted straight out of the expensive Hyatt Hotel into a dingy motel. They then bravely set off for the West Coast leg of the rapidly disintegrating tour.

'We flew from LA to Denver and then San Jose. San Jose wasn't much good, nor was San Francisco. We then got a plane right up north to the redwoods country. It was one of those places where the plane lands in the middle of a little field next to a bus stop. We got the bus and went to the gig. We were told in *no* uncertain terms that we were not wanted. They wouldn't even put us up in a hotel, so we had to drive all the way back to San Francisco, as it was too late to get a plane.'

More gigs were being pulled out, and the boys made the best of a forced lay-off for a few days in Los Angeles. A concert at Longbeach followed, but by this time all the gigs were turning sour.

'People were just shouting all the time, "Get off, where's the real Fleetwood Mac, where's Mick, where's John, where's Christine!" '

The New Fleetwood Mac however just about survived a gig in Salt Lake City where the news of the band's line up hadn't yet hit the local press and radio stations.

Dave decided he'd reached the end of the road with the New

Fleetwood Mac. He'd fallen out with Phil McDonnel, and had never got on with Craig, the hapless 'temporary' drummer. The night before the last gig, in Edmonton, he told the rest of the band of his decision.

'I rang them up and said look, that's it, I quit. I didn't go on stage with them when they played the final gig in Edmonton. I stood at the back of the hall, and boy, was I glad I wasn't on that stage. The audience weren't just throwing insults, but bottles and cans as well!'

The rest of the tour, nearly three months of dates booked by Bruce Payne and Clifford Davis, was cancelled. The whole sorry débâcle was over. The members of the band licked their wounds, flew back to London, and went their separate ways. Clifford Davis, however, did not abandon them, to his credit. He added several musicians to the basic line up of Paul Martinez, Elmer Gantry and Kirby, and formed Stretch. The band made four albums with varying line ups over the following four years and additionally enjoyed a hit single entitled 'Why Did You Do It?' allegedly written about Mick Fleetwood's actions.

Oddly, Dave Wilkinson's only real regret was that he didn't ever get to play with Mick Fleetwood. 'I would have absolutely loved to play with Mick. In fact I'd *still* like to play with him!'

In London the chaos continued. Bob Welch had heard via Bruce Payne that a 'new' Fleetwood Mac was to hit the road in the United States. He quickly rallied the band.

'I immediately got on the phone. I managed to get John and Christine who were at Benifold. I then called Mick who was in Kenya and told him that Clifford was putting a "new" Fleetwood Mac on the road for four months in the States.'

The band gathered in London. If Mick still had plans to join Clifford's 'new' Fleetwood Mac he did not mention them to Bob. They called Bruce Payne again, and began to discover that the problem was not going to be at *all* easy to resolve.

'Bruce said to us, "Well, I don't know! Clifford is the legal manager of Fleetwood Mac and he's the one who's been booking the dates. You are going to have to deal with him direct." '

They then decided to call Warner Brothers, their record company. Surely through their obvious and acknowledged presence on their own albums, the band could easily establish that *they* were the 'genuine' Fleetwood Mac? But once again, it wasn't that simple.

Bob: 'We called Warner Brothers. They said, "We love you guys, you are the band. BUT – we don't *know* who owns the name. Maybe

Clifford *does* own the name." Everybody was sitting on the fence. It
was a real nightmare situation!'

Bob, Christine, John and Mick then made the obvious next move.
They called a lawyer.

'We told him the whole situation. The immediate thing he succeeded in doing was to get a temporary injunction to stop the fake
Fleetwood Mac working. But the band did wind up doing about a
month's worth of dates. They had had a bad reaction. Sure it made
us feel good that people were shouting, "Where's Mick, where's
John," etc. But we couldn't work!'

What was really going on? David Simmons, the band's accountant,
had a view.

'I think Bob Welch, a rather manipulative person who was in
America where they had more aggressive lawyers, saw something
in the marketplace. He saw a golden-packed opportunity and wasn't
very happy that Clifford had apparently taken full advantage of it.'

Clifford certainly didn't see it that way. He felt and *still* feels that
he was treated unfairly. Particularly by Mick Fleetwood. A few dates
into the 1974 tour his phone began to ring.

'I started getting press people calling me up. I got very upset
because I was being told – rightly or wrongly – that Mick Fleetwood
apparently telephoned all the radio stations in every city in which
the New Fleetwood Mac were due to appear, saying that this band
were a lot of impostors, and that he knew nothing about what was
going on, and that Clifford Davis was a rip-off merchant. I just broke
down and cried.'

Bruce Payne, the American agent, had also phoned Clifford and
told him that the 1974 tour was collapsing.

'Bruce rang me and said, "We are going to have to . . . " and I said,
"I know, I know!" So we put the band back on the plane to England.'

Clifford agrees with David Simmons about the significance of Bob
Welch's role during the fraught and difficult period.

'Bob Welch and Lee Michael had made some tapes and submitted
them to Warner Brothers and couldn't get a deal. They were rejected.
Bob and John McVie had dinner together around this time in LA,
with Robert Simon, my sound engineer. Apparently Bob said, "I
don't think it's right that Mick and Chris should form new bands
and earn money, and *we* don't get anything out of it." Bob persuaded
John to fly to England with him. They met Chris, who had now split
up with Martin Birch: he had gone back to his wife. They then bent
Mick Fleetwood's ear, and persuaded him to throw in his lot with
them.'

Clifford felt that Mick was very wary about discussing the issue with him. This is how he remembers the events:

'I think he was terrified of the "high profile" Clifford Davis at that time. He got John McVie to ring me up the day I was leaving for the States. But I had a meeting with my lawyer that day, and I couldn't fit him in.'

Davis felt that perhaps the reason for the appointment was for John to tell him about Mick's change of heart. However, the two did not meet. Mick Fleetwood and Clifford Davis were not to meet again for another four years.

'As soon as I came back to England, he fucked off to America. The only time I met Mick Fleetwood subsequently was when the whole dispute was settled out of court. The band had to fly to England to sign the final settlement document.'

Clifford swore then, in 1974, never to manage an artiste again.

'I released everybody from their contracts. I just got out of the business there and then. My own *son* is a record producer and writer and he asked me to look after his interests. I *wouldn't*.'

The original members of Fleetwood Mac sued Clifford for passing off a group of musicians as the genuine Fleetwood Mac. Clifford counter-sued Mick for reneging on his agreement. The litigation dragged on. Neither party accepted the other's claims and presumably they finally just agreed to differ. The case was eventually settled out of court.

David Simmons: 'I sided with Clifford, mainly because I had a much stronger relationship with him, and I thought at the time he was doing the right thing. It went on for years. Clifford was a strong defendant, but it took up a lot of his time and energy.'

And more.

David: 'I was having a discussion with Clifford when the crisis was just beginning. We were looking at the ownership of songs. I said to Clifford, "This is a dangerous situation. You could be sued for millions of dollars, and that could wipe you out. You have a choice. Answer me a question. Are you more likely to go bankrupt or to get divorced?" Clifford didn't hesitate. He said, "There's a good chance of me going bankrupt, but I will NEVER get divorced." '

Simmons didn't hesitate either. He recommended Davis immediately to transfer all his assets into his wife's name. Clifford followed his advice, and battened down the hatches to prepare for the storms ahead. But the first one devastated him. The unthinkable happened within months. His wife *did* divorce him.

Clifford: 'Oh yes, I had a nervous breakdown over it, I lost my marriage over it. I gave everything to my ex-wife. She now runs the Fleetwood mobile, which I'd built with the help of Phil McDonnel, and the big mansion, and everything. It cost me a quarter of a million pounds. But I've never regretted it. I've always believed I could be successful at whatever I turned my hand to.'

David Simmons: 'The skies of fortune changed enormously over the four years the entire action took. By the end of that period Fleetwood Mac were all millionaires and the situation with Clifford became quite a small thing for them. Eventually the lawyers agreed to settle out of court. It was a reasonable settlement, not unfair to either party. Neither side was "branded". I think, with the benefit of hindsight, it's fair to say that both sides simply had quite different perspectives. It was easy to blame Clifford as the "big bad manager" duping the public, and maybe one could say he shouldn't have done that. But why not? He could easily say, "It was done in good faith, everybody knew what I was doing." At the end of the day, they simply had different points of view. That's what a *lot* of lawsuits are about. The fact that it was settled out of court recognises that. Both sides paid their own costs, and money due to the band which had been "frozen" was released. Clifford remained the publisher for the pre-1974 songs.'

There's no doubt that Clifford had a very difficult five years or so after the rift. He had very little money, and had to put his life back together. However in 1990 he looks fit, healthy and well and is married to a charming lady. He is now successfully involved in a new business venture.

'I've earned more money out of restoring property than I *ever* earned managing Fleetwood Mac or anybody else for that matter.'

However during our lengthy interview he insisted that I listened to his huge hi-fi system blasting out one track on CD re-release by his old band, Stretch. The track? 'Why Did You Do It?' Of course.

Oddly, there were two other 'fakes' involving Fleetwood Mac. The first is recalled by David Simmons.

'Yes, there was a Peter Green look-a-like! One of my secretaries told me that there was someone going around claiming to be Peter Green at a time when Peter was quite reclusive. The story kept coming back to me. One day she came running in to me while I was eating my lunch, and said, "The guy who says he's Peter Green is in a pub round the corner, and I've got his number!" I later rang him up and I said, "Is that Peter Green?" and he said yes. I said, "I am your accountant. Are you *Fleetwood Mac's* Peter Green?" When I challenged him he became quite offensive and bluffed his way out of the whole thing. He looked a lot like Peter Green. He had the same kind of beard, and even had his picture published in some magazine. He didn't run up any financial credit on the name. I suppose he just enjoyed *being* Peter Green!'

The third Fleetwood Mac 'fake' also harked back to the earlier band, but this time involved your author. In the early 1980s I began to receive phone calls from my various musician friends about the apparent reappearance of original Fleetwood Mac member Jeremy Spencer. I was intrigued. The controversy was further fuelled by stories printed in the London *Evening Standard* which seemed to support the rumours. I contacted 'Jeremy' and arranged to meet him in a pub. I wasn't wholly convinced, but he went a long way towards persuading me that he *was* Spencer with his astonishingly authentic recollection of the most intimate details of early Fleetwood Mac experiences. He certainly had far more than a passing resemblance to Spencer.

Looking at myself in the mirror at times I realise that twenty-odd years can wreak changes!

Still extremely suspicious, however, I contacted Peter Holt of the *Evening Standard*. He grilled him for two hours, then rang me, and assured me that the musician was quite definitely *the* Jeremy Spencer.

Finding myself able to suppress my nagging doubts, I went ahead and arranged a rehearsal and concert with my De Luxe Blues Band colleagues Bob Hall and Mickey Waller at London's Wimbledon Theatre. We trooped on stage, and played three numbers. My suspicions ought to have been further aroused when 'Jeremy' insisted on playing with his *back* to the audience, which unfortunately included the real Jeremy Spencer's parents, accompanied by their solicitor, who insisted, after our hasty exit from the stage, that we go back on and publicly announce that our 'Jeremy Spencer' was a fake.

Sensibly we ignored the instructions and got drunk instead. It seemed the best thing to do in the increasingly bizarre circumstances.

The following day Peter Holt and John Blake, the *Evening Standard* journalists, by now visibly rattled, hauled 'Jeremy' back into the *Standard* offices. They took the wise precaution of planting an ex-girlfriend of the real Jeremy Spencer in the front office.

She confirmed the horrible truth. We had all been taken for a colourful ride.

Andrew Clarke luridly confessed all to a popular Sunday newspaper the following week. He had been successfully impersonating Jeremy Spencer all over Europe for a *decade*! He had jammed with

Rory Gallagher at the prestigious Montreux Festival, performed countless concerts, and earned a good deal of money for the Children of God organisation. He claimed they had 'forced' him to carry out his elaborate, bizarre hoax in order to raise money for the organisation, following the real Jeremy Spencer's successful recordings and concerts for the same organisation. Or so he said. One could hardly place tremendous reliability upon his version of the extraordinary tale.

The whole affair ended with a mysterious phone call from someone who called himself 'Slipper of the Yard'. Indeed he turned out to be Detective Inspector Slipper from Scotland Yard's Fraud Squad. He interviewed me at great length about Mr Clarke's activities, constantly interrupted by his assistant's questions about my scrapbook, which I'd brought along to help with the details. He turned out to be an enthusiastic blues fan, and kept asking me questions about all the bands I'd been in. A suitably zany end to the kind of odd experience which seems to plague Fleetwood Mac!

9 Bob Burns Out

The first few months of 1974 were extremely fraught for Bob Welch, Christine McVie, John McVie and Mick Fleetwood. The main problem was the seeming lack of support from Warner Brothers, who were edgy and nervous about recording a new album. They were worried that if the 'old' Fleetwood Mac didn't own the name, and Warner Brothers put out a new album, the record company could run into costly and unwelcome litigation.

Anyhow competition was fierce from distinctly 'un-Fleetwood Mac-ish' acts. George McRae's 'Rock Your Baby' flagged the start of a disco boom that would last until 1979. Abba reared its successful Scandinavian head, and Mud, the Bay City Rollers and the Wombles dominated the UK charts.

Considering the problems the band were experiencing at the time, it says a lot for Mick Fleetwood's resilience and friendship that he again happily joined Dave and Jo Anne Kelly, Bob Hall and myself in London's Southern Music Studios to record 'Put a Record On', the second Tramp album. We were also joined on the session by old Fleetwood Mac colleague Danny Kirwan who had also played alongside Mick on the first Tramp album, back in 1969.

The band members put their heads together. Bob Welch was taking quite a lot of the initiative.

'Legally Warner Brothers were not bound to do anything. We had no agency, because they were caught up in the "fake" Fleetwood Mac litigation. We were on the phone constantly for a month. Warner Brothers wouldn't say yes or no even though their hearts were with us. There was only one way out of this mess, and I convinced everybody to go along with my idea.'

Bob's idea was simple. The whole band should move lock, stock and barrel to Los Angeles and deal with the problem on United States soil.

'Finally I persuaded everybody that the only way we were going to get out of this mess was to go to Los Angeles and deal with it there: we *couldn't* deal with it from England. The main work, all the contacts, strong aggressive lawyers, everything was based in the States.'

Of course, he was quite right.

'So we all wound up packing everything, leaving a friend of John's to look after Benifold. We all flew back out with the tiny amount of money that everyone happened to have in the bank at the time, with no one helping us financially at all. I had £65, Mick had £200.'

The band landed in LA and found apartments to rent. They then began the campaign to re-establish themselves as a working unit. Their plan contained two elements. First Fleetwood Mac had to hire an American lawyer to fight the court case Clifford had brought against them. Until that was sorted out, they couldn't *use* the name Fleetwood Mac.

Mick Fleetwood, looking back in 1988: 'The politest way of putting it would be to say that there was a great deal of confusion and misunderstanding. You can construe that in whatever way you want in terms of explaining what happened. There was a very gross misunderstanding of what the band intended to do. Clifford understood a very different thing. We lumbered through that for about ten months or so. Highly unpleasant, trying to prove that we were Fleetwood Mac, which is pretty ironic considering my name's Fleetwood and John was, er, not spelt the same, but certainly there was no misconception about where the name came from.'

They hired Mickey Shapiro, a tough and competent advocate. Bob Welch had known him from his old soul-band days. The issue was complex because the American and English law systems were (and are) different, and jurisdiction in one country doesn't apply to the other. The band certainly couldn't afford to hire an English lawyer to work in tandem with Mickey. So the litigation would drag on for four years before being finally resolved, long after Bob had left the band.

The other element was slightly more straightforward and involved the band working closely with the staff of the American offices of Warner Brothers, Fleetwood Mac's record company. The idea was that, through their American attorney, Warner Brothers would be indemnified aginst any damages Clifford Davis may bring against them in the event that he would totally win his case. The businessmen painstakingly negotiated while the band impatiently kicked their heels. Finally an uneasy agreement was hammered out and Fleetwood Mac (or were they?) went back to doing what they were best at. Making music.

However the recording sessions for 'Heroes Are Hard To Find' would prove to have long-term unpleasant financial repercussions for Bob Welch.

'I was the only member of the band who possessed both a Green Card (an essential working permit) *and* American citizenship. The other members of the band were not allowed to open bank accounts. I don't remember why I was so misinformed, but I was persuaded to put *all* the advance money paid by Warner Brothers, some one hundred thousand dollars, through my personal bank account!'

Two years later this would cause Bob immense problems with the IRS, the US equivalent of the Inland Revenue.

'Suddenly I went from never having earned enough money to pay taxes to *apparently* having a fortune in my bank. Two years later it caused me a *huge* problem.'

The album was nevertheless completed, with financial support from Warner Brothers. Fleetwood Mac's relationship with the record company was still a little uneasy, however.

Bob: 'We even made an in-house video for Warner Brothers, saying, "We are the real Fleetwood Mac," explaining all the legal stuff for the record company employees!'

'Heroes Are Hard To Find' was released on the Reprise label in 1974, and the band, having finally established their right to use their own name, went out on the usual marathon trek round the States to promote it.

But it would be Bob's last album, and his last tour with the band.

' "Heroes" was the fifth album I'd done with the band. It wasn't all that well received. It was apparent to me that something had to change. I didn't really see myself as a front man any more in the context of Fleetwood Mac. I think the other members of the band were seeing me in a particular light. They *wanted* certain things from me musically speaking, and things they *didn't* want from me. And I wanted to do things they *didn't* want from me!'

The band carried on with their four months' promotion tour, but Bob Welch continued to move further and further away from the musical ethos of the Mac.

'I wanted to do something very much along the lines of Led Zeppelin, something a little more "hard rockish". Zeppelin were becoming *huge* in the States. I really wanted to do that more hard-edged thing. But John, Mick and Chris *hated* that kind of thing. In 1974 it was fresh and they thought it was just a load of crap. I suppose there was some validity to that. Led Zeppelin were very brash and very raucous. Certainly Jimmy Page ripped off a lot of bluesmen!'

Bob tried hard to move Fleetwood Mac towards the musical direction he found attractive and fulfilling, but to no avail. Other problems were also emerging.

Christine McVie: 'A lot of people had been saying to me that Bob was beginning totally to dominate the band's sound and persona. In so far as Bob's personality was that way, maybe so. He was a speedy kind of guy, and because the rest of us were so laid back, it probably seemed as if he was somewhat running things. Bob was a great talker, and he *did* become the leader of the band without ever really desiring it to be that way. He probably felt that if he ever stopped doing that, the band wouldn't know what to do with themselves.'

Bob Welch was also beginning to feel very drained. 'I was so fried after our long, exhausting lawsuit that I practically couldn't put my shoes on, let alone write a song. I was just frazzled! I was just totally and utterly fatigued. I was burnt out. It was inevitable: my need to leave was *overpowering*.'

He didn't feel guilty about leaving.

'I think that they were a little hurt that I left. Particularly after the huge struggle over the lawsuit. But I felt emotionally speaking, that I had helped them get back on their feet, you know, rallied everybody. We had succeeded in getting rid of Clifford Davis. The band was now relocated in Los Angeles, which strategically was a much better place for Fleetwood Mac to be. I felt I was leaving them on a pretty solid foundation.'

And leave them he did in December 1974. One of the longest-serving Fleetwood Mac members, Bob went on to form Paris, a heavy rock, powerhouse trio. The band comprised old friend, former Jethro Tull bassist, Glenn Cornick (whose ex partner Judy Wong was now on the Fleetwood Mac pay roll) and drummer Hunt Sales. Management difficulties plagued the band. Nevertheless Bob and the boys managed to record two albums for the Capitol Record label. A third Paris album was planned, but the band collapsed before the session. However, success was just around the corner.

'Paris was a trio based very much on the Led Zeppelin model. *Everybody* in Fleetwood Mac hated it. They wished me well but they hated that kind of music. But Paris just fell apart. So I made the "French Kiss" album. It was supposed to be the third Paris album. I'd written all the material. It was much softer, much more melodic than the Paris stuff.'

'French Kiss' was an enormous success, selling over a million copies, and led to a new relationship between Bob and his old Fleetwood Mac associates.

'I remember flying to Dallas when Fleetwood Mac were doing a gig. I played them the album. It wasn't as radical, as hard core as the Paris stuff. Mick decided he wanted to manage me! He formed a small management company. The next thing, we re-recorded "Sentimental Lady". I did it with Fleetwood Mac. Everybody played on it and Lindsey Buckingham produced it. Capitol released it. I started to tour with Fleetwood Mac in their charter planes. They would fly into town to do a gig, and Mick and I would go to the radio stations. Mick would put on his manager's hat and flog "Sentimental Lady" and then put on his other hat and flog Fleetwood Mac! Then everything started to happen at once. My record started to sell and their new single went to number one. It was great. After all the problems, everybody was happy. They were happy, I was happy!'

Back in December, however, Mick, John and Christine were faced with a drearily familiar problem. Fleetwood Mac's fourth major front liner, singer, guitarist and composer Bob Welch had quit. Once again, echoing the departure of Green, Spencer and Kirwan, a large hole in the Mac line up needed to be filled.

This time, however, a happy coincidence would almost immediately play a part in the band's fortunes. Mick remembered a couple of very interesting musicians he'd accidentally heard recently when checking out a Los Angeles recording studio. He could not have known how fortuitous the encounter would prove to be.

10 Somewhere on the West Coast ...

Back in 1967, at almost exactly the same time as the very first line up of Fleetwood Mac, featuring Peter Green, Jeremy Spencer, Mick Fleetwood and your author, was taking the stage at the Windsor Jazz and Blues Festival, a new band was born six thousand miles away in the Bay area of San Francisco. Fritz.

One of the members of the band was Lindsey Buckingham. Lindsey was born in 1949, and was heavily influenced from around his sixth birthday by his elder brother's impeccable taste in music: unadulterated rock 'n' roll. The house was full of the sounds of the classic performers: Elvis Presley, Buddy Holly, the Everly Brothers, Eddie Cochran, Little Richard and many more. The music rubbed off on young Lindsey, and at the tender age of seven he began to fool around on guitar. He rapidly became very proficient on the instrument.

As Lindsey grew older, other kinds of music began to influence him. The gentler, folkier sounds of Bob Dylan, Peter Paul and Mary and the Kingston Trio caught his interest and he turned his attention towards learning and developing a country-style, finger-plucking technique on his beloved guitar. Lindsey also picked up a banjo around the same time, and enjoyed learning the new skills necessary to master this instrument.

However by the time he was eighteen years old, the music he heard pumping out of the airwaves of a dozen local radio stations was heady and exciting. Rock music filled his head and he energetically took off in another musical direction. Lindsey wanted to be part of *that* scene, and he looked hungrily around for a way to get into it. Buckingham soon heard about a local rock band which needed a bass player. He didn't hesitate. His finger-plucking acoustic guitar style hardly qualified him to play bass in a loud electric band. But Lindsey was self-reliant and young, and he quickly mastered the technique necessary to play the bass guitar.

He'd recently met a pretty, petite blonde girl in the High School in Arizona they'd both attended, and was highly delighted when she too was invited to join the band. Lindsey's pleasure was not entirely confined to his acknowledgement of her musical skills. He also fancied her quite a lot.

Stevie Nicks had been greatly influenced by her grandfather who loved to sing, and filled his house with music. Stevie wrote her own first song when she was about sixteen years old. She was suffering the kind of hopeless pain perhaps only adolescents experience after the break up of a shortlived romance, and discovered that writing both poetry and songs eased the misery for her. She also greatly enjoyed singing. Stevie jumped at the chance of joining a real live rock band. Here was the chance for her to develop and expose her considerable talents.

Buckingham and Nicks joined Fritz. The other members of the band were Bob Geary, drums, Xavier Pacheco, keyboards, and Brian Kane, guitar. Fritz worked around the US West Coast happily playing the bars and clubs. Occasionally the band would land a support spot with a big artiste. Stevie Nicks was particularly impressed with Janis Joplin's stage persona when Fritz opened for her, and she became determined eventually to produce the same kind of impact on audiences herself.

Fritz tried hard to break into the big league via a recording contract, but the best efforts of the band and manager David Forrester were in vain, although the band worked hard and played often. Their music didn't quite fit in with the heavily hard rock/psychedelic San Francisco scene in the late sixties. Perhaps Nicks and Buckingham's gentle, thoughtful melodic melodies were already ahead of their time.

Tenaciously, Fritz hung on for another four years, playing a succession of cheap and unsatisfying gigs. The frustration felt by Nicks, Buckingham and the rest of the band at their lack of any real success finally came to a head.

In 1971 they broke up. However Stevie and Lindsey's relationship had developed far beyond their common interest in music. They had become lovers. They were quite determined to stick together as partners through thick and thin. Stevie and Lindsey put their heads together and thought long and hard about the next logical move which might enhance their musical careers, and decided to move to where the record company action appeared to be. Los Angeles. Lindsey became ill and the move was delayed but finally the pair moved south from their native San Francisco.

They soon met someone who was to prove to have a crucial influence on their recording career. Engineer Keith Olsen. They played their original material to Keith and two other minor entrepreneurs, Ted Feigan and Lee LaSeffe. All were impressed with what they heard. There was much talk of recording an album in England. This proposition fell through, as did another recording deal.

However the pair's perseverance and basic belief in their own ability and talent was soon to bear fruit, though Stevie and Lindsey were yet to become rich. Lee LaSeffe managed to land a distribution deal with the Polydor Record company, and the duo finally had the opportunity for which they had been waiting. Lindsey Buckingham and Stevie Nicks cut their first album together.

The album, 'Buckingham Nicks', was released on Polydor in 1973. Virtually ignored by the promotional staff of Polydor at the time, it died a commercial death. But it nevertheless represented a substantial and satisfying piece of work which clearly revealed the burgeoning creative talent of the pair. Oddly, the album achieved acclaim in just one area, Birmingham, Alabama, and there Buckingham/Nicks enjoyed a heady and brief fame.

But, as Stevie recalled in 1987, 'We couldn't even find our album in the record shops in 1973, let alone hear it on the radio!'

The album was produced by Keith Olsen, ably assisted by Richard Dashunt. Both would play an important part in the duo's future musical career. Nicks and Buckingham were also joined by the legendary session drummer Jim Keltner and the lesser-known guitarist Waddy Wachtel.

The album was quickly deleted by Polydor. The two musicians pondered over the next move.

Lindsey started working as a session guitarist. He also enjoyed going on the road for the first time with one of his all-time heroes, Don Everly, of the legendary Everly Brothers. Lindsey had always been a big Everly Brothers fan. Don was doing a short club tour, and Lindsey was thrilled to be just a part of it. He stayed in Nashville for a while and met some of his heroes like Roy Orbison and Merle Travis. But these musical excursions, though fun, didn't pay the rent.

In order to finance the recording of further demos at Keith Olsen's Sandstone studios in LA, Nicks and Buckingham had to take jobs outside the music business. Lindsey worked in a tacky public relations company, and Stevie waitressed at Clementine's, an unprepossessing Beverly Hills singles pick-up joint.

She also worked for Keith Olsen. But not as a musician.

'In 1971 I was cleaning the house of our producer Keith Olsen for fifty dollars a week. I came walking in with my big Hoover vacuum cleaner, my Ajax, my toilet brush and my cleaning brush. And Lindsey had managed to have some idiot send him *eleven* ounces of opiated hash! He and all his friends – Warren Zevon, right – were in a circle. They smoked hash for a *month*. I don't like smoke because of my voice. When you don't smoke, there's something that makes you *really* dislike other people smoking. I'd come in every day and have to step over these bodies. I'm tired, I'm pickin' up legs and cleaning under them and emptying out ash trays. A month later all these guys are saying, "I don't know why I don't feel very good." I said, "You wanna know why you don't feel very good? I'll tell you why. Because you've done nothing else for weeks but lie on the floor, and smoke, and take my money!" '

Lindsey was certainly not being particularly supportive to Stevie at this time.

'Lindsey and his friend Tom used to go into every coffee shop in Hollywood, write hot cheques and never go back again! The Copper Penny, Big Boys . . . We fell into the American Dream out of nowhere. *We* were just nowhere.'

Certainly the future looked unpromising for the pair. The demo tapes carefully and painfully recorded during the evening, financed by Stevie's menial jobs and Lindsey's very occasional work, were getting them nowhere fast. They could have worked musically but they chose not to. Competent bar bands, playing current chart hits, could always get work round the extensive Los Angeles restaurant and steak house circuit.

Lindsey: 'Our then manager was trying to get us to do top forty stuff. He said they could get us all the gigs we could handle, if only we'd be prepared to play that kind of music, but Stevie and I knew that if we did, we'd lose whatever musical direction we had and we didn't want to prostitute ourselves. So we resisted that, and as a result, we got no gigs. Nobody wanted to hear us doing our own songs.'

However, as Stevie Nicks and Lindsey Buckingham morosely sat around on New Year's Eve 1974, wondering whether 1975 would be a better year for them, the phone rang. Their lives would be profoundly changed by the message it would bring.

Earlier the same month, a couple of weeks before Bob Welch was finally to quit Fleetwood Mac, Mick began to think about finding a new studio in which to record the follow up album to 'Heroes Are Hard To Find'. He wanted to change the band sound a little, following the rather lukewarm reviews which the album had received. However recording studios were far from his mind as he wandered round a Los Angeles supermarket one afternoon, picking up the groceries.

Mick Fleetwood: 'I was in a grocery store, and this guy came out whom I vaguely knew, though I couldn't remember his name. I asked him what he was up to, and he told me that he was doing public relations work, hustling for business for Sound City Studios. So I said, "Let's go!" I put my groceries in the back of his car, and we drove out to the Valley where the studios were. Keith Olsen happened to be in the studio at the time. I looked through the control room window and saw a girl working in the studio. I said to Keith, "Who's that pretty girl?" and he said, "Oh, that's Stevie. She's on the tape I'm going to play you." '

Mick also met Lindsey during the same visit.

Lindsey: 'We were in the process of gathering new material and were at the studio. It was sort of a home base for us. We were in Studio B. I was taking a break. I walked into Studio A and saw a *giant* of a man, with a beard and very long hair. He had a strong presence, but I didn't really recognise him. Keith Olsen was playing a track from our album for him at top volume. I shook hands with him. Then the song was over and I went back to Studio B!'

Keith carried on playing back the master tape of the 'Buckingham Nicks' album he'd recorded in Sound City. He wasn't remotely trying to interest Mick in Stevie or Lindsey's work. He merely wanted to show off the facilities he and the studio could offer Fleetwood Mac. Persuading them to record their new album there would bring in some welcome and lucrative work.

Mick dutifully listened to the tape, quietly noting the contribution from the guitar player, who impressed him. 'I'm a *stickler* for guitar players. I remember hearing Lindsey's guitar playing, and thought it was really good.'

However Mick thought no more about it, other than merely noting that he had liked what he heard. Two weeks later, when the burnt out Bob Welch unexpectedly quit Fleetwood Mac, Mick nevertheless remembered the work of the duo he'd heard during Keith Olsen's demonstration.

Mick: 'When Bob left, I phoned up Keith Olsen, and initially asked what Lindsey was doing.'

Mick was only interested in Lindsey Buckingham. After all, the band only needed a guitar player to replace Bob, not a girl singer. They'd already got the excellent Christine McVie very ably performing *that* role. But Keith explained that Lindsey and Stevie Nicks, the pretty girl Mick had spotted, were absolutely inseparable. They were a duo. They had a long-established musical and personal relationship. They certainly would *not* split up. Hire Lindsey and you got Stevie as well.

Mick: 'And then I truly gathered that they came as a package, and they wrote the songs *together*, you know!'

Mick Fleetwood decided to take the album 'Buckingham Nicks' to Christine and John and see what they thought. They listened carefully, liked what they heard, and made what would prove to be a momentous decision. Fleetwood Mac invited the struggling duo to join the band without even bothering to go through the formality of an audition. Mick called Keith Olsen on New Year's Eve, and asked him to telephone the pair with the invitation. Fleetwood subsequently spoke to Stevie briefly and to the point.

Stevie: 'He said, "Do you wanna join our band?" I said, "Are you kidding?" We were *destitute*! A friend of my brother's was at the Winterland Ballroom at one time, and saw them drive away in black Cadillac Fleetwood limousines, so I said, "That's it, I'm in!" The cash meant more than the band!'

Lindsey wasn't quite so sure, however. He hadn't liked Bob Welch's role within the band, and his influence on Fleetwood Mac.

'My awareness of the band was just the Peter Green stuff, which I think is *still* the best, really wonderful!'

However, his reservations, eroded by the pair's frustrating lack of both success and money, did not last long.

Lindsey: 'It was a very flukey thing. Stevie and I thought it over for a while. We were basically in need of funds and a venue through which to get our material out. We made the decision to join up. It was as simple as that!'

Simple it may have been. But not one member of the new line up of Fleetwood Mac, the tenth since 1967, could ever have imagined just how successful the new band would be.

11 The Band Regenerates

The next step was to arrange a meeting between John, Christine, Mick and the new recruits to Fleetwood Mac.

Stevie: 'We planned to meet the next night at a Mexican restaurant. Lindsey and I got there early. They drove up in these *huge* clunky white Cadillacs, the ones with real long fins and flashing red lights. They stopped outside and Lindsey and I were both going, "Oh boy, this is really Alice in Wonderland time, you know!" Mick got out of the car. He's about twenty feet tall. And then the *rest* of them appeared!'

In spite of the tacky cars, Stevie was nevertheless impressed, as Lindsey had been earlier when he met Fleetwood at Sound City. 'There was an *aura* when they got out of the car. They made me feel a little in awe, you know, like I was standing with some great people!'

Christine McVie was anxious. Mick and John, sensitive about her important role within the structure of the band, had put quite a responsibility on her shoulders with regard to the potential new girl recruit.

Christine: 'Mick and John said to me, "If you don't like the girl, then we can't have either of them, because they are a *duo.*" The *last* thing I was thinking about at the time was to have another girl in the band. I had been so used to being the only girl. We met them both. We all really got on well together. Stevie was a bright, very humorous, very direct, tough little thing. I liked her instantly, and Lindsey too.'

The new Fleetwood Mac had yet even to play together.

Mick: 'The first time we played together was in the basement of our agent's office. And it was at that point the real, true excitement came. It was very apparent that something was *really* happening. It was very much like when the band first started.'

Mick was enthused, and wanted Warner Brothers to share that enthusiasm. 'I remember going up to the record company and saying,

"Look, we want to *leave* the record company unless you really realise how excited we are about what we are doing!" Of course we couldn't leave Warner Brothers! But I wanted them to feel how excited we were about what we were doing. We weren't just making another record album and going out on the road, and paying their electricity bills. We didn't want them to think, "Oh, everything's all right, not that great. Oh, it's good old Fleetwood Mac again, they're always good, you know, nice solid following in the colleges." It just really felt truly exciting and we wanted them to feel that this was something really new, you know, in terms of what was happening to the band.'

There was no doubt that the inclusion of Lindsey and Stevie was a rejuvenating shot in the arm for the faltering Mac, shell-shocked after the series of blows it had received over the previous couple of years. Was December 1974 an all-time low point for Fleetwood Mac?

Mick: 'I don't know if I would say that. Whatever it was, the chemistry just happened to be right. Fleetwood Mac was unknown to people in Europe, who were totally unaware of our records. We had a really healthy career in the States. We were a cult band in terms of our following, and had been for many years. We had a good base to start from, which is the point we were at when Stevie and Lindsey joined. They'd been trying very hard and unsuccessfully to get their own careers off the ground. It was just one of those things that worked really well.'

Mick also felt that Fleetwood Mac were not only used to absorbing new musicians into the band, but generally made them feel welcome.

'As far as people coming into the band were concerned – and I think this is healthy – John and I never said, "You've got to fit like this, or play like that." We didn't, for example, tell Bob Welch when he joined the band that he had to do something because we were known for this particular sound. We didn't ask him to play like Peter Green. He came and did what he did; it went on for however long it did, and then ended. I feel proud that people have been able to come into this band and feel comfortable, not being intimidated to be a "certain something" because we were Fleetwood Mac.'

The new band did not waste a minute. Less than three weeks after the recruitment of Stevie and Lindsey, Fleetwood Mac headed back to the Sound City Studios in the Valley. Rehearsals had taken place, and had gone extremely well. The Mac were ready to record their next album for Warner Brothers.

'Fleetwood Mac', using material that for the most part had been written long before the new band was assembled, was quickly cut.

Lindsey recalls: 'We really didn't know each other too well when we did the album. So we mostly recorded tunes that had been worked out beforehand in our own styles. It was planned as well as it could have been in a couple of weeks!'

Short though its inception had been, 'Fleetwood Mac' was a first-class album, and an important commercial milestone for Fleetwood Mac. With the exception of the Curtis Brothers' countryish 'Blue Letter', the songs on the album were entirely composed within the band membership, and it immediately showed the impact that Buckingham and Nicks were to wield. Between them they wrote half the songs on the album. Lindsey wrote 'Monday Morning', 'I'm So Afraid' and 'World's Turning'. The three songs were melodic and evocative, echoing previous work from the classic Mac guitar players Green and Kirwan.

The Fleetwood Mac ladies however contributed particularly strongly to 'Fleetwood Mac'. Stevie looked back to the 'Buckingham Nicks' sessions and re-cut 'Crystal', which she and Lindsey had recorded previously at Studio City for their Polydor album. She also recorded 'Landslide'. The session additionally produced a beautiful Nicks song which was to become an enormous and enduring success. 'Rhiannon', a dreamy, mystical song about a Welsh witch, was to become a firm favourite with concert audiences for the next fifteen years.

Christine too was in fine commercial form. Her contributions to the album were to prove enduringly popular. 'Warm Ways' and 'Sugar Daddy' were entertaining, but the powerful 'Say You Love Me' and 'Over My Head' were eventually to match Stevie's song 'Rhiannon', as far as commercial success was concerned.

The album was produced by Keith Olsen and the band and recorded at Sound City, the fortuitous meeting-place of Mick Fleetwood and Buckingham and Nicks. Stevie and Lindsey remembered their old friend Waddy Wachtel from their 'Buckingham Nicks' days. He played rhythm guitar on 'Sugar Daddy'.

'Fleetwood Mac' was released in July 1975. It rapidly went to number one on the US album charts. Fleetwood Mac had once again turned a crisis into a triumph.

Christine McVie, looking back a couple of years later: 'I think we just had a product that everybody wanted at the time. It was a very versatile album, and on stage the band projected a kind of exciting image – a new sort of image which hadn't been seen before. It was unique to have *two* women in a band who were not just back up singers, or singers *period*. Stevie sings, sure, but she also does other musical/movement things which are aesthetic. The five characters on stage became five *characters* as opposed to just five members of a band.'

But what about Christine's initial anxieties about the inclusion of a second girl writer/composer/singer in Fleetwood Mac? Although Christine had liked Stevie when they first met (if she hadn't, neither Buckingham nor Nicks would have been in the band at all), would they get along when Stevie was a fully-fledged member of the Mac?

Christine: 'I liked her. Not because she was like me, quite the contrary, we're totally unalike, complete opposites at either end of the personality spectrum. The one thing we had in common was a good sense of humour. We have a good laugh together, you know! It is, I think, one of the primary reasons for anybody staying together, marriage, band or whatever it is. The ability to laugh at things, and oneself, is *really* important and special.'

Stevie Nicks also felt that the pair of them enjoyed a good relationship.

'Oh yes, because if anything I was like Christine's baby sister. She'd never had a little sister before. In the beginning it was truly just Chris and me. No wardrobe mistresses, no make-up artists, no hairdressers, no anybody. It was just me and her. Lots of times we even shared a room. So we got to know each other real quickly and became good friends real quickly because we didn't have anybody else. We *had* to end up being friends, because, you know, otherwise it was just "hang out with the *guys*" all the time!'

In July when the album was released the band had held its collective breath.

'We all knew it was a good album,' said John McVie, 'although we had a little bit of trouble convincing our record company and some of the people around us that we could pull it together so quickly.'

Stevie agreed: 'We all went to Hawaii after the album was finished and just laid back for about three or four weeks. When we got back to Los Angeles, I just sat down and put it on my stereo. I hadn't heard it since it had been finished, and I really enjoyed listening to it again. I figured that I should have been sick of it by then, but I really enjoyed it, and as I'm like the last of the big teeny boppers, then there wasn't going to be too much that anybody would dislike on that record.'

The same year would see Queen achieving their first taste of international success. Gladys Knight and the Pips and Minnie Riperton flew the flag for the females, but Stevie would not be left out.

Fleetwood Mac needn't have worried. Stevie's hunch was right. Like all Fleetwood Mac albums before it, the album was accorded a lot of initial Fleetwood Mac radio station exposure upon its release. But unlike the others, the album *continued* to be played on the radio. Sales steadily built up, until eventually the album reached the number one position. No less than a year later 'Fleetwood Mac' was still in the top ten (oddly repeating the English success of the band's first album). It had smashed the *Radio and Records* all-time record for sustained album air play. However, the sales of the album in the United Kingdom were far less spectacular. Once again Fleetwood Mac were far more popular in the US than in their country of origin. The band's decision to live permanently in the US, made a few months before Nicks and Buckingham had joined them, seemed to be paying off.

Mick: 'The decision to move to America permanently was not a financial one. The money wasn't the thing, we just weren't that rich and we didn't need tax relief. We were primarily interested in getting out of England altogether. The band wasn't working in England. At that point we were playing more and more over here. Also I thought England was very grey and full of depressed people. We just got out!'

Christine hadn't wanted to move away from England at all.

Mick: 'It was funny: Christine didn't want to move to America, but now she wouldn't go back to England to live if she was paid to!'

Fleetwood Mac's American audiences and record buyers certainly took the band to their hearts, and the members were hardly prepared for the overwhelming reaction that eventually greeted the album.

Stevie: 'It was really weird. We were driving back from a gig in Santa Barbara. All the way back to LA we kept hearing "Fleetwood Mac", the new album, the old ones, and even songs from our "Buckingham Nicks" record. It was really nice to hear that stuff on the radio. Especially in LA!'

'The success of the album went beyond my wildest expectations,' said Mick Fleetwood. 'I mean, we were confident that we had made a dynamite recording, and felt that Stevie and Lindsey had contributed a hell of a lot of new energy and a new dimension to the band. Our albums had always sold between 200,000 and 250,000, and we were always appreciated. We never lost anyone: the cult kept growing. But wide-scale acceptance was always just around the corner.'

John agreed: 'We've always kept a low profile, away from hype. That's the way we are. We never wanted to be viewed or reported as the biggest things since sliced bread. Me, Chris and Mick have been working together for a long time. We've eaten every day and always had money for smokes. I'm proud we pushed ahead. The success now makes some justification for the efforts of the past.'

But more success was to come. The Warner Brothers moguls listened carefully to 'Fleetwood Mac' and decided that not only was the album commercially strong in its own right, but that it would yield some more gold if carefully plundered. 'Warm Ways' b/w 'Blue Letter', released in the UK, completely bombed, but then Christine's 'Over My Head' was released.

'It was the furthest thing on the album that we thought was ever going to be a single,' said Christine.

But she was wrong. 'Over My Head' backed with Lindsey's 'I'm So Afraid' was a monster US hit for the band, the first since Peter Green's 'Oh Well' had tickled the hit parade at a modest number fifty-five back in 1969.

The band gathered momentum. They had immediately gone back on the road upon their return from Hawaii after finishing the album.

Christine McVie: 'We could tell by the first concert we ever did that it was going to be good. That first show went down a complete storm: there was something about the combination of people on the stage that was very special.'

Stevie Nicks: 'We started the Fleetwood Mac album in February 1975. That took three months. We went out for a few gigs in the summer, which was no big deal. Then we did a tour starting September 9th, coming back December 22nd. Four gigs in a row, one day off. No limousines. It started out cold and finished cold. We just never stopped. We played *everywhere*. We didn't exactly play teen clubs but we might as well have. We *sold* "Fleetwood Mac". We kicked that album in the ass. Christine slept on amps in the back of trucks. I hadn't a clue! But I decided that I was going to make it all right. There was no one going to say, "She can't cope. She should give it up."'

She didn't, and the band's relentless but well-planned touring schedule continued to pay off, supporting the record releases. The success of 'Over My Head' was repeated by the second single to be culled from the album, one which was to become a Fleetwood Mac classic. Stevie's delicate, haunting, 'Rhiannon', backed with Christine's 'Sugar Daddy' was another US hit for the band. Astonishingly, 'Rhiannon' was not the final bonus the album was to yield: Christine's 'Say You Love Me', chosen for the third single, completed the hat trick, making 1976 the most successful year in the band's history up to that point.

As usual, however, the chart success Fleetwood Mac enjoyed in the US was not repeated in the UK. 'Say You Love Me' was the only hit, and that only reached number forty. 'Rhiannon' *eventually* made the charts when it was reissued in 1978, but only just. It peaked at forty-six.

Lindsey, though, wasn't quite as happy as his partner Stevie in the Fleetwood Mac line up.

'Oh yes, I had a *lot* of adapting to do. Sometimes I wonder about that. I reflect on what might have happened if we hadn't joined. Because I had to give up a lot of my style at that point, to adapt to what was already there. I had to go out there and play Bob Welch songs, which I *hated* doing. I felt like part of a lounge act. I had to give up even the kind of guitar I played. I liked to play a Fender Telecaster, but I couldn't, because it didn't fit in with the piano, bass and drum sound that was already there.'

Conscious of sounding a little churlish, Lindsey concluded: 'There were many lessons in adaptation, but it worked out. I learnt a lot from Mick, especially.'

Minor grumbles apart, Fleetwood Mac set about acquiring some of the trappings to go along with their new-found prosperity. Stevie, who had taken the precaution of keeping on her waitressing job for two weeks after joining Fleetwood Mac, just in case it all fell through, was delighted.

'I felt lucky to have been found out of all those people. Me and Lindsey to be asked to join what we considered to be a very big band. We were rich and famous in six months. It was shocking! It was a Cinderella story which really happened! I was a waitress and cleaned house and did all sorts of things because what was Lindsey going to do? He was a *guitarist*! So I did all those things. Then six months later I had a lot of money, a great apartment, a car – I couldn't believe it! It's very surrealistic to stand back and look at it. I think a lot of people would have gone just crazy, because it's really such an adjustment. I went from absolute anonymity to the opposite over-night.'

Fleetwood Mac had caught on as a performing band as it never had before, playing in huge stadiums all summer long. This was partly due to the success of the album, but also because of the important role played by the exotically costumed, foxy-looking Stevie Nicks. Fleetwood Mac had at last found itself a strong visual image to go with the fine rock music it had always been able to provide.

However, in the midst of all the newly won success for Fleetwood Mac, all was not entirely well behind the scenes.

Rumours were growing.

12 Rumours

It is impossible exactly to pinpoint the time when interpersonal problems plaguing the band members began to affect the atmosphere surrounding Fleetwood Mac. But there is no doubt that back in September 1973, when Mick discovered to his horror that he was being cuckolded by new guitarist Bob Weston, things had come to a head. After Weston was sacked, Fleetwood Mac found themselves in a familiar situation – disarray.

Jenny Boyd fled, first to an apartment in LA with her daughters Amy and Lucy, and thence to England, where Weston claims they lived happily together for a short while. Jenny's account is rather different.

'Mick and I saw each other throughout our separation. I went home to England to be by myself. I'm very close to Mick's sister Sally and I stayed with her. I realised what was happening. The trip "cleared the cupboard out". That brought me back to reality. The love was always there! I joined Mick on the road again last summer (1976) and it's been wonderful ever since. We're much closer, more understanding.'

Mick Fleetwood had always been considered to be a kind of 'father figure' within the band, although he saw himself rather more as a 'mother hen'!

He wryly recalled: 'The band looked up to me for stability and counsel, particularly as *my* divorce failed!'

He remarried Jenny just four months after their divorce in the autumn of 1976. Sadly their marriage would eventually come to an end in 1979 after the couple's best efforts to save it were finally unsuccessful. (They actually divorced and remarried *twice*.) Undoubtedly painful though he found his personal problems, Mick Fleetwood was still seen as some kind of marriage counsellor within the band.

'When we started recording the follow-up album to "Fleetwood Mac" in early 1976, we were *all* in an emotional ditch. Everybody knew everything about everybody. But I was definitely piggy-in-the-middle, although in actual fact *my* marriage was going down the tubes too. But I was spared the in-house, up-front situation. I didn't have to actually *work* with my ex-spouse.'

John McVie did. His and Christine's marriage had been rocky for a long time. It had certainly started very well.

'Yes, it was wonderful, because we didn't know any different! Maybe in retrospect our problems might not have happened if Chris hadn't joined the band.'

But she had. Christine McVie, talking to Christopher Connelly of *Rolling Stone* in 1984:

'We just reached a point where we couldn't be in the same room together. We'd probably spent more time with one another than most couples who have lived together for twenty-five years. We had no individuality, no separation.'

John's drinking problems didn't help. Affable, witty, gentle and amenable when sober, he would become difficult and belligerent when drunk.

Although there was some discussion about whether the pair might quit Fleetwood Mac to ease the tension, it never happened. There seemed to be a kind of corporate loyalty to the band from all its members which apparently superseded the personal traumas they were experiencing.

The third part of that sad emotional triangle which existed in 1976 comprised the newest additions to Fleetwood Mac, Lindsey Buckingham and Stevie Nicks. They might not have been actually married, but they were as good as. Friends, lovers and musical partners since 1970, they were also experiencing the trauma caused by their emotional disentanglement early in 1976. However, like John and Christine, the difficulties and pain they were going through would not lead to either of them bowing out of Fleetwood Mac.

Stevie: 'Because, basically, we really like each other and once we go on stage all those problems, the fights, the arguments and disagreements, they all disappear. That two hours on stage is beautiful, and always was, even when things were at their worst.'

Other factors naturally played their part in Lindsey and Stevie's decision to hang on in the Mac.

'Really, each one of us was way too proud and way too stubborn to walk away from it. I wasn't going to leave. Lindsey wasn't going to leave. What would we have done? Sat around LA and tried to start new bands? Nobody wanted to do that. We liked touring. We liked making money, and we liked being a band. It was just "grit your teeth and bear it".'

Certainly the band was experiencing strange and difficult times. John McVie suddenly appeared with Sandra Elsdon, Peter Green's stunning ex-girlfriend. He also distantly lusted after Linda Rondstadt.

Stevie began a relationship with Don Henley of the Eagles, a month after leaving Lindsey, and Christine started an affair with the group's lighting director, Curry Grant. Gossip writers at the time had a field day. They put Christine in hospital with a serious illness and flagged up a 'Tenth Anniversary Tour' featuring original Fleetwood Mac members Peter Green, Danny Kirwan and Jeremy Spencer. To crown it all, Stevie and Lindsey suddenly became the proud parents of a baby girl (actually Mick and Jenny's daughter, Lucy Fleetwood, photographed with the pair).

They survived it all.

Christine: 'After ten years of struggling, it would have been silly to throw it all away. We proved to each other that we had a pretty strong character as a band, that we could cope with the problems and surmount them, which we did. John and I are friendly now, which at a point we weren't. The bonds were just too great to sever just because there was an emotional ruckus going on. Everyone *cared* about everyone else. There might have been problems between John and me, but that didn't mean we didn't care about Mick, Stevie, Lindsey, and vice versa. We're *friends*. And to let something that successful just fall apart, to say, "Sod the rest of you, I'm buggering off." No! There was a certain responsibility not only to the band, but to the whole unit. There were a lot of people on the payroll. And then there was the fact that we were *good*. Whatever happened, that was the overriding factor. The band was at the pinnacle of their career, and we had a responsibility not to break that up for anything as trivial as a divorce.'

Three members of the Mac would eventually remarry, and Stevie would later marry for the first time. But in 1976 a job had to be done. 'Fleetwood Mac' and the three singles taken from it were still selling very well ('Fleetwood Mac' would eventually sell over three million copies). Once again a familiar cry came from the record company, Warner Brothers. A new album was expected from Fleetwood Mac.

If Fleetwood Mac could be said to have one enduring quality as a band, it would be resilience in the face of adversity. In particular, drummer Fleetwood and bassist McVie had picked themselves up and dusted themselves down time and time again during the band's stormy career. Chris too had demonstrated her own strength and persistence during some very dramatic crises experienced by the Mac.

The emotional problems churning around within the band could well have brought them all to their knees. But Buckingham, Nicks and McVie, like many talented artistes and writers before them, each decided to dwell upon their recent traumas and use them as an inspiration. The new songs would meet their feelings and emotions *head on.*

'The outcome of the various separations and emotional upheavals in the band that caused so many rumours are in the songs,' Christine would recall, after the new album was released. 'We weren't aware of it at the time, but when we listened to the songs together, we realised they were telling little stories. We were looking for a good name for the album that would encompass all that, and the feeling that the band had given up (the most active rumour flying about). And I believe it was John, one day, who said we should call it "Rumours".'

The band went into a studio in Sausalito to begin work on the album. Richard Dashut, the co-producer, remembers the first months.

'It took two months for everyone to adjust to one another. Aside from equipment problems, there were psychological problems in that the band were going through a tremendous upheaval. There were breakdowns and realignments which had a tremendous effect on their music. Defences were wearing thin, and they were quick to open up their feelings. Instead of going to friends to talk it out, their feelings were vented through their music. It created a certain sensitivity. Our personal lives were in a shambles, and the album was about the only thing we had left.'

The work was hard for everybody.

'We were huddled up in this little house in Sausalito, working eighteen hours a day, and our only release was our work, so we were going to make sure that at least that was going to work out right. We put everything we had into that album. There was no magic to it, no key to success. Just a lot of hard work.'

The album was scheduled to be released in September that year, but production problems would delay the release date by months.

Lindsey: 'There was never a conscious delay. We just assumed that it was going to be easy, like the production of "Fleetwood Mac". We went into the studio after seven months of solid touring. We were tired. John and Chris had just broken up on the road; Stevie and I were on the verge of breaking up. We started cutting tracks, but everybody was going through so many weird personal trips on the side.'

The first two months were particularly difficult for everybody.

'The communication was very bad. It's not that anyone was fighting, it's just that no one was quite together enough to get a really healthy start.'

Frustrations grew to the point where Fleetwood Mac decided to leave the sessions for a while, and go back to the place which Mick would darkly describe as 'home': the road.

Stevie: 'We were all trying to break up, and when you break up with someone, you don't want to eat breakfast with him the next morning, see him all day and all night, and all the day after and all the next night.'

Mick announced to the band after a couple of months that they would rehearse for four days, and then go on the road for ten days for a breather.

Stevie: 'At that point, we *needed* the feedback. We needed to hear people say, "OK, we know you're having problems, but we still like you." '

The brief break over, Fleetwood Mac returned to the studios: but not to the Record Plant, Sausalito. The band moved its operation to Los Angeles. The album would eventually be recorded in at least four different locations: Sausalito, Los Angeles, the Davlen Studios in North Hollywood and Miami's Criteria Studios.

The band had dispensed with the services of Keith Olsen, the producer responsible for 'Buckingham Nicks' and 'Fleetwood Mac'. Mick Fleetwood and John McVie favoured a rhythm section sound for the new album which emphasised their playing more than Keith liked, so they decided to use Richard Dashut and his colleague, Ken Caillat. Fleetwood Mac themselves also wanted to play a greater part in their own destiny: Mick and John had already taken on the managerial duties for the band. Seedy Management, the tongue-in-cheek title for Fleetwood and McVie's management company, was already responsible for the shaping and direction of the band's career, though John would freely admit that the day-to-day work of the agency was largely undertaken by Mick rather than him.

Mick: 'We're much less insulated, because I make sure everyone knows what's going on. An outside manager has a tendency to try and make it look as though everything is going smoothly even when it's not.'

It wasn't always easy, though Mick thought it was worth the

effort. 'I'm not recommending it; I think it's a slightly unusual situation. You can imagine, when the band started to do noticeably well, I can't name how many people, including what were probably some very talented managers, approached us. We just chose not to have anyone poking their nose in; we felt we could do it on our own.'

Mick felt that their decision to manage themselves was crucial to the very survival of the band during what was an enormously difficult period.

'I think we've got complete peace of mind. I think, for instance, that if someone from outside had been handling this band, we would probably have broken up when there were problems. This band is like a highly-tuned operation, and wouldn't respond to some blunt instrument coming in. There's a trust between all of us that would make that a problem.'

He also saw his role as manager in a more traditional way.

'You *have* to have a pivot point when there's five people wandering around. No one else thinks about things like where to record, where we'll play on tour, whether we'll make a single or a double album – they don't particularly *want* to. And I *do*!'

John McVie, co-manager: 'The hardest thing for people in this business to accept is the fact that the band achieved all that it has *without* professional help. Some people still think that Mick's just a dumb drummer and I'm a dumb bass player!'

Work on the album continued painstakingly. This was not to be a hastily produced creation like 'Fleetwood Mac', however well that production had turned out. The band's approach to the actual recording technique was also very different from what had taken place before. 'Fleetwood Mac' and the albums before it had been largely recorded live, with the whole band playing together in the studio, completing a good single, basic take of a track. Much overdubbing and editing would then take place, of course, but the basis of the track would be the first acceptable original performance of the band. 'Rumours' would be different.

Richard Dashut: 'It wasn't necessary or even expedient for them all to be in the studio at once, ever. Only two tracks on "Rumours" were recorded and played at the same time. In other words, virtually every track on that album is either an overdub, or lifted from a separate take of that particular song. What you hear on the record is the best pieces assembled, a true aural collage.'

The band worked extremely hard. Stevie Nicks, always the most fragile member of the band, exemplified their attitude. The night she recorded the vocal part of her song 'Gold Dust Woman' provides a worthy example of the way the band worked. She did the first take standing up in the fully-lit studio. The song required an intense, dramatic approach. Take followed take. To help the atmosphere Richard dimmed the lights. She eventually sat down, wrapping herself in a huge cardigan to keep warm. Concentration grew. She soon became unaware of all the other people in the studio, hunched up with huge headphones to listen to the backing tracks. Nicks was surrounded by medicines, inhalers and lozenges to ease her slightly sore throat.

On the eighth take she cracked it perfectly. 'Gold Dust Woman' was safely in the can.

The writers in Fleetwood Mac were *not* going into the studio with finished songs, but were taking ideas and themes with a view to developing and honing them.

Lindsey: 'We'll never be a band like Tower of Power which goes into rehearsal and rehearses a song so that they can just go in and play the whole thing in one or maybe a few takes. The way we approach it is more like the way the Beatles used to approach their thing in the studio; having a general idea and then going into the studio and letting the spontaneity happen. There was nothing specifically worked out when we went into the studio. We didn't have demo takes like the last time. The whole thing just happened. That's where you capture the magic.'

A typical example of the result of this kind of approach was the song 'The Chain'. Perhaps no other song on the album is more symbolic with regard to the resilience and persistence of Fleetwood Mac. 'The Chain' is a dynamic, tough piece of rock music which incorporates the moods and feelings of Fleetwood Mac during those demanding and draining months.

Christine: 'The song was originally mine, but it was just a melody, and I couldn't find any words to it. So we edited Lindsey's bridge parts for use as the chorus, and made up new verse parts.'

Lindsey: 'The whole thing is like a Brian Wilson, "Good Vibrations", and they just worked.'

Their creative and delicate approach to the job of recording the collection of ten angst-laden songs would eventually lead to the release of a masterful album. However their way of working was very slow and expensive. Warner Brothers became anxious and edgy, but Mick Fleetwood, wearing his two hats as drummer and manager, managed to assuage their worries.

'We felt once we'd done the tracks that all the material the way *we* looked at it, was very strong. For us, which is the bottom line.'

His confidence in the quality of the material grew as the songs and recording developed, and Mick felt that, however long it took, this album was going to be worth the trouble, money and hassle.

'If it had been a little shaky, we might not have spent a lot of money recording it. But we felt it was warranted because we were working on making what was good better and better. And the record company was really very good. They called a couple of times about hearing things, and I said, "You're not hearing *anything* till we've finished." They said, "Do you realise how much money you're spending?" '

Mick did. He nevertheless felt that acting in his role of Fleetwood Mac's co-manager, he was doing the right thing.

'We were very aware of the money. Had there been an outside manager, I would say we would have been hassled more. He would be finding out about how much money we were spending and tending to feel a little intimidated about it. Again, as musicians and players, that's what we wanted to do. We were gonna get this thing pretty much how we wanted it, as near as you can ever get. And we did.'

It wasn't always easy. Rumours abounded around the time of the sessions about Lindsey's role within the Mac. Early on during the recording, Buckingham was certainly disillusioned.

'I'd gotten frustrated that my songs weren't coming out the way I heard them in my head. And Mick just said to me, "Well, maybe you don't want to be in the band!" It was a black and white situation.'

But the cracks were well and truly papered over, and the album began to take shape.

Christine however was having problems. 'When we went into the studio to record, I thought I was drying up. I was practically panicking, because every time I sat down at a piano, nothing came out!'

Luckily inspiration struck.

'One day, in Sausalito, I just sat down and wrote in the studio, and the four or four and a half songs of mine on the album are a result of that.'

Christine's mood at the time was far from pessimistic, in spite of all the emotional traumas which were flying around.

'Partly because I was so thrilled I was able to write some songs. I wasn't necessarily talking through my own viewpoint.'

Her songs seemed to be highly personal, but that was not always the case.

'Some songs I write *are* intensely personal. But, you know, there's always a certain amount of lying going on. They call it artistic licence, or something. Some songs I write are about people I know, into whose shoes I'm treading for a little while. And other songs are *complete* fabrications! Rarely do I stand in my own shoes and write a song that is that personal!'

'Oh Daddy' was not quite what it appeared to be.

'That's not a song about me. It's a song about Mick and Jenny. And "Don't Stop" was just a feeling. It just seemed to be a pleasant revelation to have that "yesterday's gone". It might have, I guess, been directed more towards John but I'm just definitely not a pessimist.'

'You Make Loving Fun' is generally supposed to be an earthy celebration of Christine's love for Curry Grant, the lighting technician with whom she was enjoying a passionate affair.

One of her most powerful pieces of work was undoubtedly 'Songbird'. Christine wanted to create an atmosphere of space and loneliness on the track, so Richard Dashut set up a bizarre recording session. Christine would record the song entirely on her own in the Zellerback Auditorium in Berkeley. The venue enjoyed virtually perfect acoustics; and at 7 a.m. the song was laid down. Any thoughts of adding layers of overdubs were forgotten when Christine and Richard played the master tape back.

Christine: 'The vibe was so good on the original that we left it really raw and basic.'

Oddly, another 'original' piece of work from Christine was to surface in the United States at around the time McVie and her colleagues were recording 'Rumours'. Sire Records, the company which handled all the pre-Warner Brothers material Fleetwood Mac had recorded for Mike Vernon's Blue Horizon label, woke up to the fact that they owned some potentially valuable products. Riding on the back of the ever-growing sales of Warner's 'Fleetwood Mac' they released an album recorded by Christine Perfect which had been issued in the UK back in 1969. Retitled 'The Legendary Christine Perfect Album' the record featured Christine accompanied by John McVie, Danny Kirwan, Top Topham, who'd played briefly with an early Yardbirds line up, Rick Heyward (yet another Savoy Brown link for Christine) and Christine's old band Chicken Shack. It included her highly creditable version of Etta James' 'I'd Rather Go Blind', the UK single release which undoubtedly and deservedly earned Christine the accolade of the UK's Number One Female Singer Award from the *Melody Maker* for two years running in 1969 and 1970.

Christine, however, did not welcome the re-release. She felt that it did not do her justice. Certainly she had left her UK blues roots far behind by the time it was released in the US. Nevertheless the album is by no means bad, containing as it does worthwhile contributions from husband John and ex-Fleetwood Mac colleague Danny Kirwan.

Back at the 'Rumours' sessions Lindsey and Stevie were also contributing some of the best work they had produced. Unlike Christine, Stevie found it difficult to write from anything *other* than a deeply personal point of view.

'Yes, all my songs are personal. They are all about things which did happen. The only way I can be is honest. I can't make up a song, I can't make up a story. I promised myself from when I was sixteen years old and wrote my *first* song about the break up from my boyfriend Steve that I would *never* lie in my songs. I would not say, "I broke up with him," if the truth was "he broke up with me". I would stay clearly truthful to the people.'

Occasionally the tensions became almost unbearable for Nicks.

'Yes, there were times when I thought this is too much for me. But, you know, sit me in a room with five crying people, and I'm a soft touch. It's like, I've said, I'd *never* be the one to break up Fleetwood Mac. Somebody else can do that.'

Lindsey and Stevie's songs were clearly directed at each other, even though Lindsey would claim that the album contained 'just a selection of songs'. 'Second Hand News' and 'Go Your Own Way', written by Buckingham, were obviously autobiographical, as was Nicks' 'Dreams'.

Lindsey: 'That wasn't conscious either. I mean you just write about what's happening. All the songs, really, seem to relate to each other. They're all about each other.'

The musical soap opera ground on. Lindsey remembers Warner Brothers' increasing anxieties: 'They were really paranoid. Understandably, because they hadn't heard any of the album. They didn't know *anything* about it for ten months at that point. They probably thought we were in the studio just helplessly flailing away.'

Mick Fleetwood, ever the diplomat, paid Warner Brothers a visit. Warners didn't want to issue a single from the album, because they feared that if the single bombed, it might hurt the potential album sales.

Lindsey: 'Mick went down and met with Mo Ostin and the people down there and listened very calmly to all their reasons why we shouldn't release a single. Then he played "Go Your Own Way". That was it. They went, "Yeahhhhh," and said, "Go ahead." They realised that the last album wasn't a fluke, and I think they felt that we knew what we were doing.'

Fleetwood Mac certainly did. The band was firing on all cylinders. Lindsey's guitar parts were more forceful and dynamic than on previous recordings.

Christine: 'On "Fleetwood Mac" he was more laid back, not so sure of himself, still very good. But on this album, his playing has come up much more forcefully. There's more power and dominance in the guitar and the aggressiveness of the guitar changes the characteristics of the songs.'

Lindsey: 'We just wanted to get a ballsier thing on this album. We wanted to do something *different*.'

They had. 'Rumours' had taken eleven months to record, of which six months alone had been taken up with the band's presence in the studio. Mixing and editing took a further five months. Warner Brothers had been patient for entirely altruistic reasons.

Mick: 'One reason we were able to work on "Rumours" as long as we did was because the "Fleetwood Mac" album was selling so sensationally and it allowed us to keep working on the new one. If we had put out the new album when we were *supposed* to, we would have killed the sales of the "Fleetwood Mac" album, and there was no point in doing that.'

However Mick's quiet determination to retain control of the band's career led to Warner Brothers' release of a single lifted from the album.

'The album was taking so long to get out. We wanted to put the single out before Christmas. It was a number of Lindsey's and I really thought it was great.'

'Go Your Own Way' was just one of the hit singles which would be taken from the new album, but the flip side 'Silver Springs' would not appear on 'Rumours' at all. Stevie wasn't too pleased. When she heard that 'I Don't Want To Know' was going to be put on the album instead of 'Silver Springs', she tore out into the parking lot and screamed with anger, frustration and shock that the song she wrote about Lindsey was going to be relegated to a 'B' side.

'That's Stevie's song. It's a really long song that the band features on stage. But it couldn't go on the album because it was too long. You can't start putting too many tracks on an album otherwise you reduce the quality of sound. So it was a neat way to get the song out and let people hear it.'

They heard it and they bought it. 'Go Your Own Way' would make the US top ten, and tickle the UK charts (peaking at forty); though, as always, Fleetwood Mac were largely ignored in Europe and Great Britain.

However in February 1977 'Rumours', the album born of strife, pain, emotion, angst and separation, was released. Fleetwood Mac had at last struck gold.

13 Consequences I

'Rumours' topped the US album charts for six solid months. Within ten months it had sold eight million copies and was still selling 200,000 copies *weekly* in early 1978. Statistics abound. At its peak 'Rumours' sold enough to go 'gold' (500,000 copies sold) *twice* a month and 'platinum' (one million sales) every thirty days. There was a platinum award for the associated eight-track cassette release; and a gold award for ordinary, audio cassette sales. Within the same period *four* of the album's eleven songs became hit singles in the US: 'Go Your Own Way', 'Dreams', 'Can't Stop' and 'You Make Loving Fun'. 'Dreams' would make number one in the US.

As if their record sales were not enough, Fleetwood Mac practically swept the board in the 1977 *Rolling Stone* readers' poll. They were placed first in no less than four categories: Artist of the Year, Best Album ('Rumours', of course), Best single ('Dreams') and Band of the Year. Stevie Nicks came a creditable second in the Female Vocalist section, joining the heady company of Linda Ronstadt, Joni Mitchell, Ann Wilson (of Heart) and Bonnie Rait. To round off their impressive success, Fleetwood Mac came fourth in the Producer category for their own work with Richard Dashut and Ken Caillat on 'Rumours'.

The album won the Grammy award for the best album of the year, and would rapidly double its 1977 sales to sixteen million copies. Money gushed into the Fleetwood Mac coffers, and the band set about some serious spending.

Christine bought actor Anthony Newley's old house in Coldwater Canyon. It was the kind of mansion that befitted a member of what was rapidly becoming one of America's biggest and most successful rock groups. The house boasted beautiful internal decor which taste-fully combined oriental and art deco design. There was a traditionally laid out Japanese garden, the obligatory swimming pool with a view of Beverly Hills and a well-equipped music room. Christine also installed a traditional English pub-style saloon to remind her of her Midlands roots, but an attempt to ship in some traditional, decent British beer didn't work. ('No, it just wouldn't travel that far!') Maids quietly performed domestic chores, a full-time secretary was in attendance and good food and wine abounded. Parked outside could be found a pair of matching Mercedes-Benzes – with licence plates named after her pair of Lhasa apsos. A sculpture studio was added to allow Christine to return to her creative Birmingham Art College roots.

Christine mused on the changes that the money and success had brought: 'It's enabled all of us to realise a few dreams that we never thought would happen. But I haven't egoed out. I'm pretty much of a recluse as it happens. What has this done, though? Well, the doors have just opened. Now I have the money to get my sculpture studio together, and the whole way of looking at my life has expanded over the last six months.'

The other band members followed suit. Mick, ever the band dandy, indulged himself with some beautifully tailored suits to fit his 6ft 6½ inch frame (Mick is *officially* classed as a giant). He then bought a huge, elegant, cliffside home in Malibu to hang them all up in. Cars too became something of an obsession.

'I really don't have any hobbies at all, unless you count collecting cars.'

He quickly amassed a 1966 Ferrari 275 GTB, a 1966 Jensen CF V8, and a rather obscure 1965 Alvis.

'Well you don't see them much over here. The Duke of Edinburgh has an Alvis. It's the typical snob English car that is so snobbish that they don't make them any more.'

He acquired an MG, a Porsche and a Mercedes.

'Believe it or not, I use them all. It's quite scientific, actually. I use whichever one has most gas!'

Mick had always lived with style and panache even when he was poor.

'I truly enjoy making money, but even when I was on the dole, I still used to save up for a pair of tailored trousers (occasionally lengthened by his long-suffering sister Susan). In fact I used to go and collect the dole money in a vintage Jaguar! I've *always* had a lot of cars!'

John McVie set about equipping himself for what would become a very serious hobby indeed. Sailing. He quickly acquired the first in a series of ever-lengthening boats, as well as an attractive Beverly Hills house. Lindsey set up home in a spacious white stucco house which he shared with Richard Dashut and the Curtis Brothers' drummer, Bob Agurra.

Stevie Nicks bought a big house in Scottsdale near Phoenix, where she had been brought up and where her parents still lived. However she rarely spent much time there and would eventually sell it and base herself in Los Angeles where the rest of the band lived. Life became luxurious for the members of the Mac, although following the release of 'Rumours' none would have a great deal of time to enjoy their new-found wealth. They almost immediately set out on the first of a series of gruelling tours to promote the album. Fleetwood Mac could hardly have been accused of laziness.

However the huge income generated by 'Rumours' meant that touring could become a lot more comfortable.

Christine: 'The way we conduct the tours is a lot nicer for sure. When you have the money to charter your own plane and stay in nice hotels, it makes life on the road infinitely easier.'

The band had mixed feelings about touring. Mick Fleetwood had always enjoyed it, as did John McVie.

'John adores it, he's always first on the plane. Christine is a real trouper, she's adapted to all the rigours. Lindsey, on the other hand, can do without it. As for Stevie, she doesn't really like travelling, but she's an audience addict, so she rises to the occasion.'

Mick thoroughly enjoyed the contrast between the band's early tour experiences and the post-'Rumours' situation.

'We're just not that money conscious. There's enough money to go around for a while and I have a feeling that there will always be more. You should remember that most of the troupe came up the hard way. When we were in the early British blues band, we spent virtually every night of our lives driving up or down some horrible British motorway. It was an extremely primitive way to make a living. Christine may like to enjoy a bit of luxury now, but I can remember when she used to have to sleep on top of a Hammond organ for weeks on end because no one could afford a hotel room. So we've all worked hard for what we've supposedly got.'

Things didn't go entirely smoothly however. The first fifteen dates of the 1977 tour had to be cancelled due to Stevie Nicks' throat problems. Additionally Lindsey needed to have his wisdom teeth extracted, leaving him with two beautiful black eyes. Just in time for the band's photo session for the cover of *People* magazine.

'Panda' imitations apart, Lindsey and the rest of the band waited until Stevie was quite well, and they started their marathon tour. It was to criss-cross the United States and last six months. *Crawdaddy*, the well-known American rock magazine, ran a review of one of the 'Rumours' concerts. Their gig in San Diego took place just weeks before the release of 'Rumours', but the set already heavily featured the contents of the album and was typical of the concerts to come. A local reviewer would report:

San Diego gave Fleetwood Mac a tumultuous heroes' welcome as the group walked to its stage positions in darkness, opening in a shower of lights with Christine's 'Over My Head'. 'Station Man' followed immediately with John stepping forward to churn out the song's classic bass line as Mick grinned at him from behind a formidable drum kit. Lindsey, looking very relaxed in jeans and white kimono jacket, grabbed the lead, layering in sparkling riffs and fills that drew applause. Halfway through, Stevie, a sultry witch in black suede boots and midnight chiffon, took centre stage with 'Rhiannon' and brought the arena to its feet in a screaming peak of excitement, Christine followed with excellent vocals on 'Why' and 'You Make Loving Fun'. Then Stevie moved behind Mick's drum kit during a vintage favourite, 'Green Manalishi', as John and Lindsey worked out on a ballsy bass–guitar exchange.

In 'World Turning', a sizzling highlight of the set, Christine moved out from the keyboards to play marracas and power a three-voice chorus as Mick's drumming gradually gained solo domination with a cracking tempo shift. He polished off a beer with one hand, then leaned out from behind his kit holding an African talking drum beneath one arm. For the next minute this goateed beanpole in black vest and skinny plus-fours bounced amazing sounds around the arena, then rushed back to pump to a high-kicking finale. The ninety-minute set closed to a roaring ovation after 'Don't Let Me Down' and 'Hypnotised', the two encores.

Hot stuff indeed. The band was fully exploiting Stevie's natural flair and ebullience. She looked good, with her foxy, diaphanous black chiffon and lace outfits, and she loved to dance and prance. Her high energy on stage could be misleading.

'It's not like I just go on stage and sing every night. I *scream*. And crash a tambourine on my leg and dance around a lot. It's almost an athletic trip for me because I've never been very strong. In fact I'm like a snake all day, just grooving along slowly. Then for two hours on stage I have all that energy. Afterwards I'm a basket case. I've got to be practically carried away immediately.'

Stevie had *always* enjoyed dancing:

'As for the dancing, it's nothing I haven't done my whole life. I decided from the beginning that if I didn't have something visually interesting to do I wouldn't just stand out there. I leave the stage when Lindsey or Mick has a heavy solo. ''Rhiannon'' is the heavy duty song to sing every night. On stage it's a real mind tripper. Everybody, including me, is just blitzed by the end of it. There's something to that song that touches people. I don't know what it is but I'm really glad it happened.'

The song was certainly to become an enduring classic for the Mac. Stevie still receives letters from people who claim that it 'changed' their lives and several parents have told her they named their baby after the song's title. There is even a UK produced Stevie Nicks fanzine called 'The White Witch', based on the song's lyrics.

Stevie's sassy image, though good for the band, would have an unwelcome backlash for Nicks herself. Finally painfully free from Lindsey, Stevie next found herself labelled by the press.

'For a while it was funny. Then I really started to get angry. I mean, I'm supposed to be having all these relationships with all these guys that I don't know that maybe I've met once, that I don't *want* to know and there's nothing I can do about it. All of a sudden I'm picking up these papers and I'm the ''Siren of the North''!'

The reality was quite different.

'In the last year, I've begun to realise what a tremendous power trip rock 'n' roll people are on. I don't *like* rock 'n' roll stars. I especially don't like *men* rock 'n' roll stars, mainly because of the size of their egos. I don't need it. I've gone through it and I didn't like it and I won't do it again. I'm really a very *quiet* lady. I love being at home!'

She might not have generally liked rock 'n' roll stars, but Stevie was developing a soft spot for one in particular. The Eagles drummer Don Henley called her out of the blue, asking to meet her. Both were busy touring, and so the friendship developed at long distance over the phone. Eventually Fleetwood Mac and the Eagles found each other on the same bill. Mick and John, knowing her interest in Don, played a mischievous joke.

Stevie: 'It was weird, and fun. We arrive at the gig, and the Eagles are in the next dressing-room, right? Now, I would *never* go in there and say, ''Hi, I'm Stevie.'' *Never!* I would *die* first. So I go into our dressing-room and there's this *huge* bouquet of roses with a card in it. So I open up the card and it reads, ''The best of my love, dot dot dot. Tonight question mark, Don.'' And I said, ''That's about the uncoolest thing I've ever seen in my whole life! I mean how could he possibly pre-conceive something like that? And I'm *dying*, right. My face is red and I'm fuming. And then, finally, Christine grabs me and takes me aside and says, "Don didn't send that. Mick and John did." They were in hysterics!'

Proper introductions were made however and Stevie and Don started a friendly relationship. But life on the road was demanding for both Nicks and Henley. Anyhow Stevie had strong feelings about mixing personal relationships with rock 'n' roll.

'I certainly couldn't take an old man on the road. Egoistically a man couldn't handle it. You *can't* drag a guy on the road. In Lindsey's new position he could. I can't. I'm stuck. I've been going out with Don, the drummer in the Eagles, and we've talked about it a lot. And even him, who does it too, and who's much more famous and rich than I am, it's even hard for him to handle. He doesn't want to sit around backstage, and I don't want to put him through it. It's the same with me. When I go to his gigs I feel out of place.'

Stevie wryly recalled her own ambivalent feelings. 'It was real funny. I drove him once to the airport when he was leaving for a tour and I said, "I wish you weren't leaving." And he looked at me, threw up his hands in mock despair and raised his eyebrows. He said, "She does just the same thing I do and *she* doesn't even understand!" '

Stevie understood the dilemma experienced by many people who work long and hard in the music business.

'How can you have a relationship with someone who is in a band, and yet how can you have a relationship with someone who isn't? How many doctors or lawyers are going to look at you and say, "Sure, Stevie, I'll see you in three months, I'll read about you every day." Then when you come home on vacation, you're doing an album which means you'll be in the studio all day and half the night, until four o'clock in the morning, when you roll in and say, "I'm *so* tired." Then when you finish the album you get a call saying you've got two weeks off. Then you're going on the road to *promote* the album!'

How were other members of the band coping with their post-relationships 'Rumours'-documented blues? John McVie had mixed feelings about the relationship between him and Christine after they split. John could sometimes laugh about it.

'It's a saga! It's a mobile Coronation Street!'

However the all-important friendships within the band had endured:

'Well, because we're friends first and everything else second we were able to accept it all. I can accept Christine being on the road with her old man and she can accept me being on the road with my lady. The same applies with Stevie and Lindsey and Mick. About the only relationship that hasn't happened is between me and Lindsey. But there's still time!'

Christine McVie felt that John did *not* bounce back after their relationship ended as much as his brave front might suggest.

'I still worry for him more than I would ever dare tell him,' she told *Rolling Stone* in March 1974.

'I still have a lot of love for John. Let's face it, as far as I was concerned, it was *him* that stopped loving me. He constantly tested what limits of endurance I would go to. He just went one step too far. If he knew that I cared and worried so much about him, I think he'd play on it. There's no doubt about the fact that he hasn't really been a very happy man since I left him, I know that. Sure, I could make him happy tomorrow, and say, "Yeah, John, I'll come back to you." Then *I* would be miserable. I'm not that unselfish.'

How did Christine think John could cope with her new boyfriends?

'John can't handle Curry (Grant) too well, even though he's more at ease with other women around me than I am with men in front of him. But if I was the kind of girl who wandered in with a new boyfriend every week, enjoying my new-found freedom, I don't know how he could handle that. But I'm *proud* of having been John's wife. Maybe we don't feel the same about each other any more, but I wouldn't like to wipe that off the board.'

John McVie: 'Yeah, it still affects me. I'm still adjusting to the fact that it's not "John and Chris" any more. It goes up and down.'

McVie's quiet, laid back, non-pretentious attitude to life would occasionally make him feel inhibited.

'It's difficult to tell someone, "Yeah, I'm *this* kind of person." The *quiet* thing is fine. If I had anything that I thought was world shaking or profound, I'd say something. I really can't come up with anything on politics, the state of society, the relationship between music and society. It's just horseshit. I play bass.'

And how.

Lindsey was beginning to feel a lot more positive about his break up with Stevie. Christine, spending a lot of time with Nicks, felt that Stevie was occasionally finding it harder than him.

'Stevie and I spent a lot of time together. She was going through a bit of a hard time too because she was the one who axed it. Lindsey was pretty down about it for a while, then he just woke up one morning and said, "Fuck this, I don't want to be unhappy," and started getting some girlfriends together. Then *Stevie* couldn't handle it . . . !'

Lindsey Buckingham: 'I came back from the tour feeling really cleansed. All the things that had been happening between me and Stevie, and between John and Chris, mellowed into the situations as they are now. And it was important that I met a lot of beautiful women who I like a lot. Because, y'know, with the exception of one intervening summer, for the past ten years I've been tied up with just two ladies. Now here I am at twenty-six realising capabilities about myself, being a little more aggressive socially and having a good time.'

How did Lindsey cope with her new man?

'For Stevie, someone like Don Henley is good for her. It's strange. It's one thing to accept not being with someone and it's another to see them with someone else, especially someone like Don, right? I could see it coming, and I really thought it was going to burn me out, but it was really a good thing just to see her sitting with him. It actually made me happy. I thought there was something to fear but there wasn't.'

Lindsey felt that the whole situation had actually helped him. 'The whole break up has forced me to redefine my whole individuality — musically as well. I'm no longer thinking of Stevie and me as a duo. That thought used to freak me out, but now it's made me come back stronger, to be Lindsey Buckingham.'

Mick and Jenny Fleetwood were quietly struggling behind the scenes with their own marriage. But, sadly, things weren't going too well, in spite of the tremendous common interest they had in their two lovely daughters, Lucy and Amy. They had remarried in the autumn of 1976 following the divorce which almost immediately followed Mick's discovery of Jenny's adultery in 1973. The painstaking struggle continued, but within two years every member of Fleetwood Mac would be with a different partner. 'Rumours' might have been an enormous success for the band, richly deserved on artistic merit, but the emotions and angst which were responsible for its lengthy and troublesome birth had created reverberations which would continue for many months yet.

Before then, an important, nostalgic trip had to be made.

London was calling.

14 Back to Blighty

Fleetwood Mac had briefly returned to the UK after the move to Los Angeles in 1974. In October 1976 the band purportedly flew over to promote the album 'Fleetwood Mac' with a press call. But the real reason was to sign the final legal papers concerning their long-standing dispute with Clifford Davis. It had recently been settled out of court at terms agreed by both sets of protagonists. The sorry business following the 'fake' Fleetwood Mac tour of 1974 was finally over.

Ironically things even went wrong for part of the bid to promote the band during its short trip. During a lavish reception thrown by the UK arm of Warner Brothers, a film designed to show the band's exciting stage show was marred by poor sound quality and speeded up projection. Mick found it rather embarrassing. Typical of the ill luck that had dogged the band in Britain.

However in 1977 the band undertook their first tour of the British Isles for over six years. Oddly, the British members of the Mac were the *least* keen to come 'home'. In spite of their great success in the United States in the 1970s, Fleetwood Mac had long been unable to really crack it in the country where it all began – with Peter Green, Jeremy Spencer and Danny Kirwan. Albums which would shift 250,000 to 500,000 units in the US would be lucky to sell 4,000 to 5,000 copies in the UK. The sales of the singles told a similar story. Mick, John and Christine had completely settled themselves in the US, with homes, friends and careers, and had no wish to change things. Mick spoke to a *Sounds* reporter in England in April 1977.

'I think I can speak for Christine and John when I say that we wouldn't ever want to base ourselves in Britain in the future. Certainly not for financial reasons. There is not a healthy situation over here. Opportunities are far more available in the US.'

The first press call in the Holiday Inn, Birmingham was a little fraught. Christine and Curry were tired, but Chris was nevertheless moderately enthusiastic.

'We only got a few hours' sleep in the four days before we left and I feel really wasted. But it's nice to be back on the map. I hear "Rumours" has already sold 80,000 copies. That's great!'

John, however, wasn't in the mood for idle chatter during the call, and ended the evening by inexplicably hurling a glass of vodka and tonic in Lindsey's face. Lindsey oddly took no offence whatever at this gesture. John then retired with ill grace to bed after what had certainly been a long and tiring haul for the band.

The problem that always dogged Fleetwood Mac in England was the UK public's wish to wind back the clock to the time when Fleetwood Mac were a wonderful home-grown blues band. People found it hard to accept that the band could dramatically change its feel and style, as new and talented musicians provided fresh input. However Mick and John had never clung tenaciously to one particular type of music for the band but had always sought out innovative, creative and exciting musicians to join Fleetwood Mac when gaps occurred in the line-up. As long as those musicians were original and talented it didn't really matter that the band's musical ethos changed.

Mick: 'The success here in England is great, and I'm really pleased. But we are all worried about being labelled as the "Blues Band gone wrong". Stevie and Lindsey keep asking me what it's going to be like and I have to keep saying, "I don't know." We've been in a whole different world over in the States. Perhaps people will say, "What about Peter Green, then?" We hope not.'

Peter, nevertheless, wouldn't entirely go away. During the same afternoon Mick, wandering around Birmingham to see if he could find a 1966 Jensen to add to his impressive collection of cars (he did), popped into a music shop, only to find a young guitar player hammering out a Peter Green song!

Green did indeed surface during the band's visit. The Mac had previously met him during their brief October 1976 visit. They bumped into him again in the lobby of their hotel in 1977.

Christine: 'I didn't recognise him! He was fat and flabby and looked "slept in". He was carrying a big cassette machine blaring out disco music. I heard this voice say, "Hello, Chris." I turned round and saw this rotund little guy with a big beer gut and a pint in his hand. I couldn't believe it. I said, "Aren't you embarrassed?" "Naw," he said, "fuck it, what the hell." We gave him a room at the hotel for a few nights. He'd knock on your door, come in and just sit there on your bed, not saying anything. He wouldn't volunteer anything. He'd just sit there and laugh.'

The first Fleetwood Mac concert was a success, and augured well for the rest of the tour. The British fans were surprised and pleased to hear Peter's 'Oh Well' played with affection and power by the Mac. The song wasn't just included as a sop to the UK, however. Pre-'Rumours' material that the band remained fond of would often be included, and the Peter Green song would survive in the set for many more years. More importantly, the crowd loved all the contemporary Mac songs, and gave the band a deserved standing ovation.

Stevie said at the time, 'I think it was a success tonight, which doesn't mean to say I don't think we could have done better. But I really felt some love and some good energy, and I needed that because I don't like to lose and I don't like to fail.'

Stevie had certainly experienced a sense of failure at the end of her previous visit to the UK.

Backstage, the band were relieved and tired. Christine talked animatedly to her father, to whom she'd dedicated a song during the set. Stevie talked to the press.

'I felt like the very first night we played in El Paso, Texas. Nerved *out*! Christine was the most nervous, it being her home town, and she was making me nervous!'

Stevie's desire for the band to do well in the homeland of three-fifths of its members stemmed from a kind of loyalty.

'Tonight was a challenge, an ego challenge, which is healthy. We don't *need* England from a financial point of view. I didn't want to come! But we need to do well in England for our *hearts*. Because this is *home* for John, Mick and Christine. And if it's home for them, it's home for us too. It's our proxy home.'

It wasn't surprising that Nicks had not wanted to return to England after her 1976 visit.

'That was very bad. I just wanted to go home. Nobody was interested at all. The crowning glory was on the last day of interviews when I was sitting with John. This guy talked to John for a whole *hour*, and then he turned to me and said he was sorry but he didn't really have anything to ask me. I said, "Well, OK," and I walked out. I was so bummed out I got on a plane by myself and went home. I didn't really want to be in a place where nobody wanted me.'

This time round, however, the UK *did* want Fleetwood Mac and 'Rumours'. The tour was a success, and helped the singles, 'Go Your Own Way' and 'Don't Stop', leap into the UK top forty. 'Rumours' went on to sell extremely well in the UK, though the band were still not to enjoy the record success they experienced in the United States. The short, enjoyable tour over, the weary band flew home to contemplate the next move.

15 Consequences II

Normandy, France, 1978. Mick Fleetwood, weary like the rest of the members of Fleetwood Mac after their gruelling touring schedule following the 1977 release of their massive hit album 'Rumours', was visiting his mother for a brief holiday. He stayed in a small hotel overlooking the town square. One morning, suffering a monumental hangover, Mick's befuddled senses were dragged from sleep by the sound of music coming from the square.

'I was in a room in the town square with a horrific hangover, and I was woken up by the sound of the local brass band that relentlessly went round and round the square. As the day went on, *they* got drunker and drunker. But one thing was apparent. *Everyone* followed the brass band around the town, and I thought, "What a good idea!" ' The idea would remain with him.

Months earlier, during that relentless post-'Rumours' tour, Mick had talked to *Rolling Stone*:

'We'll start recording when we finish this tour, probably about March. Everybody's already got quite a lot of material loosely together. Stevie's always got tons and tons of stuff. She writes songs all the time. So basically, we're gonna get down and do some very extensive rehearsals before we go into studios this time and pick material that we feel is strong. You never can tell. Sometimes things that you think are gonna turn out great in the studio don't. And on a very loose level, we're thinking about doing a double studio LP. We feel that we've got enough material. If there's any filler, then we wouldn't dream of doing it. But that's an exciting thing at least to attempt. It stimulates everyone and it's a challenge. You don't just knock out another album. It's like a real commitment.'

Mick could hardly have known just what a commitment the recording of the follow up album to the arguably unfollowable 'Rumours' would become.

Naturally, the more success any band receives in the commercial marketplace, the more pressure their record company exerts upon them to produce a new 'piece of product' (the term commonly used by the music business moguls hints very strongly at the way *they* see the work produced by musicians). And 'Rumours' was a roller-runaway, monster, mega commercial success. Sales neared eighteen million copies, and had by no means stopped.

So, paradoxically, the pressure was on. The band had to come up once again with the goods. Lindsey, responsible for much of the success of 'Rumours', with his partner Stevie, felt anxious. He didn't want the band to be forced into producing a kind of 'Rumours II'.

'One of the things I've always tried to do is to go "against the grain" of what the group as a whole represented at a given point of time. When "Rumours" was running rampant, with sales of sixteen million, I had a *real* problem with that scene. Because to me, you know, the way I felt, "yes, it's a good album. It's got a lot of good things about it but . . . ?" '

Lindsey felt that the album's reputation was almost becoming unhealthy.

'It seemed to me at some point that there was a major discrepancy between what the work was, and what was going on outside of that. And I found that to be sort of dangerous ground. You know, Michael Jackson land. You're walking on *thin ice* as far as how you define yourself and what you are and what is *expected* of you after that!'

Dangerous ground and thin ice were familiar territory for the members of Fleetwood Mac. If the follow up to 'Rumours' would be recorded by Buckingham, Nicks, Fleetwood and the McVies, it would be the first time in the band's history that a particular line up had produced three albums in a row. None before had lasted long enough in Fleetwood Mac's eleven-year history. They had survived 'Rumours' by the skin of their collective teeth, though had hardly emerged unscathed. Relationships were crashing, blood and tears were being copiously spilt, and band members locked in post-split-up misery were occasionally hardly communicating at all. Long-distance touring had followed the 'Rumours' release. But in 1978 the band finally had a few months to catch its breath before turning to the next project.

However in 1978 the personal fortunes of four of the band members began to change for the better. Lindsey met beautiful model Carol Ann Harris and began a happy relationship with her which would last six years. He had finally got over his traumatic split with Stevie, which had been followed by a brief 'bachelor boy' lifestyle during which he'd enjoyed his new-found freedom. Protective of Carol, Lindsey had learnt the importance of respecting his partner's individuality and space.

'She doesn't much tour with the band. I want to give Carol the chance to express herself through her modelling without tearing too much from our relationship.'

She would nevertheless occasionally join the band on the road in future years.

Christine and John had bowed to the inevitable and divorced, having separated as partners some time previously. John moved out of the house to live on his forty-foot luxury ketch for a while, and dated various girls. Still distantly lusting after Linda Rondstadt, and hearing that Fleetwood Mac and Linda would be at the same rock awards ceremony the previous year, John had rushed out and bought a beautiful crushed velvet suit to impress her, but, alas, she hadn't shown up.

However, luck was eventually to be on his side. He began a serious relationship with Julie Reubens, whom he met through some business connections. Their friendship changed into romance, and finally love. The couple married at a star-studded wedding in 1978. Mick Fleetwood was naturally chosen to be John's best man, and guests included Ronnie Wood from the Stones, old Bluesbreakers boss John Mayall, and various family members. Ex-Fleetwood Mac guitarist Bob Welch, and even Peter Green showed up. Christine McVie and Stevie were happy to see John settled. Christine noticed an immediate change for the better in John's personality.

'Oh yes, John has mellowed since marrying Julie. He's become a gentle person.' She nevertheless found it just a little odd that he asked to borrow *her* house in which to perform and celebrate the happy deed! John and Julie would subsequently divide their time between their Beverly Hills home and John's sixty-three-foot sloop.

Christine herself had ended her relationship with Curry Grant, the lighting technician with whom she'd been enjoying a protracted fling. Soon after her divorce she met the mercurial Dennis Wilson, legendary drummer with the iconoclastic sixties heroes, the Beach Boys. The relationship would last three years during which time life with Dennis, a larger than life figure, would never be boring. They split their time between Christine's house and Dennis's sixty-eight-foot boat moored at Marina Del Rey. Marriage was discussed but children were ruled out.

Dennis: 'I'm thirty-six years old and my lifestyle is pretty much settled as far as sacrificing and accommodating myself to children.'

Christine: 'Dennis lived life with such a raw passion that he wanted to do everything. It was as if he was always trying to cram ten pounds into an eight-pound bag. He awakened things in me I'd have been scared to experience and made me feel the extremes of every emotion.'

Dennis Wilson introduced Christine to the excitement and exhilaration of speedboating and water-skiing, and wrecked McVie's Rolls-Royce so many times that it was finally written off. He would not tour with Christine, however.

'It didn't suit his personality to be a guest, to have to say, "Oh, I'm with the piano player." '

A creature of impulse, Dennis once dug and planted a heart-shaped plot in their front garden, filling the space with red roses as a birthday surprise.

'He was an impulsive, passionate man: a multifaceted jewel,' Christine would say after their split three years later. 'I loved him very much. Let's just say he was too radical for me, a total extremist. I couldn't keep up with the pace. All the time I was with him he was burning the candle at both ends . . . *and* in the middle.'

Dennis would sadly die by drowning as the result of a boating accident some years later.

Life hadn't been easy for Mick Fleetwood. Democratically elected by the other members of the band to be Fleetwood Mac's own guidance counsellor and social worker, he had also been coping with his own problems. Sadly, after twelve years of marriage, interrupted by the brief 1973 divorce, the relationship seemed to be finally over.

'Yes,' Mick said in late 1979, 'the second split seems permanent, but luckily we get on well.'

Jenny obtained custody of Lucy and Amy, and returned to her native England with them. However Mick would be able to see the children quite freely during the holidays, although of course that wouldn't be quite the same.

'I quite miss the fact that I can't be a father. I happen to be one of those men who adores that thing of "all right, kids, let's go and do something *now*".'

As if marital difficulties weren't enough to contend with during this period, Mick discovered that he had a medical problem.

'I had been feeling burnt out. My eyes were going wild. I started drinking like a fish, and I'd hyperventilate while talking.'

His doctor suggested that the problem might be psychological rather than physical. After all, Mick had already packed more drama into his short life than most people do in a lifetime. However Mick found the suggestion hard to accept.

'My ego couldn't accept the fact that I was going round the twist. But I was manic-depressive. One minute I'd be happily eating some ice cream, and the next I'd be convinced I was going to die from a brain tumour. I had eighteen months of hell.'

Luckily for Fleetwood the problem was diagnosed. It was not a psychological trauma at all. Mick was suffering from a relatively mild form of diabetes. Once an appropriate diet was devised which would meet his body's complex sugar requirements, he recovered. So did his emotional fortunes. He met attractive and intelligent model Sara Recor.

'Bless her – she was there to hold my hand and look after me.'

Interestingly, Lindsey had also recently discovered that he had a medical problem. During the 1978 tour Buckingham blacked out in the shower of his hotel room. He was rushed to hospital and given all kinds of tests. It was discovered that he had a mild form of epilepsy, now quite under control through mild drug dosage.

The fifth member of the Mac was more cautious about hurling herself into a new affair of the heart. Stevie was enjoying her relationship with the Eagles' Don Henley, but didn't feel ready to settle into a tight, cosy, one-to-one relationship. Subsequently she found herself rather lonely on tour.

'I'm the only one in the band that's on their own! There's three ladies that design my clothes, and I bring one of them along with me. She'd keep me from going crazy because I'd have to have someone to talk to after gigs. Everyone else would hit the bar, but I can't do that, my health can't stand it. So Christy and me, we'd just go back and order tea. She meditates and talks to her old man on the phone and I'd read. There was the presence of someone being there, so it's very serene. We were like two nuns doing our thing, and she became one more member of the band. The band is all there is room for in my life. It's just as well. Security is so tight that no one can get within ten feet. I hardly ever meet any new men.'

Stevie even changed her home because of her disillusionment with her current lifestyle. Nicks' large Tudor-style house above Sunset Boulevard was put on the market because it attracted hangers-on who overstayed their welcome.

'Any man I ever went out with called the place "Fantasy Land". I won't always be in a rock band, and I don't want to come off this absolutely helpless.'

Stevie moved into a modest condominium instead. Displaying her occasional tendency to bite the hand that fed her, Stevie said at the time, 'Some people thrive on being a rock star. I *hate* it. I don't like being waited on all the time, people following me around saying,

"Let me do this, let me do that." I don't need doctors, nurses and babysitters. I need love.'

She would find it. Of a sort. Marriage *was* awaiting Stevie in the future. But it would be a shortlived and misadvised affair.

The Mac, with at least some of the pressures off them at last, turned to the job in hand. The next album.

And it had to be a *killer*!

Peter Green, the founding father of Fleetwood Mac. (Harry Goodwin)

Fleetwood Mac's first gig at the Windsor Jazz & Blues Festival, 1967; left to right: Peter Green, Jeremy Spencer, Mick Fleetwood and Bob Brunning. (Max Browne/Dave Peabody)

The Mac become a quintet: Fleetwood, Green, John McVie, Danny Kirwan and Jeremy Spencer. (Harry Goodwin)

Exit Peter Green, the 1970 quartet: Jeremy Spencer, John McVie,
Danny Kirwan and Mick Fleetwood. (Harry Goodwin)

Christine McVie joins the band: Danny Kirwan, Jeremy Spencer,
Christine McVie, John McVie and Mick Fleetwood. (LFI)

The 1972-74 band: Danny Kirwan, Bob Welch, Mick Fleetwood,
Christine McVie and John McVie. (LFI)

The California Fleetwood Mac of the mid-Seventies: Christine McVie, Mick Fleetwood,
John McVie, Stevie Nicks and Lindsey Buckingham. (Barry Plummer)

Christine McVie, Lindsey Buckingham, Stevie Nicks,
Mick Fleetwood and John McVie. (Barry Plummer)

Christine and Stevie. (Barry Plummer/LFI)

Bob Brunning and Mick Fleetwood recreate the Mac's original rhythm section in a north London pub, 1984. (Bob Brunning)

The 1987 Fleetwood Mac with Rick Vito and Billy Burnette: Vito, Christine McVie,
Mick Fleetwood, Stevie Nicks, Burnette and John McVie. (LFI)

The reformed *Rumours* era line-up in 1997: Mick, Stevie, John, Christine and Lindsey. (LFI)

Back from the wilderness: Peter Green in 1997. (Brian Rasic/Rex)

16 Tusk

'Rumours' was certainly a hard act to follow. As the band prepared to record its all-important follow-up album, 'Rumours' was still selling by the truck load. The album would shortly become the best selling LP of *all* time, a record it would hold until Michael Jackson's 'Thriller' came along. Warner Brothers were both expectant and anxious. What would Fleetwood Mac pull out of the hat to follow such a phenomenal success?

Mick had already decided that the new album would be a double. After all, the band contained three talented and prolific writers, all of whom naturally wanted to see their songs produced and recorded. A single album would allow Nicks, Buckingham and McVie on average just four tracks each, and all three writers had many more compositions which they would like out on release. Clearly, however, such a project would be lengthy and thus costly, if the time it took to record the two sides of 'Rumours' was anything to go by.

Fleetwood donned his manager's hat and came up with a radical solution. Surely it made sense to buy their own studio, rather than incur the massive hourly costs that an inevitably lengthy period of recording would entail? After the initial outlay the band could relax, free from the insidious and niggling pressures of the hourly-based studio bill ticking away. He went along to Warner Brothers to float the idea. The cautious executives immediately sunk this plan with a very large bucket of cold water. Uncharacteristically, Mick backed down, failing to follow his usually reliable convictions. It was a rare slip for the Fleetwood/McVie managed band. If he had followed his instinct Fleetwood Mac would have ended up with a self-owned studio *and* a double album.

Mick: 'I told the group we should just buy the entire studio. And sure enough we could have done it easily.'

An observer would later wryly comment that they could have bought *Cleveland* for what they paid in studio costs. But they didn't follow Mick's advice. Fleetwood Mac joined Richard Dashut and

Ken Caillat in the Village Recorder Studios to begin the mammoth and costly task of recording the new double album. The name for the project was soon selected. Mick would coyly claim that, one, the title stemmed from the 'sound' of the song which would eventually become the title track and first single from the album, and two, it sounded like a 'herd of elephants'. John McVie earnestly attributed it to the band's enduring interest in ecology and wild life. The truth was a little more bizarre, and was directly connected with Mick's long-time habit of emphasising his own genitals by means of a couple of wooden balls hanging from his crutch. 'Tusk' was his own slang word for his male member.

Work on the album progressed. An early track to be produced was 'Tusk' itself. Mick recalled the idea which had struck him back in France when he was listening to the local brass band through the fog of his ghastly hangover. With typical panache, Fleetwood decided to combine his idea of using a brass band with a riff which he and Buckingham played during the band's lengthy soundchecks. The brief guitar and drum riff pattern Mick and Lindsey punched out through Fleetwood Mac's vast PA system to aid their mixing engineers to balance the sound stuck in Mick's head. A marching band was required. It would have been easy enough to record the track in the Village Recorder studios but, typically, Fleetwood Mac decided to do it the hard way.

Wally Heider's mobile recording unit was hauled over to the Dodgers' baseball stadium, and no less than 112 members of the University of Southern California Trojan marching brass band were recorded live. Their contribution was painstakingly added to a studio concoction. The original drum riff from the soundcheck repertoire eventually found its way on to another song which never got completed. Instead, Lindsey Buckingham and co-producer Richard Dashut took a twenty-second section of the drum track, speeded it up, played around with it, and repeated it over and over again to form the heart of the track. Lindsey remembers that the short drum section which formed the core of the song occupied a piece of recording tape long enough to go round the studio control room about twenty times.

Suitably doctored, dubbed and edited, the song 'Tusk' was completed. Mick was enthusiastic about it and ambitiously planned a novel future gimmick for the band's performances.

'I was hoping to invite the local brass marching band out of *every* town we played in all over the world to come out and play the song with us. It would engender a really warm feeling for the town, and would create a good rapport between us and the audience if they knew that *their* local band was playing.'

It was a nice idea, but it never came off. The video later produced by the band to promote 'Tusk' also had a novel touch. It featured a cardboard bass player.

John McVie: 'We had the idea that using the USL brass band with Fleetwood Mac would make a good promotional film. Except that I was 120 miles out to sea on the way to Tahiti in my boat at the time. So they had to use a six-foot cardboard cut-out of me for the filming. I saw the video when I got back and thought it worked very well. Very appropriate!'

And symbolic. John McVie, ever the least patient Mac member in the recording studios, had insisted on recording his bass parts very early in the proceedings, and had then sailed off leaving the rest of the band to work on the album's endless overdubs, vocal parts, mixing and editing tasks. Costs were rising by the day. Creativity did not come cheap and Fleetwood Mac's new-found wealth encouraged extravagance.

Christine McVie: 'Recording "Tusk" was quite absurd. The studio contract rider for refreshments was like a telephone directory: exotic food delivered to the recording studio, crates of champagne – the very best, obviously, with no thought of what it cost. Stupid, really stupid. Somebody once said that with the money we spent on champagne in *one* night, *they* could have made an entire album, and it's probably true!'

Mick Fleetwood, though acknowledging that there were occasional band excesses, would later justify the expense.

'It was our money, money we spent on *artistry*, if you like. If someone wants to call it an indulgence, well, I don't consider it such. It would have been if we had been sitting around farting down a microphone, but not if you worked in the way we have always done, in various states of mind. There was *always* a sense of purpose and *work*. Even when we were pretty, er, well, *loaded*!'

Stories abounded. It was rumoured that the studio would be booked for days on end with little music being produced and much time being wasted. Fleetwood saw it differently.

'We've *never* wasted huge amounts of time when recording. Don't get me wrong. You are not clocking in and clocking out. You can't just say, "Uh oh, it's ten o'clock, I'm off." If you are finishing off a track, you stay up until you get it! It took *that* amount of time because *that's* what we chose to do. We were very lucky to be able to do it. If we had wanted to be really chintzy, we would have gone and made an album for about a hundred thousand dollars, and pocketed the rest of our advance. I don't ever consider that we wasted time in the studio. We spent our advance money, which we were very lucky to have. I feel that putting that money back into your craft and spending the amount of time which we do in the studio is our business. If that is indulgence then it is an indulgence in the healthy sense of the word as far as I'm concerned.'

Work continued on the album. A leading figure was emerging within the Mac as far as 'Tusk' was concerned: Lindsey Buckingham. He dominated the project. Not only had he written almost half the material, he also produced much of it too. He spent months working quite alone both at the Village Recorder and in his own crude basement apartment studio. His maverick, loner approach to 'Tusk' caused anxieties and some bitterness within the band.

Christine McVie: 'At that point, Lindsey was starting to get very experimental in his own studio and was veering a little left of centre. He had already decided that he wanted to make a solo record. In order to keep him within the fold we all said, "Well, look, let him do his experimenting and incorporate it in the album somehow." That's how in essence it came to be a double album. There was all this experimentation flying around, especially from Lindsey's point of view.'

Certainly some of Lindsey's ideas were off the wall. He became obsessed with the project. His elder brother had won a silver medal in the 1968 Olympics, and Buckingham remembers being awed by his strict routine. 'He'd get up at six in the morning, work out, go to school, work out till dinner, go to sleep and start all over again.'

Buckingham's routine when working on 'Tusk' was not dissimilar. He would get up early, work on the tapes at home before going off to the Village Recorder to carry on through the afternoon, evening and night.

'I'd come out of my basement studio after about six hours and Carol would be sitting in the living-room watching TV or something, and I just wouldn't have much to say. My mind would be *racing* with the "Tusk" songs.'

Several of his 'Tusk' contributions were recorded almost entirely in his crude basement studio, with Lindsey playing all the instruments, including Kleenex-box drums.

'Oh yes, we broke down a few barriers at the time! "The Ledge" was crazy. There are about four or five vocal tracks on it which are not particularly tight. All of them were sung in my bathroom. I stuck the mike on the floor and did them down on my knees. I did a *lot* of the vocals like that, because I liked it. Because it sounded weird!'

Although the recording costs incurred during Lindsey's bathroom squats must have been relatively small, the bills nevertheless mounted. Lindsey, feeling increasingly responsible and anxious, would later go on the defensive.

' "Rumours" took *longer* to make than "Tusk". The reason that "Tusk" cost so much was that we happened to be at a studio that was charging a *hell* of a lot of money. It took ten months to make "Tusk". "Rumours" took the same amount of time for *half* the amount of tracks. There's no denying what it cost, but I think it's been taken just a little bit out of context.'

The album briefly featured a guest guitarist from the band's illustrious past. On 'Brown Eyes', one of Christine's songs, could be heard Peter Green.

Mick Fleetwood: 'That's right. He plays literally about eight notes at the end of one of Chris's songs. He just wandered into the studio while the track was being done.'

Recording dragged on. Warner Brothers started to become nervous. They felt that the delay between 'Rumours' and its successor was too great. The record company moguls had a brilliant plan. The first LP of the double album set should be released as soon as it was completed. That idea was firmly rejected by the band. So was a heavyweight, but dumb advertising campaign dreamed up to publicise 'Tusk' by a sharp New York agency presented by Warners to Fleetwood Mac.

Finally 'Tusk' was completed. Christine and Stevie's contributions remained faithful to their clearly-defined styles. They mixed a little uneasily with Lindsey's unusual and experimental tracks. The pot-pourri very much illustrated the rather fragmented approach which the whole band had adopted to the production of the double album. Christine would darkly describe it as a 'non-communal rotation system'. Warners, eager, yet unsure about the package they'd been handed, pushed out 'Tusk' as a single in September 1979 to herald the album.

Stan Corwyn, surely representing the views of the Warner Brothers' executives rather than Fleetwood Mac, said at the time, 'They are understandably nervous about greeting the public with it. It's not often that a group has a ten-million unit album to follow up on. It's become more of a media event than necessary. So while a hysterical start may be helpful, we'll know within a month what our sales figures are. The campaign will be modestly keyed. All we are saying to the public is, "Are you aware this is here?" '

'This' was here in competition with some heavy acts. Blondie, the Police, Abba, Earth Wind and Fire, Art Garfunkel, Gloria Gaynor and Donna Summer were all achieving high chart placements.

The album had cost a staggering $1 million to produce. Was it worth it? The band and Warner Brothers nervously awaited reaction from the media.

Lindsey remained defiant: 'My reaction to following up "Rumour" was to instigate the "Tusk" album which was like *total* flip-flop on what *that* album had been. It was a far softer, commercial thing, and it was not at all well received by Warner Brothers at that time. There was a funny story about all the executives listening to it and seeing their Christmas bonuses flying out of the window, which I thought was a great equation, you know! But I think that I've always been the sort of "wild card" in the group. I am not shackled by being perceived as any *one* thing, as other members of the group might be.'

Out came the single. The ever-familiar Fleetwood Mac curse again descended. Discovering extraneous surface noise on some of the 'Tusk' singles, Warner Brothers were forced to recall the entire initial shipment. Nevertheless, after a period of corporate breath-holding, the single nudged its way into the top ten. October 1979 saw the long awaited release of the double album, straight on to a somewhat depressed market. Retailers, caught in a sales slump, had awaited it eagerly, licking their lips in anticipation of a repeat of the till-jangling success of 'Rumours'. They were disappointed. It sold well, but not spectacularly. Neither the single nor the album was played as much as 'Rumours' material on the all-important AM Radio stations, and clearly there was not to be an immediate repeat of the runaway success of its predecessor (which was still selling a healthy 20,000 copies a week).

Lindsey spoke to the press just before the release of the second single to be culled from the album: 'In a way, this is a difficult time for us as a band. People are still making their minds up about the album. That goes for radio stations too. It has only been out a few weeks and most people just haven't heard a lot of it on the radio. I think that when we put out another single or two they will respond to what we've done.'

Mick Fleetwood had mixed feelings.

'We couldn't help but know what was going on out there, outside the studio, but that was Warner Brothers' problem, not ours. We tried to isolate ourselves from those matters as much as possible. The record company *did* point out the state of the economy and tell us how much more difficult it would be to sell a double album than a single album. But they didn't try to get us to change our mind about doing a double album. They just wanted to make sure we were aware of the situation, which was proper.'

He felt that Warner Brothers had been honest with them.

'I am sure what they said was true. We might have hurt ourselves commercially by sticking with the decision to do a double album. "Tusk" may not sell as many copies as "Rumours" but we are prepared to accept that. The important thing to us was that we should be pleased with the album. And we are.'

Lindsey felt in retrospect that Fleetwood Mac might have misjudged the level of conservatism to be found within their record-buying fans: 'It's been a strain for me personally in that I can't believe in myself as much as when I put the album out. I was just busting out to do something that I felt had a little more depth to it, something that didn't have a lead guitar solo in it like every other song you ever hear. But then over a period of time you realise that people aren't really getting the message. You wonder whether you've been deluding yourself or what, especially when the rest of the band start telling you that it's maybe time to get back to the standard format.'

However more trouble was looming. The next blow came with the release of the second single from the album, Stevie's haunting 'Sara', one of her five songs on 'Tusk'. It had been written about her old flatmate, Sara Recor, now Mick Fleetwood's new flame, and later his wife.

Almost immediately after the release of 'Sara', a woman living in Grand Rapids, Michigan commenced court proceedings in order to sue Nicks for plagiarism. She announced that *she* had written it, not Stevie. She claimed that she had sent a photocopy of her lyrics to Warner Brothers in 1978. Despite the fact that Stevie Nicks had numerous witnesses willing to testify on her behalf, the legal hassles continued for months. Stevie was able to produce a crude demo she had cut of the song way back in July 1978. In 1981 the claimant's lawyers finally conceded that their client was wrong, but the whole affair had angered Stevie.

'There *were* some great similarities in the lyrics, and I never said she didn't write the words she wrote. Most people trying that one on think that the other party will settle out of court, but *she* picked the wrong songwriter! To call me a thief about my *first* love, my songs, that's going too far.'

Amid the controversy 'Sara' was released, and gave the band another hit single. Sales of 'Tusk' and the two singles inched upwards. Two subsequent singles, 'Think About Me' and 'Funny', would just about scrape into the top twenty. Oddly, reversing the usual pattern, 'Tusk' did better in the UK than in the US, reaching number two in the British charts as opposed to number eighteen in America. 'Sara' reverted to type, reaching number seven in the US compared to number thirty-seven in the UK. 'Think About Me' scraped into the US charts at a high of twenty, not showing up at all in Great Britain's record charts. 'Tusk' had been very much Lindsey's baby, and compared to 'Rumours', it was a turkey. If anything, this was to bring the band closer to breaking up than all the previous fractured personal relationships had done. The band were very disappointed in the public's reaction to the follow up to 'Rumours' and blamed Lindsey for going too far in the opposite direction with his 'Tusk' input.

Stevie: 'Lindsey is *absolutely* against duplicating anything. So if he even *thinks* that people are gonna think he's trying to duplicate something he will go *so* far the other way. So the best thing to do with Lindsey is not to even remind him, so that he doesn't get too radical. Cause, he's one of those men, he'll get *totally* radical, you know, he'd say, "I'm not going to do anything *like* the last one, for my own cultural growth and the pursuit of art . . . !" '

Though the band had been behind him during the recording of the project, they did not conceal their displeasure as sales reports began to filter back to the Mac.

Lindsey: 'Oddly enough, no one in the band really made a judgement about it until it became apparent that it wasn't going to sell sixteen million copies.' Lindsey additionally noted, 'It was a double album and certainly confounded everyone's expectations – which is what it was meant to do. Once it became apparent that it wasn't going to be a massive commercial success, then the band members . . . Mick would say to me, "Well, we went too far, you blew it." And it was very hurtful. We were out on the road and I'm going, "Oh, my God, how am I gonna react to this?" '

By April 1980 the awful truth finally dawned. 'Tusk' was a comparative failure.

After all, it had only sold five million copies.

17 Live!

As usual, the new album needed to be promoted. And, as usual, the tour would be a mammoth affair. Messrs Fleetwood, Buckingham, Nicks and the McVies, joined by Ray Lindsey (guitar), Tony Todaro (percussion) and Jeffrey Sova (keyboards) all doubling as road crew members, rehearsed for six weeks in September 1979. On October 27th the band performed the first of no less than 113 concerts. The tour would last very nearly a year, and take Fleetwood Mac all over the world. It is worth reproducing in full the 'Tusk' itinerary, if only to understand and comprehend the kind of trek Fleetwood Mac were prepared to undertake to promote and sell their wares.

October 1979
26 Pocatello, Id. – Mini Dome
27 Ogden, Ut. – Dee Events Centre
28 Salt Lake City, Ut. – Salt Palace
31 Denver Co. – McNichol's Sports Arena

November 1979
1 Denver Co. – McNichol's Sports Arena
2 Albuquerque, N.M. – Tingley Coliseum
5 St Louis, Mo. – Checker Dome
6 St Louis, Mo. – Checker Dome
7 Cincinnati, Oh. – Riverfront Coliseum
10 New Haven, Ct. – Veterans Memorial Coliseum
11 Uniondale, NY – Nassau Veterans Mem. Col.
12 Uniondale, NY – Nassau Veterans Mem. Col.
15 New York, NY – Madison Square Garden
16 New York, NY – Madison Square Garden
17 Boston, Ma. – Boston Gardens
20 Rochester, NY – War Memorial

21 Philadelphia, Pa. –
    The Spectrum
22 Providence, RI –
    Civic Centre
25 Largo, Md. – Capital
    Center
26 Pittsburgh, Pa. –
    Civic Arena
29 Ann Arbor, Mi. –
    Crisler Arena
30 Champaign, Il. –
    Assembly Hall

December 1979
 1 Cedar Falls, Ia. –
    Uni-Dome
 4 Los Angeles, Ca. –
    The Forum
 5 Los Angeles, Ca. –
    The Forum
 6 Los Angeles, Ca. –
    The Forum
 9 San Diego, Ca. –
    Sports Arena
10 Los Angeles, Ca. –
    The Forum
11 Los Angeles, Ca. –
    The Forum
14 San Francisco, Ca. –
    Cow Palace
15 San Francisco, Ca. –
    Cow Palace
16 San Francisco, Ca. –
    Cow Palace

February 1980
 3 Tokyo, Japan –
    Budokan
 4 Tokyo, Japan –
    Budokan
 5 Tokyo, Japan –
    Budokan

 8 Kyoto, Japan –
    Kaikan
 9 Gifu, Japan – Shimin
    Kaikan
11 Sapporo, Japan –
    Kuseinenkin
    Hall
13 Yokohama, Japan –
    Kenmin Hall
14 Sendai, Japan –
    Sports Center
16 Osaka, Japan –
    Festival Hall
17 Osaka, Japan –
    Festival Hall
21 Perth, Australia –
    Entertainment
    Centre
22 Perth, Australia –
    Entertainment
    Centre
25 Adelaide, Australia
    – Tennis Stadium
27 Sydney, Australia –
    Hordern Pavilion
28 Sydney, Australia –
    Hordern Pavilion

March 1980
 1 Melbourne,
    Australia –
    Festival Hall
 2 Melbourne,
    Australia –
    Festival Hall
 3 Melbourne,
    Australia –
    Festival Hall
 6 Brisbane, Australia –
    Festival Hall
 7 Brisbane, Australia –
    Festival Hall

8 Brisbane, Australia –
Festival Hall
11 Melbourne,
Australia –
Festival Hall
12 Melbourne,
Australia –
Festival Hall
15 Sydney, Australia –
Hordern
Pavilion
16 Sydney, Australia –
Hordern
Pavilion
17 Sydney, Australia –
Hordern
Pavilion
20 Wellington, NZ –
Athletic Park
22 Auckland, NZ –
Western Springs
27 Honolulu, Hi. –
Neil Blaisdell
Center (HIC)
28 Honolulu, Hi. –
Neil Blaisdell
Center (HIC)
29 Honolulu, Hi. –
Neil Blaisdell
Center (HIC)

April 1980
30 Portland, Or. –
Coliseum

May 1980
1 Seattle, Wa. – Hec
Edmunson Pavilion
2 Vancouver, BC –
PNE Coliseum
5 Edmonton, Canada
– Coliseum

6 Edmonton, Canada
– Coliseum
9 Minneapolis, Mn. –
Met Center
10 Minneapolis, Mn. –
Met Center
11 Madison, Wi. – Dane
County Arena
14 Chicago, Il. –
Rosemont Horizon
15 Chicago, Il. –
Rosemont Horizon
16 Indianapolis, In. –
Market Square
Arena
19 Buffalo, NY –
Municipal
Auditorium
20 Richfield, Oh. –
Richfield Coliseum
21 Richfield, Oh. –
Richfield Coliseum
23 Detroit, Mi. –
Joe Louis Arena
24 Detroit, Mi. –
Joe Louis Arena

June 1980
1 Munich, Germany –
Olympic Horse
Riding Stadium
3 Bremen, Germany –
Stadhalle
4 Cologne, Germany –
Sportshalle
8 Frankfurt, Germany
– Betzenburg
Stadium
9 Zurich, Switzerland
– Hallenstadion
Zurich

12 Brussels, Belgium –
Forest National
13 Rotterdam,
Holland – Ahoy
14 Paris, France – Palais
de Sport
16 Stafford, England –
Bingley Hall
17 Stafford, England –
Bingley Hall
20 London, England –
Wembley Arena
21 London, England –
Wembley Arena
22 London, England –
Wembley Arena
25 London, England –
Wembley Arena
26 London, England –
Wembley Arena
27 London, England –
Wembley Arena

August 1980
5 Lakeland, Fl. – Civic
Center
6 Miami, Fl. –
Sportatorium
8 Atlanta, Ga. –
Omni
11 Mobile, Al. –
Municipal
Auditorium

12 Birmingham, Al. –
Jefferson Civic
Center Coliseum
13 Baton Rouge, La. –
Riverside
Centroplex
16 Dallas, Tx. Reunion
Arena
17 San Antonio, Tx. –
Convention Center
Arena
18 Houston, Tx. – The
Summit
21 Omaha, Nb. – Civic
Auditorium
22 Oklahoma City,
Ok. – Myriad
23 Wichita, Ks. –
Kansas Coliseum
24 Kansas City, Mo. –
Kemper Arena
27 Las Cruces, NM –
Pan Am Center
28 Tucson, Az. –
McKale Center
29 Phoenix, Az. –
Compton Terrace
31 Los Angeles, Ca. –
Hollywood Bowl

September 1980
1 Los Angeles, Ca. –
Hollywood Bowl

The crew involved in such a jaunt was very large. The entourage included karate black belt bodyguards, masseurs, make-up artists, drum, guitar technicians, personal secretaries, catering manager, lighting and sound engineers, road crew and so on. The tour manager for this epic trip was one John Courage, a charming Londoner with lengthy Fleetwood Mac connections who would later play an even more important role in the band's set up. The lighting director for the tour was Curry Grant, Christine's friend. All twenty-six members of the Fleetwood Mac Flying Circus worked and played hard, and the world tour was by and large a great success. However, Fleetwood Mac, never afraid of a challenge, took a chance on the tour. They decided to include no less than nine new songs from 'Tusk' in the band's repertoire. Because fans respond to the familiar, there was a real risk that the momentum of the show could be lost by including more than two or three completely new songs in a set. Buckingham admitted that the large number of new tunes had cut into audience response on early tour dates, but he defended the practice.

'It would be easier for us to get a quick audience response. If we wanted more "mania" out there, we could stick in "Never Going Back" instead of "Save Me A Place" or "Don't Stop" instead of "Over and Over". We could also have made the show more up-tempo. But I think audiences will appreciate the freshness of what we are doing. We can't allow ourselves to stay in the "Rumours" framework on stage any more than we could in the studio. It has been *three years* since then. We've all gone through a lot of new experiences and influences.'

The tour was not only seen as an opportunity to present Fleetwood Mac's new material to the great American public, it also presented the band with an opportunity to finish a project it had started way back in 1977. The production of a truly 'live' album would surely demonstrate the band's great strength as an exciting and entertaining concert attraction. Richard Dashut, the recording engineer who had been involved with his colleague Ken Caillat on the production of both 'Rumours' and 'Tusk', had had very strong feelings in 1977 about such a project.

'We will *not* do a "live" album because we believe that "live" music and studio sound are two different things. I personally do not *like* "live" albums. I would rather go to a concert and *feel* it rather than hear a recording of it.'

He would change his mind.

Fleetwood Mac were hardly strangers to live recordings. Of course, bootleggers had done that job for them many, many times over the years. The first of many such recordings must have been the one which led to your author receiving a cassette tape in 1985 of the entire one and a half hour set recorded at the band's second *ever* gig, at the Marquee Club, back in 1967.

The following year Fleetwood Mac taped one of the many BBC Radio One shows they would record. The band comprised Green, Kirwan, Spencer, McVie and Fleetwood, and all five members were on blisteringly good form. The session included 'Rattlesnake Shake',

'Tiger' (one of Jeremy Spencer's rock 'n' roll parodies) and 'Green Manalishi'. An enterprising bootlegger carefully linked his tape recorder to his FM tuner and one side of 'Merely A Portmanteau' was captured for posterity. The other side of the bootleg album was badly recorded two years later in 1970 at the tail end of a Fleetwood Mac concert, and was truly dreadful. Wimpish, out of tune recordings of songs from 'Kiln House' featuring a newly Green-less Fleetwood Mac, it included also a stupefyingly boring nineteen-minute version of 'Tell Me All The Things You Do'. The package added up to a very forgettable mixed bag. Released very much against the band's wishes in 1975 on Kornyphonic Records, 'Portmanteau' is a must only for die-hard fans of the original Mac line up.

A far better live recording of Fleetwood Mac was made in 1970. Dicky Dawson, who worked for the band, used a professional mobile recording unit to record three Fleetwood Mac concerts, which featured such never-released numbers as 'Jumping At Shadows' and 'Only You' plus a stunning version of 'Green Manalishi' sung by Peter Green. This set of recordings was eventually released on an album titled 'Fleetwood Mac Live At The Boston Tea Party', once again without the band's approval. Recordings of various US radio shows could also be found (at a high price!) by collectors on specially pressed albums. The band, both playing and being interviewed, regularly surface. However these ventures did not represent the band as they really wanted to sound on a 'live' release. So they decided to beat the bootleggers at their own game and produce the 'definitive' live Fleetwood Mac album.

The process had started during the 'Rumours' tour.

Mick Fleetwood: 'We've recorded some gigs on this tour. We do it every tour, and the recordings just get put away. Who knows? Live, these songs are very different. Without all the overdubs, they really kick ass. You can't get all those little tinkles and cymbals and tom-tom overdubs. You play the *gut* out of the number. A good live album can be great and a very easy thing to do!'

John McVie also liked the tension produced by recording live performances by the Mac.

'To me, that's the excitement of it, cause you're out there, and there's no chance to say "Stop this number! I want to re-do that last bit". You're out there being a working musician and *that's* what it's all about!'

Clifford Davis, Fleetwood Mac's first manager, had felt the same way.

'My feeling about good live albums is this. Sometimes you can get an artist who, no matter how they sound in the studio, simply *excel* live! And Fleetwood Mac made their *name* as a live band!'

Live albums are also relatively cheap to produce. After the stunning million-dollar bill for 'Tusk' the cost of recording the band live would seem reasonably modest. The musicians' and road crew's expenses were covered by the income from the concerts, and with skilful on the spot engineering a minimum of post-production studio work would be necessary.

Nevertheless Fleetwood Mac typically still managed to haemorrhage money by recording over four *hundred* performances spanning a period of four years in order to produce the eighteen tracks which would eventually comprise 'Fleetwood Mac Live'. Why was Dicky Dawson able to get a whole LP out of just three shows by a band that was, in its own words at the time, 'at the bottom'?

Christine: 'You look back on it, and the best times are when you had to *struggle* a bit. It's a different kind of exhilaration that we get from playing now. We no longer get the thrill of wondering how we're gonna go over. We don't get the same kind of jitters as we did, because we're established now. We know we don't have to worry about monitor problems, and we know that everything works like a well-oiled machine. If we don't sound good, it's our own fault!'

But, of course, they did sound good. Four of the songs on the live album dated from the 1977 'Rumours' tour: 'Monday Morning', 'Dreams', 'Don't Stop' and 'Don't Let Me Down Again'. Not all the tracks were recorded in front of live audiences. 'Dreams' and 'Don't Stop' were taped during the band's soundcheck before a Paris gig. 'Monday Morning' was recorded in Tokyo, and 'Don't Let Me Down Again' in Passaic. Later tracks would be recorded in Wichita, St Louis, Oklahoma, Cleveland, Tucson, London, Santa Monica and Kansas City.

The rich sound of Fleetwood Mac was not always easy to attain away from the sophisticated facilities of the studio. Roadie-cummusicians Ray Lindsey, Tony Todaro and Jeffrey Sova helped to thicken the sound, and faithful cohorts Richard Dashut, Ken Caillat and Trip Khalaf beefed up the on and off stage mix.

Nevertheless the album, despite sophisticated post-production by Ken and Richard at the George Massenburg Studios and Soundstream Incorporated, remained a warts-and-all job. 'Don't Stop' and 'One More Night' were impeccable, but Lindsey's charming, gauche and off-key version of the Beach Boys' 'Farmer's Daughter' hardly represented the band's best work. There were also some startling omissions. Although the double album did not pretend to be a 'Greatest

Hits' collection it was surprising that not one good live version of
tried and trusted band favourites like 'You Make Loving Fun', 'The
Green Manalishi', 'The Chain' and 'Station Man' could have been
found by sifting through the four-hundred-plus tapes. The only
reminder of the good old days which did appear on 'Fleetwood Mac
Live' was a truly terrific version of Peter Green's soulful, sad, yet
rousing song 'Oh Well'. Ably performed by Lindsey Buckingham,
the powerful song had richly deserved its permanent place in the
Mac's repertoire for over eleven years. Lindsey certainly did the song
justice on the live album.

'Over And Over' and the tough 'I'm So Afraid' further contributed
to a surprisingly strong release. Considering that the double album
was expensive, and essentially a recap of two previous Fleetwood
Mac albums, 'Fleetwood Mac' and 'Rumours', plus just four new
songs, its success was surprising. Selling at $13.98, with no tour to
promote it 'Fleetwood Mac Live', released in November 1980, made
the top fifteen in the US, and managed a respectable number thirty-
one in the British charts. 'Farmer's Daughter', Lindsey's quirky
tribute to the Beach Boys, was released as a single in both the
United States and Britain. It was not particularly successful in either
territory, and 'Fireflies', the follow up in the US did not even merit
a release in the UK.

Nevertheless Mick once again had hit the nail on the head.

'Fleetwood Mac has never done a live album before with any form
of this band. It seemed to me that after a year on the road, there was
no better time to release one.'

He was right.

But, once again, rumours were spreading. This time they were
even more serious. The word going around the music business was
that, finally, the crunch had come.

Fleetwood Mac were going to split up. For good.

18 Solo Flights

Finally the 'Tusk' tour was over. On September 1st, 1980 the band played the final, 113th, concert close to home, in the Hollywood Bowl, Los Angeles. The band and crew were suffering from severe battle fatigue. Nerves were raw. Fleetwood Mac members had been spending as little time together away from the stage as possible. Lindsey in particular was still smarting from the criticism he had suffered from the other members of the band following the relative failure of 'Tusk' in the marketplace (a failure that hundreds of groups would have given their right arm for: well over five million double albums shifted). Stevie was totally whacked. Never a touring and party animal, her poor health and frail physique had taken its toll during the year-long trek. Even the robust Christine was feeling the strain.

'After the Tusk tour we were just *flattened* and exhausted, physically and mentally. We felt that we deserved a break, and we *took* that break. We took a *long* break!'

Many observers at the time thought the break would be very long indeed. Perhaps even permanent. The band retired to their various havens and licked their wounds. Thoughts of a new album from Fleetwood Mac were very far from their minds. In particular, Mick Fleetwood, Lindsey Buckingham and Stevie Nicks had other plans. The time had come to turn their backs on Fleetwood Mac and concentrate on their own needs. By the end of 1981 all three musicians would have new albums on the market. Fleetwood Mac was going to take a back seat.

Founder-member Mick Fleetwood was certainly no stranger to the inside of other artistes' recording studios. His immense skills as a drummer were very well known and had resulted in many invitations to occupy the drum stool from a wide variety of musicians. Way back in 1968 Mick had backed Blue Horizon stablemates Duster Bennett, Eddie Boyd and Gordon Smith on their albums, along with other Mac members, and 1969 saw Fleetwood in the studio with your author's band 'Tramp', along with fellow-Mac Danny Kirwan,

Dave and Jo Anne Kelly and pianist Bob Hall. Mick rejoined old boss John Mayall for two albums around the same time, and 1973 saw him working on a project which, coincidentally, involved two other ex-Bo Street Runners, Mike Patto and Tim Hinkley. Brother-in-law George Harrison also came along for the ride, and the four helped out Alvin Lee on his album 'Road To Freedom'.

1974 saw Mick back in London's Southern Music Studios to record the second Tramp album, again with Danny Kirwan and Co. Three years later Mick Fleetwood would work on a very successful album with the ex-Fleetwood Mac musician he was managing. Bob Welch's 'French Kiss' featured Mick and Bob who joined current Mac members Lindsey and Christine. The next couple of years would see various Mac members joining Mick in the studio with other artistes. John McVie played bass along with Mick on Warren Zevon's album 'Excitable Boy' and Stevie and Lindsey helped Mick on Walter Egan's 'Not Shy'.

Fleetwood and Christine McVie next worked with Bob Welch again on 'Three Hearts' and in the same year, 1979, John and Lindsey joined up with Eric Clapton to record Danny Douma's 'Night Eyes'.

The same year John McVie, Lindsey Buckingham and Mick worked with Rob Grill on 'Uprooted'. In 1980 Mick Fleetwood worked again with Todd Sharpe. Todd had played guitar on 'Three Hearts' and 'Night Eyes' with Mick, and the musician was beginning to impress the lanky drummer. They joined Turley Richards and Bob Welch to produce 'Therfu'.

However, in 1981 Mick Fleetwood decided the time had come to stop guesting on other people's albums. So, apart from a brief involvement with Ron Wood's super-stars-stuffed studio session which would result in the LP '1234', he turned his attention to a project dear to his heart.

'After our "Tusk" tour marathon, which lasted nearly a year, we agreed to take six or seven months off. I decided to "renourish my soul".'

Mick Fleetwood was a born wanderer. The son of a pilot, in his youth he had lived variously in England, Egypt and Norway. By 1981 he had spent over thirteen years on the road all over the world with Fleetwood Mac. However, one trip had really stood out.

'I went to Zambia. I had a *marvellous* time. The people were remarkably honest, with no illusions or false egos. Since then I've always wanted to record in Africa, using African drummers.'

This would come as no surprise to anyone who listens carefully to Mick's drumming style. His influences clearly include the rich, moving, powerful African drumming rhythms. His own percussive power and strength reflected the admiration he had for those countless performers to be found in that vast continent. However, before his dream could be realised, a few minor practical details had to be sorted out.

First of all the trip needed financing. Mick Fleetwood bowled along to the Warner Brothers office, confident that they would back him all the way. They wouldn't. Perhaps wary after the huge cost incurred by 'Tusk' they balked at the estimated four hundred thousand dollars Mick's new, non-Fleetwood Mac album would cost. Undeterred, Fleetwood phoned around and finally persuaded the giant RCA record company to underwrite the ambitious project.

The odds against the successful completion of the scheme seemed high. For a start, Ghana had *no* recording studios. Mick, ever the optimist in the face of adversity, saw no problem. Simple. Two twenty-four track portable mixing desks, plus all the associated Ampex tape machines, monitor speakers and software could be shipped out to Africa. It was perhaps unfortunate that half the equipment accidentally ended up in Switzerland. A minor hitch; followed by another. One truck and two cars suffering from blown-out tyres and brake problems stranded the gear somewhere in the middle of Ghana. And another. His romantic, idealistic plan to wander all over the country picking up percussionists who inspired him was torpedoed by treacherous and dangerous road conditions. Eventually Mick solved the problems. Instead of hauling the expensive equipment around the dirt roads of Ghana, he would transport all the musicians to Accra.

Mick loved it: 'I consider travel to be one of the best forms of education, and this was a particularly uplifting experience. Working with the local musicians, with the master drummers was a *humbling* experience. We all need to be humbled once in a while. It kindles the essence of living.'

Mick didn't want the experience to be simply a one-way cultural exchange.

'I went there hoping to *leave* something behind, not just to rip off the African musicians. I wanted to put something into the country, not just "take out".'

Idealistic perhaps, even rather grandiose aims, maybe, but Fleetwood assuaged his sensitive feelings by arranging a February concert in the city's Black Star Square. All the musicians would play for nothing, and all the concert proceeds would be donated to the Ghana branch of the Musicians' Union.

The raw, exciting sounds taped in Ghana were carefully shipped back to LA. Loyal producer and friend Richard Dashut began the work of editing, mixing and adding to the African work. The album would turn out to be an odd, but hypnotising mixture of cultural styles. Ghanaian music would sit awkwardly alongside Buddy Holly's 'Not Fade Away' and a couple of Fleetwood Mac songs. 'Walk A Thin Line' was one. 'Rattlesnake Shake' was another. Mick Fleetwood, ever loyal to his old Mac friend Peter Green, decided to involve him.

'There was *no* way I could cut that track without Peter. It was *his* song.'

(Mick also negotiated a new recording contract for Green with Warner Brothers at around the same time, reputed to be worth a million dollars. Green declined. Once again, he felt that he was potentially being bought by the devil.)

Fleetwood's other musical companions on 'The Visitor' included Todd Sharpe, George Hawkins and ex-Beatle George Harrison. Asked by a gauche young reporter during the press launch for the album whether the inclusion of Harrison on the venture had been in the form of a 'Lennon tribute', Mick replied simply, 'Nope. He's my brother-in-law.'

What did he think about the album?

'It's weird, but highly listenable. How it will sell, I don't know. A Fleetwood Mac record is fairly assured of success because of our track record. But an album like this, which is a new concept, *completely* off the wall concept, is very much a question mark with regard to commercial success.'

It wouldn't achieve it. Nevertheless the group of musicians would survive to play another day. 'Zoo', as they were subsequently titled, would become thoroughly intertwined with the life of the Mac. Bassist George Hawkins and guitarist Todd Sharpe would eventually play alongside Vince Denham, Steve Ross, Ron Thompson, Lindsey Buckingham, Jan Clarke, Christine McVie and Don Roberts on Mick's second solo album, 'I'm Not Me', released in 1983.

The connection would not stop there. Hawkins and Sharpe would also work again with Christine and Lindsey.

Mick: 'She got to know them when she played on my second album, and they've all become great friends.'

The two musicians would feature on Christine's own solo album.

Far more significantly, they would be joined by another guitarist, both for Fleetwood's 'I'm Not Me' and as a pick up band put together by Lindsey Buckingham for his appearance on 'Saturday Night Live',

the prestigious, networked US TV show. The Choloes featured Steve
Ross, Hawkins, Sharpe . . . and one Billy Burnette.

'I hope it's going to be an ongoing situation,' said Mick at the time.
'I suppose it depends on how things go with the album and on the
road. We have worked as a band, so I know for sure it's happening
musically.'

Zoo would work sporadically, but Billy Burnette's Fleetwood Mac
connections were already forged, and would not be forgotten.

Lindsey Buckingham had precisely the same needs as Mick in
1981. A break from the road, followed by the chance to channel his
creativity into a solo project. Buckingham had a backlog of song
compositions which he wanted to see released. Like Mick, he had
also worked on other recording projects outside Fleetwood Mac,
including several with Mac colleagues Christine McVie, John McVie,
Mick himself and Stevie Nicks, but the chance now presented itself
to record his work as an entirely free agent.

Even on the gruelling 'Tusk' tour, he had been preparing for the
project. Preferring to stay in his hotel room with his two loves,
girlfriend Carol and his Teac tape recorder, working on songs and
sounds, Lindsey was busy composing and creating. Finally he was
ready. 'Law And Order' was born. Why that title?

'Someone said, "Why did you call it 'Law and Order'?" and I said,
first of all it has nothing to do with the contemporary context in
which that term is used now, it has nothing to do with the society
aspect. It's more specifically the theme of how to retain innocence
and how to keep your innocence while experiencing pain. Everyone
is born with innocence, but as you get older, you tend to close off
your feelings more, you tend to become more cynical, more self-
aware, less giving and the album is in some ways asking the question
– how do you keep those innocent eyes through which real beauty
is seen? It comes down to choices – do you reject a situation, or a
person, because you are confronted with pain, or do you accept pain
as part of the whole, and learn to get through it to the other side?
I've experienced a bit of that in the last year and I'm getting through
it, and I think in order to keep that sense of innocence, you really have
to instil a sense of discipline in yourself and a sense of commitment –
commitment is a key word – to something you care about, and that's
how the title came about.'

In spite of the fact that Lindsey's relationship with the rest of the
members of Fleetwood Mac had certainly somewhat soured, his
choice of musical partners for his musical venture spoke volumes
with regard to the strength of 'family' ties. With the cream of the

rich field of Los Angeles session players available at his bidding, who did Lindsey choose? Christine McVie and Mick Fleetwood of course. Plus associate George Hawkins and Buckingham's girlfriend Carol Ann Harris.

The musical collaboration between Lindsey and Mick could even survive a swipe. One track, 'Bwana', seemed to refer to Mick's album 'The Visitor' in a none too complimentary way. Was there a reference?

'Well, there is, actually – Mick and I were having a little tiff one day. This particular song was almost recorded, all those crazy, cartoon-background vocals. At that point it really had no reference to "Bwana". Richard Dashut, who was helping me through the second phase of the album said, "Why don't you go out and sing it sort of fifties style?" I went out and started singing a different way, and a whole new melody evolved and at that point the lyrics went with the new melody. There's really nothing negative about Mick in there – it was just on my mind at the time! Mick and I are real close – close enough to make references to one another in songs without having to worry about it.'

'Trouble', one of the tracks on 'Law And Order' would be released as a single. Mick Fleetwood's drum contribution, as usual, was important.

Lindsey: 'Mick and I recorded for several hours but nothing seemed quite solid enough as a whole track, so we picked a short section, cut the kick drum into itself, took it out of the machine, shut the motors off so it wouldn't be spinning and looped it around a microphone stand – and put the parts on to that. It still sounds like Mick – still has a certain tension, something to do with where he places his kick, he always lays the snare further back than the kick – and it has that creep to it.'

That 'creep' not withstanding, 'Trouble' was not a hit, and neither was the album.

Like Mick before him, Lindsey was undeterred by the disappointing sales of his solo venture. Two years later Mercury would release his second project, 'Go Insane'. Following the painful break up of his relationship with Carol Harris, the album was at least partially inspired by the angst-ridden emotions Lindsey was experiencing at the time.

Never a man to use one-syllable words when lengthier ones would do, Lindsey commented: 'The lyrics were to some extent inspired, if that's the right word, by the slow disintegration of a six-year relationship I had with a young lady. I tried everything I could to maintain a commitment to this person, but she began to display non-constructive behavioural patterns and I just reached a stage where no more allowances could be made. So, a lot of the songs on ''Go Insane'' have something to do with various aspects of what happened.'

There was another interesting track on the album: 'DW Suite' dedicated to Dennis Wilson of the Beach Boys. It addressed itself to the parallels between Dennis's role within the famous sixties West Coast band, and Lindsey's own role within Fleetwood Mac, as he perceived it. Yet another connection existed. Dennis had been Christine McVie's lover.

Lindsey: 'I wrote ''DW Suite'' as a personal tribute to Dennis Wilson, the Beach Boys' drummer, who drowned last December. It's divided into three distinct segments and contains a number of musical themes, both traditional (''Loch Lomond'' is one noticeable strand) and modern. I also did it as a way of tipping my hat to Brian Wilson who was the driving force behind the band. I've always identified with Brian because he has spent years attempting to take what was essentially a successful early sixties pop band into a more adventurous and challenging direction. Yet the pressure put upon him by the other members of the BBs and even his own family because of the desire to experiment and change has been incredible. In fact the only way he's been able to handle it is to revert to a childlike mental existence, which is tragic. Maybe by including this track I've managed to exorcise a demon that's been haunting me for years concerning my own position with the Fleetwoods.'

The album was produced by Roy Thomas Baker. (Richard Dashut, Fleetwood Mac and 'Law and Order' producer declined the job, saying after his protracted work on Mick Fleetwood's 'Visitor', 'I am so burnt out that I just cannot bring myself to go back into the studio.') Lindsey, in an overtly theatrical gesture, had flown to London to present his demo tapes to Baker, who was embroiled in his Queen and Cars projects at the time.

Lindsey's second album had proved to be an interesting, thoughtful and in many ways innovative piece of work. But it fared little better than its predecessor in the record racks of the world's music shops.

Only the third member of the Fleetwood Mac trio seeking wider horizons would achieve huge success outside of the band. Stevie Nicks, in 1981, was preparing to spread her wings and fly. High.

19 Stevie Soars

In 1976 Stevie Nicks had attended a music industry convention in Acapulco, Mexico. There she met the president of Bearsville Records, a New York based record company. His name was Paul Fishkin, and he was to become an extremely important figure in Stevie's life, in more ways than one. At the time, Fleetwood Mac were beginning to take off following Stevie and Lindsey's recent addition to the band.

Paul Fishkin: 'Although she was having a great time with the Mac, and they were extremely successful, there was a natural desire for her to express herself in other areas. In those days Fleetwood Mac were far too successful to be enthusiastic about the individuals in the band doing solo projects. I don't think any of them really considered it apart from Stevie.'

Paul decided that he could be the person to perhaps facilitate such a project: 'Stevie and I periodically talked about the idea of making a record. And we then became *really* good friends.'

Paul, Stevie and publicist Danny Goldberg decided to form Modern Records and the three began the long drawn out process which would lead to the production of Stevie's first solo album. It would be a long wait for Paul and Danny, but they were patient. Other Nicks projects were mooted and subsequently quietly dropped or shelved: 'Rhiannon' could form the basis of a movie, for which Stevie would compose a soundtrack; her fairy tale based on Beauty and the Beast could be turned into an animated film; another of her ideas for a film apparently featured the love affair between a goldfish and a ladybird, which she rather extravagantly claimed later could become 'The Dr Zhivago of children's cartoons'. None of these projects came to fruition. Danny and Paul waited. And worked. First they needed to set up a distribution deal for Modern Records, which took some considerable time. When that task was satisfactorily completed their patience again had to be sustained.

Paul: 'We had to wait *two* years after we completed the distribution deal with Atlantic Records. We didn't get an album from Stevie for a further two years. We knew that that would probably be the case, because of her obligations to the Mac. She would *not* antagonise the band. She felt very close to them and in no way, shape or form did she want to hurt Fleetwood Mac.'

Stevie certainly *didn't* want to damage Fleetwood Mac, but, exhausted like the rest of the members of the band, she had had enough after that gruelling year on the road. She compared the experience to a marriage.

'Because we have certainly spent more time than most married people will ever spend together! And we have gone through more incredible experiences than most married people will ever go through, and you know we've travelled the world. We've danced across the stages of Europe. We've been everywhere together, we've done everything together. If my mum and dad had one twentieth of the time with me that Fleetwood Mac, even with my solo career, has with me, they'd be totally happy. Because they feel they never ever get to see me. But if somebody from Fleetwood Mac calls and says "I need you to be here," you go! You don't call in *sick* to Fleetwood Mac!'

The break from the band would at last give Nicks the chance to spread her wings. The shelves of her apartment were certainly piled high with material. A prolific writer from her early teens, Fleetwood Mac had only afforded Stevie limited opportunities to see her songs recorded, produced and released on albums. The reason was simple. The band happened to be blessed with not one, but *three* talented writers. This meant that Nicks could on average expect to see about three or four songs released every two years, a frustrating experience for such a productive writer. However her solo career could throw open some doors

She was anxious about the project: 'I'm *always* nervous about doing something new! I was particularly anxious about making this album because I knew I wouldn't have four other people to blame if it didn't do well. In Fleetwood Mac, if I fail, I fail with four other people. Here, if I fail, I fail alone. It's always scarier to be alone.'

Stevie knew that one way to minimise the risk was to surround herself with talented people in whom she could trust. Old friend Don Henley was one. Guitarist Waddy Wachtel also went back a long way with Nicks. In addition Paul Fishkin and Stevie hired top session man Russ Kunkel on drums plus 'Professor' Roy Bittan, Bruce Springsteen's pianist; Don Felder of the Eagles, Elton John's guitar player Davey Johnstone and Bob Welch's David Adelstein came along for the ride; and Tom Petty and the Heartbreakers were also heavily involved in the recording. The use of such talented and busy players ruled out marathon Fleetwood Mac-type sessions.

'We did it in a sort of piecemeal way because we'd only get people in for a few days at a time. Tom Petty and the Heartbreakers don't exactly sit around waiting for the phone to ring for session work! Russ Kunkel and Waddy Wachtel also have *impossible* schedules. So we scheduled the album around them. We'd get them for a couple of days and work *fast*.'

Nicks was initially worried that she would miss Lindsey's arranging skills.

'That's one of the reasons I wanted to see if I could do it myself. When you work with somebody who is that much in control and who has always been that much in control – from, like 1970 on – you forget that you're even capable of doing something yourself. I'd write my song and then Lindsey would take it, fix it, change it around, chop it up and then put it back together. Doing that is second nature to Lindsey, especially on my songs. He does better work on my songs than on anybody's because he knows that I always give them to him freely. It's a matter of trust.

'So it was interesting to work without him, because my songs pretty much stayed the same, the only difference was what happened after I'd written them. When I write a song I sit down at the piano and play it front to back. For "Bella Donna" I would do that, or have a demo like that, and the other musicians would just listen to it, getting their own ideas of how to fill in the rest. Usually after a couple of times listening to the song they had a good idea of what they could do with it. My songs aren't complicated to say the least. The sessions went very quickly really.

'It was exhilarating! Instead of just sitting around hour after hour I got to be a part of it. Working with Lindsey, it's so easy to just let him take charge. On this album I didn't have to fight to do my songs the way I wanted to. The other players just did them the way I wrote them and they came out great. We didn't do a ton of overdubs. We didn't put on 50,000 guitars because we didn't have Waddy around long enough to do 50,000 guitar overdubs. We were lucky to get him to do one guitar part!'

Work certainly proceeded at a spanking pace. Stevie had ten years' worth of songs to get out of her system. 'After the Glitter Fades' dated back to 1972. 'Highway Man' written about the male members of Fleetwood Mac and the Eagles, 'Leather and Lace' and 'Think About It', an ode to Christine's marital difficulties with John McVie, were written in 1974–5. 'Edge of Seventeen' was an example of Nicks' most poignant work.

'That song is all about how no amount of money or power could save John Lennon or my favourite Uncle Jonathan, who died at about the same time. I felt very angry, sad, helpless and hurt.'

The prophetic 'After the Glitter Fades' was written in 1974.

'Believe me, I'd seen a *lot* of glitter fade by the time I wrote that song. It was about the two years before Lindsey and I joined Fleetwood Mac. That was a *tough* period for us, because we were very serious about wanting to be professional musicians. I didn't have any friend in LA and he did. And while he was making friends and playing music, I *had* to work!'

Sixteen songs were eventually recorded, and then the painful choice had to be made.

'I wanted *all* of them to get on. I agonised about it! If I had put them all on, though, there wouldn't have been enough room for a label!'

Stevie had enjoyed being in charge of the project.

'In Fleetwood Mac I'm one of six. In the "Stevie Nicks" organisation I'm the *boss*. I never wanted to be boss of Fleetwood Mac. Mick's the chief and that's OK, because we *gave* him the title.'

Her choice of songs to appear on the album was immaculate.

By September of the same year Stevie Nicks' first ever solo album, 'Bella Donna', was sitting comfortably at number one on *Billboard*'s album chart. As if that wasn't enough, no less than *three* tracks from the album would become hit singles. The first two made the top ten. 'Leather and Lace', a duet with her old friend Don Henley, ended up at number six. 'Stop Dragging My Heart Around', Tom Petty's song on which she dueted this time with Tom himself, made number three. Early 1982 would see her own 'Edge of Seventeen' peaking at number eleven. The album itself rapidly attained platinum status.

Stevie had achieved something which had evaded her Mac colleagues Lindsey and Mick. She had indisputably proved that her songwriting and performing talents were impressive enough to support a highly successful career outside Fleetwood Mac.

However another bridge had to be crossed. Performing on stage without the 'safety net' of the Fleetwood Mac family to catch Stevie if she fell. She was nervous, but she coped.

'Nervous? Are you kidding? Terribly! I hadn't been onstage alone before. It's a whole different can of beans to realise that if you're not out there – if you have to run to the wings for some powder or to get your hair brushed or because you're dripping wet – there is no one onstage who'll talk to the audience. But we had some truly spectacular moments, when the band and I were blown away at the response. At one Los Angeles show, I must have looked like the bag lady of "Bella Donna". I was bent over because I had so many roses to carry. I was crying. Another great thing was that no one in the audience ever yelled out, "Where's Tom Petty? Where's Lindsey? Where's Fleetwood Mac?" '

The finer details of Stevie Nicks' solo career, and the success it would bring her, could easily fill the pages of another book. Suffice it to say that Nicks would go on to make three more successful albums following the three million plus sales of 'Bella Donna'.

'Wild Heart', released in 1983, would once again combine her talents with those of Tom Petty, Waddy Wachtel, Roy Bittan and producer Jimmy Iovine. By now Jimmy was also occupying a place in Stevie's heart as well as behind the mixing desk, like Paul Fishkin before him.

The song 'Wild Heart' had been previously written with the help of Nick's friend Sandy Stewart. Stevie had decided upon the title of her second album *before* she had even recorded 'Bella Donna'. An uncredited guest on 'Wild Heart' (upon his own insistence) was Prince.

Stevie: 'He was in LA and I just called him up and said, "I'd like it if you could come." He said, "Yes, ma'am" and he actually showed up, and put on this awesome part. He can be heard on keyboards on the beginning of "Stand Back".'

Once again, the album additionally spawned hit singles. 'Stand Back' hit the number five spot in the charts, and 'If Anyone Falls' attained the number fourteen position. Stevie was learning the importance of video promotion by this time, and the accompanying promos achieved wide MTV coverage. The album itself didn't do quite as well as its predecessor. Nevertheless it once again included Stevie performing with Tom Petty and the Heartbreakers on 'I Will Run To You!'

Two years later, Nicks released her third solo album, 'Rock a Little'. Waddy Wachtel was just about hanging on from his involvement with the previous albums, but producer Jimmy Iovine was to fall by the wayside during the sessions. Their romantic relationship was getting in the way of business.

Paul Fishkin: 'I think there's a moment when you do *better* because of a personal relationship and there's a period when there's *less* creativity because of it. Jimmy started the record. They cut a lot of tracks but then they decided it wasn't working musically. It happens. They were together for two albums, they were still friends, but they just both felt it was time for a change.'

Another old friend was subsequently winched in. Keith Olsen knew Stevie from the 'Buckingham Nicks' album sessions way back in 1973, on which he had worked. Olsen, a musician as well as a producer, was able to guide Stevie through the demands made by the intricacies of the recording studio. Rick Nowels also helped out as a producer, and the combination of Nicks' performing and writing talents with those of the three producers bore fruit. 'Rock a Little' was declared to have achieved gold and platinum status *simultaneously* on the same day in 1985.

'Talk To Me' and 'I Can't Wait', lifted from the album, both became hit singles for Stevie. She received various awards and achievements during her prolific solo career: the Best Female Artiste of 1983, *Rock Magazine*'s Sexiest Woman In Rock award in 1984, and several others.

1989 would bring her fourth solo venture. Her work on 'The Other Side Of The Mirror' would bring her to producer Rupert Hine's Buckinghamshire studio in the UK. He was chosen on the basis of some rather tenuous evidence, according to Stevie Nicks.

'I don't know many producers. When I went to do my first solo record I picked Jimmy Iovine simply because I'm a *terrific* Tom Petty fan, and I *loved* the sound he'd got on Tom's "Damn The Torpedos". This time I met two other producers I liked very much, but I ended up choosing Rupert simply because I liked him the most. It was just a look in his eye, and a feeling about him that I trusted. I knew we'd probably get into a row or two along the way but above all I could *respect* him.'

Once again her instinct was to serve her well. 'Rooms On Fire', the single lifted from the album, would give Stevie her biggest ever UK solo hit.

Clearly she could have left Fleetwood Mac several times over since her 1981 solo success. But she didn't.

'We have *no* democracy in Fleetwood Mac. Mick is the King, and that's it. I accept that. I've accepted it for fourteen years. I'll continue to accept it until the day I die. I know I can leave, but I *love* that band as much as I love doing my own music, there's always been a part of me that has said I'll *never* be the one to break up Fleetwood Mac. I won't do it.'

She didn't.

Eight years earlier, in 1981, Fleetwood Mac, in dangerous disarray following the numbing 'Tusk' tour and the solo flights (ominously unsuccessful for Fleetwood and Buckingham), took a hard look at future prospects. It didn't take long for a corporate decision to be made. The band *would* continue. *With* Stevie Nicks.

And that meant they had to get busy. A new album was required. Fast.

20 Mirage

The band regrouped. Initial awkwardness and unease between band members was inevitable. Mick's solo album had hardly set the charts alight, nor had Lindsey's. Stevie, however, was well on the way to carving a very substantial career for herself following the massive success of 'Bella Donna'. In addition the band were smarting from the relative failure (*extremely* relative; upwards of nine million double units sold) of 'Tusk', the thirteen-month, million-dollar project which had been so close to Lindsey's heart. He felt particularly hard done by. No doubt if the release had been a massive 'Rumours' type success the whole band would have basked in its glory, but with its failure, four fingers seemed to be firmly and accusingly pointing at Buckingham.

However a deep breath was collectively taken, and Fleetwood Mac jumped on a big jet plane to take them to Europe. Their destination? An ancient château outside Paris. Not just any old château. Le Château, Hérouville. The very same 'Honky Château' featured on Elton John's eponymous album.

Christine: 'We decided that we wanted to be outside of Los Angeles because we wanted to be without any distractions. We wanted to be just the *five* of us, and work something out.'

Plus Richard Dashut, Ken Caillat, Ray Lindsey, Tony Todaro, Dennis Dunstan, Wayne Cody, Dwayne Taylor, Debbie Alsbury, Dennis Keen, Jimmy Iovine and various other members of the Fleetwood Mac entourage. The band never travelled light.

This time, however, there was to be no limitless budget, and no experimenting. Far from it.

Additionally the new album would very definitely attempt to recreate the massively commercial feel and sound of their monster album 'Rumours'.

However, the recording schedule would hardly see a return to the heady days when Fleetwood Mac could cut an album in a couple of days. Nevertheless the initial sessions at Le Château which provided the raw material for the new album were laid down in just two months; quick by 1980s and Fleetwood Mac standards. There was also another advantage in being far from the distractions afforded by Los Angeles. The band *worked* together. Members would not adopt the fragmented approach to the recordings which had typified the Fleetwood Mac's 'Tusk' recording routine, where little of the material was produced as a result of the five guys in the band actually recording *together*.

Christine: 'One common bond on "Mirage" is that the band is actually playing on everybody's songs the whole way through. Also there are no messages to one another on this album. This is *not* a diary like "Rumours". It seems like a happy record to me. We all enjoyed making it. The tracks are self-explanatory in that way. "Mirage" is more cohesive than "Tusk".'

Certainly some of the best songs were born of genuine, deep feeling.

Stevie: 'There is a *lot* about returning to San Francisco. "Gypsy" was written when my very best friend died of leukaemia, and was all about the fact that she wasn't going to see the rest of her life. I used to see her bright eyes. It was obvious she wasn't going to make it, and so I was going to be a "solo" gypsy. This was my *best* friend from when I was fifteen years old. So I was a solo gypsy all of a sudden. That was very sad for me. Sometimes that's when I write my very best songs. When I'm *really* sad.'

The basic tracks laid down, the large Fleetwood Mac party packed its mountains of bags and flight cases and headed off home. The job of producing the album was just beginning however. Ever faithful Ken Caillat and Richard Dashut, helped by Carla Frederick and Dennis Mays, spooled the massive master tapes through the giant desks in Larrabee Sound and the Record Plant, Los Angeles. The complex task of editing, mixing and overdubbing ploughed on. Finally, ten months later, the all-important follow up to 'Tusk' was released. What did the band think of the final result?

Christine looked back in 1987. A journalist asked her whether she thought that 'Mirage' had seemed to be rather a 'let down'.

'Oh, yes! All of us feel that, definitely. That album was really a result of pressure, not just from the periphery, but from ourselves. We had decided we'd go in and do something that was expected from us, and it failed. From all our points of view, I think I can say that we were all disappointed. It reeks of insincerity to me.'

In the same year, she would say: 'The "Mirage" album seemed to be something that was expected of us at the time. It was a little superficial. We'd really only made four albums with this particular configuration of band members. Of them all, I think "Mirage" is probably the weakest. After the huge success of "Rumours", the *phenomenon* and the complete swing to the left with "Tusk", the making of "Mirage" was an effort to get back into the flow that "Rumours" had. But we had missed a very vital ingredient. That was the passion, the desire to *do it!*'

Lindsey also felt that the album did not feature the band's best work.

'We should have progressed, but instead we just reacted against "Tusk". It was pleasant but *much* too safe. "Mirage" was quite reactionary after "Tusk", I think, because forces within the band and without were saying to me, "You went too *far* on 'Tusk'." That was kind of hard to deal with, taking the flak over "Tusk".'

Christine floated one theory for the somewhat lack-lustre, *déjà vu* feeling about 'Mirage'.

' "Rumours" had been born out of strife and tensions. During the recording of "Mirage" the band members were boringly friendly again. We were no longer the musical soap opera we used to be!'

Pundits within the music business at the time put forward another explanation. Perhaps Christine (just about to begin work on her own solo project), Lindsey and Stevie were keeping back their best songs for their own albums? One could hardly blame them if it were true. However all three would strenuously deny it.

'Mirage' eventually surfaced in July 1982. As always the British rock press either ignored or castigated it. Christine's songs were deemed to be particularly strong, however, and Stevie's powerful 'Gypsy' was supported by an innovative and appealing promo video when the song was released as a single.

'Mirage' might not have quite equalled the success of 'Rumours' but Christine remained philosophical at the time.

'We don't let "Rumours" intimidate us any more. We just accept it as a phenomenon that cannot be repeated. I know "Mirage" is selling well, but I don't think for a moment that twenty-five million people will buy it. I don't think twenty-five million people could *afford* it!'

As always, the performance of 'Mirage' in the marketplace, though perhaps disappointing to the ever-hungry Warner Brothers moguls, would have afforded other bands the excuse to go out and celebrate on the finest champagne for a week. The album topped the US charts and made number five in Britain. 'Hold Me', just one of the three singles lifted from 'Mirage', made number four in the US but bombed in England. Oddly Lindsey's 'Oh Diane' once again reversed the usual pattern. Supported by a shaky live performance on prime time British TV, it climbed to number nine, wihout even denting the US top 100. 'Gypsy' reverted firmly to type: number twelve in the US, as opposed to a top fifty scrape at forty-six in the UK. Christine's 'Hold Me' did the best in America of the three singles. The record made number four there, but paradoxically didn't get near the British top fifty.

Had the solo ventures taken some kind of toll? Christine didn't think so.

'The solo albums have actually brought us closer together. They've served as an outlet, letting us get things out of our system. There is not much opportunity to display your wares on a group album. Not that that was ever a cause of our disagreements. If we screamed at each other, it was nearly always for personal reasons. But we're working together much more strongly these days. People can't believe we can be friendly together. They are amazed when they see John and me having dinner together.'

Cosy though the image might be, as presented by Christine McVie, the post-'Mirage' tours, solo ventures and other band issues would result in the longest-ever gap between the release of albums that the band had experienced. Five full years would pass before another Fleetwood Mac album would appear.

21 Fleetwood Mac – Who?

The release of 'Mirage' was followed by the obligatory promotional tour. Rehearsals had started in mid-July 1982; and September 1st saw Fleetwood Mac stepping on to the boards in Greensboro, North Carolina. This one wasn't going to be a marathon. The tour ended on September 30th in Oakland,California: a bare two months, short by Mac standards. During the jaunt a feature-length concert video was produced by David Putnam, who had been responsible for the multi-Oscar-decorated *Chariots of Fire*.

Lindsey and Stevie's appetite for the road, however, was diminishing.

Lindsey: 'Stevie doesn't really want to go out on the road. I enjoy playing live, but it's not *nearly* as much of a learning thing or a growing thing as staying home and working on new tunes.'

In the autumn of 1982 the band members went their separate ways. Fleetwood Mac was about to experience its longest-ever lay-off from the recording studio and the road. However the next few years were not to be uneventful.

John McVie and Julie were still smarting from the events of 1981. The Honolulu Police Department's drug-sniffing dog had singled out a package addressed to the McVies' fashionable Napili area house in Maui, John's long-established Hawaiian haven. The subsequent search of the McVie household revealed the contents of the parcel: four and a half grams of pure cocaine. Other goodies found in the house included no less than seven guns: three loaded pistols, three rifles and a Remington 570 riot shotgun. To add to the McVies' problems, according to the police, John's wife Julie had attempted to destroy some of the evidence during the search.

The situation was potentially very serious for John who was a resident alien in the USA, not a national. The charges resulting from the bust were 'possession of cocaine', 'possession of firearms', and Julie's 'hindering prosecution'; and so there was a chance that John would be deported if convicted. The McVies waited anxiously. John claimed that he had no knowledge whatever of the presence of cocaine in his house. A lie-detector test supported his statement, and convinced the court that McVie was unaware that the drug was in his home. He hadn't known that the possession of guns was an offence. After all he lived in the good old USA, a society which was proud to protect the rights of its citizens to possess firearms: 'It was a stupid thing to do. If I had known what the law was, I would have complied.'

John was fined a thousand dollars, and Julie was ordered to stay out of trouble for a year. They heaved a huge sigh of relief, and set about making plans for some pretty extensive sailing trips. Mac duties seemed far away.

Stevie was very busy. Her solo projects were time-consuming and rewarding. However, a major event was about to take place in her personal life. Marriage, no less. But for all the wrong reasons.

Stevie's father, Jess, had been anxious about her lengthy single status:

'When Stevie passed thirty and had not got married I honestly did not think she ever would. When a woman goes that long being single, particularly when she's hugely successful, usually her career is so important that she *won't* get married.'

Stevie had highly valued her friendship with her 'Gypsy' school-friend Robyn. It was in 1982 that disaster had struck for Robyn and her husband Kim Anderson, with the awful news that Robyn was diagnosed as having leukaemia. Then, rarely for someone with the fatal disease, she became pregnant, and was delivered of a baby boy by emergency Caesarean section just three days before her tragic death.

Kim and Stevie were understandably distraught. Racked by her love and loyalty to the tiny Anderson family, and desperate to help, Stevie made a radical and emotional decision. She vowed to marry Robyn's widower and help bring up her best friend's baby. On January 29th, 1983 Stevie Nicks married Kim Anderson. Following a brief Big Sur honeymoon, Stevie went back to work on her album, 'Wild Heart'.

Nobody approved, but Stevie was invincible.

Jess Nicks: 'We met Kim a number of times when he was married to Robyn. He was a very nice young man, but I can't say we were overly pleased with the marriage. Frankly, we felt that Stevie was possibly marrying Kim out of love for Robyn, and a feeling that *somebody* had to be a mother to a new baby. We felt it was too *early* for her to marry Kim: Robyn had been dead for only four or five months. But Stevie has tremendous internal fortitude, and when she makes up her mind to do something, *nobody* can change it.'

Stevie's long-time friend from the Mac, Christine McVie, also strongly disapproved.

'I found the marriage very bizarre. She thought it was what Robyn would have wanted. But they'd known each other for a long time, and it didn't seem like "crazy love" to me. I didn't even buy her a wedding present.'

Nicks became stepmother to baby Matthew. Problems surfaced fast.

'It's tough, because I'm *never* home. But Matthew is a very special baby. He'll see this thing through and he'll be fine. Matthew is here for a definite reason. He has his own little path to follow from here.'

He would follow that path without Stevie. Just eight short months later the Andersons would divorce. Matthew would survive and prosper. But Stevie's personality and behaviour were beginning to worry those around her.

Christine: 'Ten years ago, she really had her feet on the ground, along with a great sense of humour, which she still has. But she seems to have developed her own fantasy world somehow, which I'm not part of. We don't socialise much.'

The disastrous marriage, coupled with the pressure associated with the demands of her solo career, was pushing Stevie ever closer to an emotional cliff edge. Nicks was becoming dependent on drugs, and her vulnerability was growing.

Meanwhile Christine was organising the recording of her second solo album. Her first, recorded way back in 1969, had been subsequently released in the US against her wishes.

'I didn't have *one* finger in the pie except that I wrote a couple of weedy songs!'

Like Stevie before her, she was anxious about her new solo work.

'I was *really* scared about the project to start with, but my fears have been completely dispelled.'

Why? She chose to surround herself with a mixture of old friends, proven colleagues, and highly respected session players for her all-important solo venture. The Average White Band's drummer Steve Ferrone was joined by bassist George Hawkins and Todd Sharpe. Hawkins had played with Mick Fleetwood's band Zoo, as had guitarist Todd Sharpe. Hawkins in particular, joining Christine and the rest of the band in the recording studios in Montreux, Switzerland, played an important additional role within the project. He co-wrote five songs with Christine for the album, and wrote two on his own.

Other old friends joined Christine. Stevie Winwood and Eric Clapton helped out. McVie flew back to the UK to collaborate with Winwood. They sang together on 'One in a Million' and co-wrote 'Ask Anybody'. Winwood also played synthesiser on four tracks. The British connection was completed when Eric played guitar on 'The Challenge'.

'Got a Hold of Me', the first single from the album, would make the USA top ten. The follow up, 'Love Will Show Us How', was not successful, but her collaboration with producer Russ Titelman, Sharpe, Hawkins, Ferrone, Winwood, Clapton and Mac colleagues Fleetwood and Buckingham was a satisfying and rewarding venture. Christine had proved, like Fleetwood, Buckingham and Nicks before her, that she could produce a worthwhile and creative piece of work outside the constraints of Fleetwood Mac.

Back in the Stevie Nicks camp, all was certainly not so well. Despite her solo success, demons were getting to Stevie. The pressures and pain of her unfulfilling, shortlived marriage to Kim Anderson, plus the demands imposed by her solo career, were causing her huge problems.

'It crept up slowly over a number of years, but it finally got to a point where I was being so overworked by everyone that I realised I couldn't go on without dropping.'

Stevie made a brave and courageous decision. She needed help desperately. That help could be found at an internationally renowned centre for addicts of all kinds. The Betty Ford Clinic.

Stevie explained why her addiction was tied up with her relationship with the Mac.

'I guess I got paranoid about the way Fleetwood Mac simply died. I couldn't understand it. We'd been one of the hottest properties for *years*, but suddenly it all fell apart when the others wanted to start doing their own thing. I recorded a couple of solo albums, but I was always aching to get working with the Mac again. I suppose I've always been the most dedicated Mac member, and it never made any sense to me that such a vibrant group could be allowed simply to drift apart.'

Her brave decision paid off.

'It was the best move I've ever made. It worked wonders for me, and now I'm strictly an orange juice girl. I'm enjoying life to the *full*!'

Stevie had not noticed that alcohol addiction had been creeping up on her.

'See, I never really thought about drink as a kind of drug, like cocaine. But it is. You can get hooked on it just as easily, and it can destroy all your ambitions. I guess I just didn't realise that at the time. I've always been anti-drugs, but I thought drink was harmless, just a relaxation. I can't tell you how wrong I was. I have to tell you that the Betty Ford people were marvellous.'

Marvellous they were, but it certainly wasn't easy for Stevie. She found herself in the clinic at the same time as country star Tammy Wynette, who was trying to kick her dependency on the pain-killing drugs she used to take to get through recurrent bouts of severe ill health. In a regime that required getting up at six and working, studying or attending therapy sessions all day, celebrity status presented its own problems for the pair.

'That was my only gripe. They were a little *hard* on you for being famous!'

The routine was tough. Stevie shared a spartan cubicle with an elderly alcoholic woman. All domestic chores were undertaken by inmates: bed-making, cleaning, dusting, mopping and vacuuming. But she stuck it out. Nicks left the Betty Ford Clinic with her head held justifiably high. Stevie had gone as low as she could ever have imagined. Now there was only one way left for her. Up.

Meanwhile Mick Fleetwood was experiencing some difficult personal problems of his own. Mick, displaying his usual resilience, had survived the sad breakdown of his marriage to Jenny Boyd, and his illness. But another problem loomed. In spite of – or perhaps because of – the vast amount of money pouring into the Fleetwood Mac coffers, Mick had found himself in an extraordinary situation. He was bankrupt! Accountant Dave Simmons found it hard to believe.

'I said, "This *cannot* be for real. Mick Fleetwood *cannot* have gone bankrupt." He said, "David, if you earn six million pounds, and you spend eight million pounds, you go bankrupt. Believe me!" '

Trevor Dann, interviewing Mick for the BBC 2 *Twenty One Years On* programme about Fleetwood Mac, asked him where all the money went.

Mick: 'It went on real estate. I bought *too* much real estate, and I had a very bad business manager who will remain nameless. It was not only me who went down the tubes. There were several friends that were part of the company who went down. I none the less take the blame. But in retrospect, the grand foray of foolishness was not part of it. The drug binges and everything else were not part of it. I had a *lot* of property in Australia and a *lot* of property in Los

Angeles. But the bank came knocking on the door! That's what *really* happened!'

He would later add: 'I've no idea how much I spent on drugs, but it was definitely not enough to have made me bankrupt. I bought *too* many properties and made *too* many investments. I was earning two million pounds a year and wanted to *do* something with it. It was my fault, but there were also a lot of people around who had not given me their best advice.'

He survived. And so would Fleetwood Mac, against all odds, during those turbulent post-'Mirage' years. Although the band members had largely drifted apart the old family ties were still pretty strong.

Christine: 'Yes, we kept in touch. We didn't exactly go and have tea with each other. Mick tended to be the link between all of us. I also saw quite a bit of John. Lindsey played on my solo album in Montreux, and we all live quite close to one another. We were in touch, have been and have always remained friends throughout the gap between records.'

Christine herself was to accidentally become the catalyst which would bring the Mac back into the recording studios after their lengthy sojourn. She was asked to contribute a song to the *A Fine Mess* movie soundtrack. The film people gave her freedom to record with whoever she chose. The song required for the film was the Presley classic 'Can't Help Falling In Love With You'. Recalling Lindsey Buckingham and Richard Dashut's long-time devotion to Elvis, they seemed the obvious choice as co-producers. She didn't think twice about the bass player and drummer for the session.

'We thought we'd get *the* rhythm section in at the same time. It was actually the first time that the band had been in a playing or recording environment for something like five years. The chemistry and atmosphere in the studio was such that we ended up playing a lot of other things. Then we started thinking about getting into the studio again.'

Mick: 'It went very smoothly and everybody had a lot of fun, so from that point we just took the bull by the horns and actively organised ourselves to get back into the studio.'

Momentum grew. Even Lindsey, increasingly reluctant to declare his undying loyalty to the Mac line up, responded to the optimistic mood.

'I was halfway into my third solo album, but at some point it became apparent that the needs of the many outweighed the needs of the few. When we did the "Mirage" album a lot of things had been left out on a limb. Emotional things and even financial things. A new album was a way to bring everything back together.'

Lindsey temporarily abandoned his solo project. The emotional pull exerted by Fleetwood Mac once again eschewed the band members' personal problems.

'Tango in the Night' was born. But it would herald a major change within the band's line up. Lindsey was on the move.

22 Tango in the Night

The year 1986 augured well for Christine McVie. Following the release of her successful solo album by Warner Brothers in 1984, Christine had been quietly developing her relationship with keyboard-player-composer-engineer Eddy Quintela. She had met Eddy while she was recording the album in Montreux.

'It's the most fun relationship I've had in a long time.'

Christine was nevertheless understandably cautious about the future, wary after her tempestuous relationships with first husband John McVie, Curry Grant and Dennis Wilson.

'I'm not saying we'll get married, but I won't be pessimistic. It depends *so* much on the man. Eddy is very different from my first husband John. He's ten years younger than I am, but he's stable, mature and fun. We're *very* good friends and we laugh together. I'd probably be irritated by an unintelligent, immature younger man, but an amusing, sensitive thirty-year-old is wonderful! We've known each other since I made my solo album. He's Portuguese, and a great musician.'

Christine and Eddy decided to take the plunge. In October 1986 they married. Eddy would become involved in the recording of the new Fleetwood Mac album, co-writing one song each with McVie and Buckingham.

The Mac 'family' was back in action. Unsurprisingly for them, things didn't go entirely smoothly. Mick would describe the recording sessions as being like 'pulling teeth'.

He would add: 'Stevie was the victim of some in-band gripes.'

Lindsey would confirm this: 'We had a *very* hard time getting her into the studio, and when she did arrive, she would be in a world of her own.'

The lengthy lay-off also hadn't helped much.

Lindsey: 'We hadn't worked together for four years and we weren't really used to seeing one another. When that happens there's pressure from Warner Brothers of course, and the people on the periphery. The lawyers and managers started to move in to initiate the production of an album. There *was* a group need to record, but all our individual managers and lawyers had to talk, because there was no one else to put the thing together logistically. The band as such didn't *have* a manager since Mick stopped doing that job.'

The 'men in suits', as John Lennon sarcastically called business-men involved in the industry, met. The discussions tended to be long and complex.

Lindsey: 'The meetings were a little chaotic. More people than I've ever seen! But . . . that's show business!'

Christine also felt that the long separation might create problems: 'We hadn't seen each other for a *long* time. I had seen John briefly in Montreux, and I hadn't seen Stevie for at least two years. She's been on the road. I couldn't even remember the last time I had seen her: I think it was when she got married.'

Stevie's personal problems had not gone unnoticed by Christine.

'Stevie was on the road for a *long* time. She went to Australia, and then she toured the States, so she was simply not here. Yes, that was definitely causing problems. For sure.'

However, McVie admired Stevie's determination to overcome her drug and alcohol addiction.

'She's wonderful. I have a *lot* of respect for the girl. She went to the Betty Ford Clinic and is now absolutely terrific.'

Hopes of recording the album quickly faded fast.

Christine: 'It ended up taking longer to record than most of the others! The people at the record company, lawyers and people on the periphery thought it might be a good idea to bring in an outside producer. I don't know how we got lulled into believing them, but we did. It just didn't work out. He lasted about three weeks. It was a disaster. I think he felt just a little bit intimi-dated.'

Fleetwood Mac immediately reverted to a winning formula: Richard Dashut, almost a band member by now, and Buckingham. Whatever the external problems, the writers in the band certainly came up with the goods. Lindsey contributed 'Caroline', 'Tango in the Night', and 'Big Love'. He also collaborated with Richard to produce 'Family Man', and worked with Christine on 'Isn't It Mid-night', 'Mystified' and the oddly titled 'You And I Part II' ('You And I Part I' would be released as the 'B' side of the single 'Big Love').

Christine and Eddy Quintela came up with 'Little Lies' and McVie wrote 'Everywhere' on her own. Additionally, Nicks certainly didn't let Fleetwood Mac down. She had always claimed that she did *not* keep her best songs back for her solo ventures, and her contributions to 'Tango in the Night' were clearly no lightweights. Stevie's old friend Sandy Stewart had written 'Seven Wonders'. With a little refinement from Nicks herself, the song was one of the strongest on the album. Nicks additionally came up with 'When I See You Again' and 'Welcome to the Room . . . Sara'. A powerful collection of material indeed.

At last the basic tracks were laid down at Rumbo Recorders. Lindsey and Richard took the raw tapes over to 'The Slope' and began work on what was by now a familiar task for the pair. The lengthy and arduous process of turning the basic recordings into a glossy, commercial product began. Aided by engineer Greg Droman, they began producing the all-important and long-awaited album. After all, babies born on the day 'Mirage' was released were already starting school.

Christine: 'Time has gone so awfully quickly. It's quite amazing to us when people say it's been five years. Five years in this business is almost the kiss of death.'

The album, dedicated to old Mac friend Judy Wong, finally surfaced in April 1987. The band held its breath. Had the old magic deserted the five members?

Certainly not. Once again Fleetwood Mac proved that they possessed the perfect ear for pleasing the public's taste. 'Tango in the Night' quickly attained the number one position in the album charts on *both* sides of the Atlantic for a change. 'Tango' would relinquish and return to that position no less than three times. Naturally the Warner Brothers moguls quickly plundered the album for singles. There were plenty to choose from. In one year alone four would make the US top twenty: 'Big Love', 'Little Lies', 'Seven Wonders' and 'Everywhere'. The first two appeared in the top ten in both the UK and the US. A fifth single, 'Family Man', would however hardly dent the charts on either side of the Atlantic. Nevertheless an imaginative and appealing video helped 'Little Lies' in particular. The band was learning the importance of this kind of promotion for their singles, and quickly became adept at using the medium.

The success of the album in Europe as well as the US surprised Christine.

'The album went to number one in *Sweden* of all places, which is quite bizarre for us. Usually our albums are successful in America, then Europe and *then* England. But "Tango" and "Big Love" were both huge hits when they first came out in England. I think they've forgiven us now for not having Peter Green in the band!'

The next item on the agenda for Fleetwood Mac was obvious. The obligatory world-wide promotional tour. No real problem. Except that one rather important member of the Mac would *not* be coming along.

Lindsey Buckingham.

23 Behind the Masks

Lindsey had been a member of Fleetwood Mac for nearly thirteen years. He had made no secret of the fact that he was disenchanted with touring, and wanted to develop his solo work. Indeed the production of 'Tango in the Night' had interrupted his efforts.

'Back in 1985 I was working on my third solo album when the band came to me and asked me to produce the next Fleetwood Mac project. At that point I put aside my solo work, which was half finished, and committed myself for the next seventeen months to producing "Tango in the Night". It was always our understanding that upon completion I would return to my solo work in progress.'

And he meant just that. A globe-trotting promotional tour was completely out of the question. Mick Fleetwood respected his decision.

'We knew that it was not something that he really wanted to do. He wasn't pulling the wool over anybody's eyes. I think he showed a lot of strength in a strange kind of way in being able to turn round to four other people and say, "I'm out." And I'm glad he did it because it would have been hell for him. All in all, yes, I was disappointed at first. But very shortly afterwards I was not at all disappointed. I was actually relieved that he'd had the strength to do that.'

Stevie: 'Lindsey really felt from the beginning that the "Tango in the Night" record would be his last Fleetwood Mac record. Everyone believes in dreams and fairy tales, and everyone believes that everything will work out so I think that in our hearts we all just hoped that he would change his mind. I knew he'd never change his mind. Well, I had already given Lindsey up. Lindsey was a thing of my past.'

Buckingham was pleased that his swan song with Fleetwood Mac was 'Tango' rather than its predecessor, 'Mirage'.

'I will say that the "Mirage" album would not have been an album that I would have felt comfortable ending the situation with. "Tango in the Night" I would certainly feel is a much stronger piece of work. *If* it were to be left at this, *if* we were to say that it was our last production together I think we'd all be happier than if it had been "Mirage".'

Christine was also philosophical: 'This is an end of an important era for us. I'm obviously saddened by the fact that Lindsey can't work with us any more. But people change direction, and don't always grow together after twelve years.'

Once again the tabloids had a field day. One of them had Lindsey leaving the Mac because of his unrequited love for . . . Christine McVie!

Lindsey bore Fleetwood Mac no grudges: 'Of course, I wish them all the luck in the world on the road.'

He had no reason to bear grudges. His involvement in the band had given him the creative outlet he had only dreamed of back in 1975 when he and Stevie were scuffing around with Fritz. He was a multi-millionaire and virtually a household name in the music business. The Mac had been good to Lindsey.

His departure ended the longest period Fleetwood Mac had gone through without personnel changes. However, Mick, John and Christine were thoroughly familiar with the situation. Having lost Green, Spencer, Kirwan, Walker, Weston and Welch along the wayside, they were hardly about to panic.

This time, recruitment to the Mac was not to be so fraught. Mick, Christine, Lindsey and Stevie had been working on and off with a couple of guitarists.

Billy Burnette and Rick Vito.

Stevie had worked with Billy on Red Sovine's 'Are You Mine' for her 'Rock a Little' album. Burnette, son of the legendary Dorsey Burnette, had also played with the Choloes, a pick up band assembled by Lindsey Buckingham for his appearance on *Saturday Night Live* consisting of Mick Fleetwood, George Hawkins (who would work with Christine on her solo album) and Steve Ross.

Rick Vito also had an impressive pedigree.

'I'd been working with Bob Seger and the Silver Bullet band. I did the last album, which was called "Like a Rock", and went out for about a ten-month tour with him. When I got back off that tour I was playing clubs. Mick Fleetwood happened to come in one night and jammed.'

Mick and Rick went back a long way.

'We met in 1982 at a Dick Clark twenty-fifth year anniversary convention. We sat at the same table. We talked, and became good buddies. I was a *fan* of the original Fleetwood Mac. In fact I have some photos that my friend and I had taken of Fleetwood Mac in

Philadelphia in 1968 from the front row. That band was a *big* influence for me at that point. I immediately went back and started a band like Fleetwood Mac. I started writing songs like Fleetwood Mac. Peter Green was a *tremendous* influence on me. The original group was especially inspiring for me.'

Billy had toured and recorded with Zoo, Mick's part-time fun group, and co-wrote a song with Christine McVie for her 1984 solo album. He had released his own album, and his songs had been recorded by Roy Orbison, Ray Charles and Jerry Lee Lewis.

Rick also enjoyed a previous Fleetwood Mac connection. He and John McVie had recorded with John's old boss John Mayall, back in the mid-1970s. Vito had also worked with Jackson Browne, Bonnie Rait, Roger McGuinn, John Prine, Todd Rundgren, Rita Coolidge and others.

Mick Fleetwood, Christine and John McVie and Stevie Nicks hardly hesitated.

Stevie: 'We didn't really audition them. We went out to dinner! I walked into the restaurant. Billy and Rick were sitting there with Vito's manager Dennis Dunstan. I sat down and they introduced me to Rick, whom I'd never met before. Of course I'd known Billy Burnette for a long time. We didn't talk about music that much. We talked about our lives and our friendship. And how nice it would be to be able to be in a band together.'

The next day Burnette and Vito rehearsed with Fleetwood Mac. At the end of the rehearsal Christine, John, Stevie and Mick briefly put their heads together. Mick, the acknowledged leader of the band, made a proposal.

'The lads are in?'

No one disagreed. Rick and Billy were hired.

Did they feel they had instantly to take over Lindsey's previous musical role within the Mac?

Rick: 'There was *no* pressure in any way to become like Lindsey, to become a Lindsey clone, or anything like that. I think the initial thing was for us to come in, step right in, and be able to fill the space that was left by his departure.'

Nevertheless it is interesting to note that Fleetwood Mac deemed it necessary to hire *two* guitar players to replace the huge void left by Lindsey's departure.

Stevie: 'Rick does what Lindsey did. Billy plays all the parts Lindsey did rhythm-wise, but couldn't do in concert.'

Billy and Rick felt very comfortable about joining Fleetwood Mac.

Billy: 'Well, they are great people to work with. I'd known them for about five or six years. They made us feel very welcome. It was that family kind of feeling for me.'

Rick: 'It's an honour, you know. Very exciting and completely unexpected. But I'm really enjoying it. I'm loving it.'

Trevor Dann asked Billy whether he thought Fleetwood Mac would change following the inclusion of him and Rick Vito.

'God, I'll guess we'll know that when we write the songs and go into the studio. I remember Stevie when she came to rehearsal one day. She said that she thought the whole thing sounded really great in a small rehearsal room.'

Stevie Nicks: 'It sounded like Fleetwood Mac! If you walked outside and listened from out in the parking lot, the first thing you would say is *not*, "Ah, I don't hear Lindsey." What you hear is Fleetwood Mac!'

Was Stevie right? The new line up would rapidly put the hypothesis to the test. Fleetwood Mac, Mark Eleven, were about to hit the road.

Fleetwood Mac assembled for the 'Shake the Cage' tour. The band decided to augment the line up, and took along four extra musicians, Asante, Lori Perry, Sharon Celani and Eliscia Wright.

Asante was born in Kotoridua in West Africa, and started drumming at the age of four. By the time he was ten years old he was acknowledged to be a master drummer. After leaving college he immediately became a professional musician. He worked both as a solo artiste, recording two albums, and toured and recorded with some extremely well-known people, including Hugh Masekela, the Crusaders, Third World, Lonnie Linston Smith, Miriam Makeba and Paul Simon.

Mick had met Asante when he visited Ghana in 1981 to record his solo album 'The Visitor' and much admired his percussion skills. The two became firm friends and Asante happily joined the Mac for the 'Tango' tour.

Lori Perry, Sharon Celani and Eliscia Wright had been working with Stevie Nicks as her backing vocalists during her solo work. Their harmony skills certainly beefed up the overall Mac sound.

The McVies, Nicks, Vito, Burnette, Fleetwood, Perry, Celani, Wright and Asante set off for the first US leg of the tour with a vast, fifty-strong entourage. The huge Fleetwood Mac circus was on the road again after a lengthy lay-off. How did the new band sound? Stevie Nicks was enthusiastic right from the word go.

'Every night I felt more comfortable! Every night you feel better about it! Every night it sounds better! Every night it's more fun because the easier it gets to play, the more you can actually just have fun playing and singing. I love it when I don't have to worry about whether I'm going to remember the second verse, when I know the songs so well that it's just like silk.'

Nicks felt that the new band gelled together remarkably quickly.

'I saw an *incredible* improvement within two weeks, from Texas to Phoenix. It was amazing to watch. I don't know what it really was, except that we were just together so much, and we played so much, and everybody was intent on making these songs sound so good for the people who loved Fleetwood Mac. We strove to make it a great show. With or *without* Lindsey. With or *without* me, with or *without* Chris. Not without Mick or John though. You couldn't have Fleetwood Mac without them!'

Billy Burnette agreed that John and Mick constituted the rhythmic and spiritual heart of the band.

'They are a *great* rhythm section to say the least. And they've been real good friends for *ever*, you know. A sort of magic seems around them. I remember somebody said something about "Little Lies" going through the roof, being a big hit. And John said, "It's unbelievable, there's *another* one!" I guess it's just a lot of magic!'

The on-stage vibes between Stevie and Billy were pretty strong: embarrassingly so for him sometimes.

Stevie: 'When I sing things like "Go Your Own Way" to Billy, the *looks* I give him. Well! I *have* apologised! The fire, you know! I'm amazed he just doesn't blow up!'

Billy: 'And there's nowhere to go on such a big stage!'

Billy and Stevie had already started collaborating on songs, both on the road and at Stevie's house.

'Oh yes, we've already started. In the car, writing songs. I also love nothing more than when Billy and Ricky show up at my house with a guitar. A lot of that goes on now, and it hasn't gone on for twelve years since Lindsey and I split up. We actually sit around and play music. I love that. It's the best thing in the world. Guitar, drum pads and a small recording studio. That's just the most fun part of all.'

Back on the 'Shake the Cage' tour, however, Stevie Nicks' health was again beginning to cause concern. So much so that the Australian leg of the tour was cancelled, and the European dates were pulled back to accommodate her health needs. Nevertheless Fleetwood Mac hit Europe on a real high. The band performed at sold out performances in Ireland, Germany, Sweden and Holland, and the visit to England included ten sold out nights at the huge Wembley arena. The success of the band in London was important to Fleetwood Mac.

Rick: 'The *highlight* of 1988 was playing ten sold out nights at Wembley. That was a real thrill!'

Nicks: 'Since Lindsey and I had joined Fleetwood Mac it seemed that the Europeans and the English weren't crazy about the fact that these English people had picked up these two Californians, you know! So to return to England and have the audiences as loving and sweet and kind as they were was *wonderful*. Because it was different from any time we'd been there before.'

The band also had some fun in London. The first night of the Wembley concerts brought a royal visitor backstage. Prince Andrew. The band (particularly the American contingent) were impressed. This gave Christine McVie an idea. An elaborate hoax was set up.

'We decided to set up one of the road crew during one of the ten shows at Wembley. We told everybody that the Princess of Wales was also going to visit us backstage. We laid out the whole protocol thing. Everyone was told where to look, not to take their eyes away from the princess when she was talking, not to talk to her unless she talked to you. The whole proper protocol thing, you know!'

Christine then hired a professional look-alike, an actress who had been successfully exploiting her resemblance to the Princess of Wales for some time. The jolly jape worked well.

A less than royal visitor backstage during two of the Wembley concerts was your author. It was great fun to talk to the band again, particularly John and Mick. I had met Mick briefly in 1986 when he came to London. On that occasion we played together again after a trifling lay-off of twelve years. John Dominic, Mick's old Bo Street Runner colleague, set up a gig in a London pub at Christmas. For an enjoyable hour or so Mick, John and I pounded away some heavy r'n'b, recreating half the old Bo Street Runners and the original Fleetwood Mac rhythm section for a bemused but enthusiastic audience.

Rick Vito and Billy were interested to talk to me about Peter Green. (Rick also insisted that I passed on his regards to Danny Adler, the American guitarist in my current De Luxe Blues Band. They knew each other quite well.) Rick felt quite a responsibility, stepping into Peter's shoes. The band were still including Peter's 'Oh Well' in the set.

'It's an *honour* you know. It's very exciting and completely unexpected.'

Did he feel that the spectre of previous wrecked and wasted Fleetwood Mac guitarists haunted him?

'I don't. We're not kids any more. That's the one thing we have over the other people who rose to prominence in Fleetwood Mac. They were all in their twenties, just basically starting out in the business. We've both been in this business *all* our lives. So we've *already* survived the most difficult parts.'

The Wembley shows were a great success. The set included an amusing and crazy element. Mick, all gangling six foot six of him, strode out from behind the huge drum kit to perform an unusual solo. Secreted about his person was a whole range of small electronic percussion drum pads, all hooked up via radio mikes to the massive PA system. Leering lasciviously at the huge crowd, suggestively patting and pounding various parts of his anatomy, Mick performed what was possibly the first ever walking-drum solo. The sounds bounced around the vast arena, and constituted a witty and original addition to a strong show. There were some odd omissions: 'Rhiannon', 'Go Your Own Way' and 'Tusk' only featured sporadically, due to Stevie's throat problems.

The band's European success would spill over into their record sales. In the first week of September 1988 'Tango' retained the number one spot in the UK for the second week running. It was joined by no less than four Fleetwood Mac albums in the UK top hundred: 'Rumours', 'Live', 'Mirage' and 'Tusk'.

The tour ground on. Finally the vast Fleetwood Mac party hit the Birmingham Exhibition Centre for the last 'Shake the Cage' concert. The familiar post-tour party wearily over, everybody limped home to the United States. 'Tango in the Night' had once again proved that Fleetwood Mac were not a band to write off in the face of adversity.

Back home in the US the band relaxed, caught up on sleep, and considered the next move. As always the next album loomed. But this time Fleetwood Mac could afford to relax. Because, quite legitimately, the time seemed to be right to release a collection of their most successful singles. The release would also present Ricky and Billy with the opportunity to contribute to Fleetwood Mac in a tentative and modest way. They would both play on just two tracks of the album. A new era was beginning for the band.

Christine: 'In a sense it's the end of an era and the beginning of another. We've never had a "Greatest Hits" album before. It's a collection from our Lindsey and Stevie period. There's no padding. There are also two introductory songs with Billy and Rick. It just seemed perfect timing to clean the slate and start the next chapter with these two guys.'

Christine wasn't quite correct about the new album's originality.

1971 had seen the CBS album release of the same name, featuring the first classic line up of the band.

Rick and Billy were also pleased to ease their way gently into the Fleetwood Mac recording routine.

'It kinda takes the pressure off us for coming up with a new album. It makes it easier to play on two tracks instead of ten. After all, we're going to be on an album which is probably going to be pretty successful.'

1988 was to be a particularly happy year for Mick Fleetwood. He finally got around to marrying his long-time girlfriend, the stunning Sara Recor. The couple exchanged their vows at Fleetwood's home on a bluff overlooking the Pacific Ocean on April 24th. John McVie (unsurprisingly) was the best man, and the two-hundred-plus wedding guests included Christine McVie, Bob Dylan, Stevie Nicks, George Harrison, Ali McGraw, Dick Clark, Dave Mason, Jeff Lynne, Chubby Checker, Billy Burnette and Rick Vito. The biggest surprise however was the appearance of Lindsey Buckingham. Mick was pleased to see him.

Buckingham: 'I thought it was a good time to break the ice. I hadn't seen anyone since we'd had a little confrontation at Christine's house some months previously, when all of the touring stuff was being thrown back and forth. It was an ugly scene for a short time.'

John McVie was also to have a pleasant surprise in the same year. His long-standing application to become an American citizen was successful. More pleasure was round the corner. On February 28th, 1989 Julie and John would become the extremely proud parents of a baby daughter. Molly Elizabeth McVie was born in the Cedars Sinai Hospital in Los Angeles. John assured me on the phone shortly afterwards that he was definitely doing his bit as a dad, including nappy duties!

Mick Fleetwood decided to branch out during the same period. Always a theatrical and imposing figure, he turned his attention to an area in which his talented sister Susan had excelled. Acting. Michael Brokaw, Lindsey's manager, suggested it, and Mick dutifully performed in the movie *Running Man*. The beard went for a subsequent role as a fish-like alien from the distant planet Antede in an episode of the long running cult series *Star Trek*. February 1989 would also see Mick co-hosting the UK Television awards show, the 'Brit. Music Awards'. The show was a complete shambles, and neither Fleetwood nor his co-host Samantha Fox emerged with much credit from the débâcle.

On January 15th, 1989 the band, with new members Rick and

Billy, went into the studios to start work on the next, post-'Tango in the Night' album. John McVie told me that the new album was even better than "Tango", and so it proved to be. "Behind the Mask" was released in April 1990, and immediately went to the number one spot in the UK. The album peaked at number eighteen in the States. Fleetwood Mac had done it again. But, as always, triumph would be followed by disaster. Surely this time, the band could not possibly survive the next blow?

In November 1990 Christine McVie and Stevie Nicks both decided to leave Fleetwood Mac.

24 Adrift

Why did Stevie and Christine decide to leave the band? Certainly they felt outraged at Mick's revelations contained in his autobiography published in 1990. Nicks felt particularly aggrieved with regard to his "kiss'n'tell" account of their earlier affair. She also wanted to pursue her solo career. Nicks had always been the most successful of the five when it came to commercial success in her own right. As a prolific and talented songwriter, she had often found it terribly frustrating that only two or three of her songs ever appeared on Mac albums.

Christine was simply tired of the madness which seemed to have surrounded the Mac for the previous two decades. After all, John would wryly comment that "the only two people in this band who haven't had an affair are Mick and me!" Although Mick would put up a brave front to the press, claiming that Fleetwood Mac had not *really* broken up, but were merely "taking a break", few believed him. After all, the true architects of the band's success from the mid-Seventies onwards had been the writers: Nicks, Christine McVie and the departed Buckingham. John and Mick rightly prided themselves on their respective roles within the band. Their resilience and stamina had kept the often beleaguered group afloat for years, but neither of them claimed to be any more than highly efficient members of one of the best rhythm sections in the world. They *needed* talented singers and writers if Fleetwood Mac were to survive.

All Mac members retreated into solo mode, with varying degrees of success. Fleetwood Mac would be placed on hold for a while. Stevie Nicks' estrangement intensified when, to her fury, Mick Fleetwood would not allow her to place her beautiful song "Silver Springs" on the "Greatest Hits" package she was carefully compiling ("Timespace – The Best Of Stevie Nicks"). It wasn't quite his fault. Mick, who owned the rights to Fleetwood Mac songs, had signed a deal with Warner Brothers, who would not give permission for "Springs" to be released on another record label. Stevie dramatically announced that she would never again have anything whatsoever to do with Fleetwood Mac.

Mick Fleetwood reluctantly resigned himself to the loss of the two major players in the Fleetwood Mac organisation, and started to do what he had always done best. Pick himself up, and look to the future. Just to add to Fleetwood Mac's problems, Rick Vito also left the band. Good old musical differences were cited. Only Billy Burnette remained from the "Behind The Mask" line up.

The various Fleetwood Mac members then went their different ways. In 1992, Rick Vito released *his* solo album, "King Of Hearts" on Modern Records, but even the presence of Stevie Nicks on a couple of tracks did not help sales, and the album was rather less than successful. John McVie also had a try, helped out by various members of the Fleetwood Mac extended family. Billy Burnette happily joined John, Mick Taylor and Lola Thomas on his unpretentiously titled "John McVie's Gotta Band With Lola Thomas". It fared no better than Vito's album.

Even Lindsey Buckingham's album, "Out Of The Cradle", released almost four years after his dramatic departure from the Mac bombed. It was an excellent piece of work, and attracted terrific reviews, but this was insufficient to encourage record buyers to actually buy it.

Tellingly, Mick Fleetwood's solo album, the second with his beloved alter-ego band Zoo, hinted at a possible new direction for Fleetwood Mac. His instinct for spotting potential Mac members had not deserted him, although he really wasn't thinking about that at the time of recording.

Nevertheless, the choice of Bekka Bramlett as singer was to be prophetic. The daughter of the acclaimed musicians Bonnie and Delaney Bramlett joined various members of the Mac family to record "Shaking The Cage". Fleetwood and Bramlett were joined on various tracks by Billy Burnette, Christine McVie and Lindsey Buckingham. The Mac members seemingly could not stay away from each other! Mick, however, was now maintaining that Fleetwood Mac was dead in the water. Nevertheless this did not prevent him working closely with John McVie to produce a major CD box set to celebrate the band's twenty fifth anniversary. "The Chain" would be released in November 1992, and surprise, surprise, Mick and John went back into the recording studio with Lindsey Buckingham, Stevie Nicks, Christine McVie, Billy Burnette and Rick Vito to work on four new songs. A rather familiar line up for Mac followers. The decree absolute did not seem to be forthcoming quite yet.

During the same month, fate dealt Fleetwood Mac a very unexpected hand. Bill Clinton had been elected as the President of the United States of America. All candidates had run high profile campaigns, using T.V. as a crucial part of their attack. Clinton had chosen Fleetwood Mac's "Don't Stop" as his campaign song, and it had been played incessantly during his relentless pursuit of the voters. When he won the presidency, there was only one band he wanted to play at his pre-inauguration January 1993 ceremony, which was to be broadcast coast to coast on national T.V. Fleetwood Mac. And not just *any* old Fleetwood Mac. The "Rumours" line up, no less. Not all the band were enthusiastic, however. Lindsey Buckingham: "I thought it was touching that for the first time you had a president who was openly professing his alliance to rock and roll." However, Buckingham went on to say: "That gave off a sense of possibility that maybe *didn't* really pan out."

Christine seemed to have no illusions, either. Interviewed after the brief reunion, she declared: "It was a one-off thing, and I don't think anyone thought much beyond that show. At the airport as we left to come back to L.A., it was pretty much, 'Well, see you around'."

Nicks also felt that in spite of all their personal differences, unless Buckingham was to be a *permanent* member of a re-formed F.M., she didn't really want to be a part of it.

However, Fleetwood Mac were quite enjoying their return to the spotlight, and the band played a few more gigs, albeit without Stevie Nicks. Nevertheless, the dream of a completely stable Mac line up was still to elude Mick Fleetwood and John McVie. The next departure? Billy Burnette. He wanted to make his solo album, although the failure of other Mac members solo efforts might have sounded a warning note for him. Out came "Coming Home", enjoying no more success than other post-Mac projects for ex-members. It seems that Fleetwood Mac's whole would always be greater than the sum of its parts.

John and Mick were by now thoroughly used to coping with the roller coaster personnel problems in the band. The choice of new singer seemed obvious. In came Mick's "Zoo" colleague, Bekka Bramlett. Mick: "The most noticeable move is that we have a new girl singer out front. Her name's Bekka Bramlett, she's the daughter of Delaney and Bonnie, whom a few people might remember. And she comes from great musical stock, is extremely talented, and she's the lead vocalist. She doesn't play an instrument on stage. She's a soul singer in many ways, but she has a great sense of harmony."

The choice of a new singer/guitarist seemed less obvious. Mick, ever the gracious host, had been offering hospitality to Dave Mason in his Los Angeles home. Mason was a quirky, talented and accomplished singer/songwriter who had played in the legendary British band Traffic alongside Steve Winwood, Jim Capaldi and Chris Wood. He had written Traffic's biggest UK hit, the haunting "Hole In My Shoe", and, though dogged by a succession of poor recording deals, also played or recorded with Jimi Hendrix, The Rolling Stones, Family, and Delaney and Bonnie and Friends. The latter band featured the Bramletts and Eric Clapton, who after the rigours of Cream and Blind Faith was enjoying the opportunity to play as a sideman instead of being the leader. Mason, by virtue of being on the spot, thus became Fleetwood Mac's latest recruit.

Billy Burnette ate a slice of humble pie, and asked to rejoin Fleetwood Mac. Mick, ever expansive, agreed. Christine McVie decided that although she didn't want to return to the relentless grind of life on the road with the band, she was prepared to record with the "new" Fleetwood Mac, the twelfth line up of the band. They produced a song, "Blow By Blow" for the 1994 World Cup soundtrack, and then F.M., minus Christine, hit the road for the umpteenth time.

Stevie Nicks was doing the same. Demonstrating her same old inability to entirely separate herself from Mac members, however, she had invited Rick Vito to join her on her tour to promote her 1994 "Street Angels" album.

After some more time in the studio, Fleetwood Mac returned to the road. Their involvement in a "revival" package show, with Pat Benatar and R.E.O. Speedwagon was somewhat undignified and not a great success, although, much to everybody's surprise, original Mac member Jeremy Spencer popped up to make a guest appearance during the band's visit to Japan.

Lindsey wasn't impressed: "That last incarnation of Fleetwood Mac on the road with Dave Mason and Bekka Bramlett had gone out as a nostalgia package. It was with Pat Benatar and R.E.O. Speedwagon, stuff you don't like to see the name Fleetwood Mac associated with. I think it was hard on Mick Fleetwood." Back in England, however, there was some extremely exciting and heartening news for Fleetwood Mac members and fans alike. After two decades in the wilderness, founder member Peter Green was alive and well, and back on the music scene!

25 "Time Will Tell"

It had taken a long time. Peter Green, the undisputed leader of the original Fleetwood Mac, and one of the very finest British blues guitarists of his generation, had suffered greatly since he walked out of the band on the 31st of May, 1970. Although Peter did not immediately abandon his beloved music, it wasn't long before his illness badly affected not only his playing, but his whole life style (see chapter three for details).

Mick Fleetwood had stayed in constant touch with Peter during the wilderness years, and every member of post Peter Green Fleetwood Mac line ups had freely acknowledged his pivotal and fundamental role within the band, and were greatly saddened by his illness. Stevie Nicks: "When we got the phone call from Mick Fleetwood asking us if we wanted to join the band, Lindsey and I went out and bought all those records from the beginning of Fleetwood Mac. We listened to them *very* carefully to see if we could add anything to the band, or if *they* could add anything to what Lindsey and I were doing. We wanted to know if this was something we were gonna do just for the money, or if we were gonna do this because we could improve upon it in some way. And what we connected to, of course, was Peter Green. It was his mystical influence that drew us in, that made it OK to *stop* doing Buckingham Nicks and join Fleetwood Mac!"

Mick Fleetwood felt equally strongly: "I have to say that I learnt from Peter Green. I looked to Peter Green and thought, there's someone I know who is *really* talented. There's someone who taught me a helluva lot about the way I think about music. The real goods is Peter Green. He's not just a talented player, he's a wonderfully powerful, deep thinking person. That's what I'm attracted to."

All that talent had apparently gone to waste following Peter's illness. But, miraculously, in the mid nineties, Peter began to recover. Helped by various people, he slowly began to discover his love of music again. Michelle Reynolds, Nigel Watson, Neil Murray and Cozy Powell helped him form Peter Green's Splinter Group. No one would claim that he immediately hit his top form, least of all Peter. "No, I still don't have the technique I had. I get it sometimes. But I'm not worried because I can develop another technique. I'm in no hurry. Just taking my time." Tellingly, when B.B. King invited Peter to jam with him on stage in Manchester in late 1997, and reminded him that they need no rehearsal because "it's the blues", Peter replied that he didn't *play* blues guitar. The Splinter Group's set certainly contained very little blues material.

The demand for Peter Green's early Fleetwood Mac recordings had never abated however. In 1992 a distinctly lo-fi, but nevertheless historically interesting CD was released on both the Receiver and Sunflower record labels. "Peter Green's Fleetwood Mac: Live At The Marquee" was crudely recorded at the band's *second ever* gig at London's prestigious Marquee Club in Soho. The recording featured the *original* Fleetwood Mac line up of Peter Green, Mick Fleetwood, Jeremy Spencer – and your author!

In September 1995, a much more interesting collection of vintage Mac recordings emerged; "Fleetwood Mac: Live At The BBC". The band had recorded many live sessions for the British Broadcasting Corporation between 1969 and 1971. Unlike the United States with its thousands of local stations, the entire UK population could at that time receive only the BBC's four radio stations: Radio One, Two, Three and Four, and a few foreign stations. Many famous bands recorded sessions for the Beeb, including both the Beatles and Led Zeppelin who have released similar collections of their historic BBC recordings. The Mac recordings were interesting for the same reason: the recording budgets were tiny, and the bands were recorded fast and very live. The lack of sophisticated recording techniques, and complete absence of complex post-production work, meant that the listener heard the band in much the same way as they would by attending a live concert, warts and all.

Peter Green was asked two questions by journalist Julia Ficken in 1997 about his comeback. "Were you happy when you weren't playing?" Peter: "No." Julia: "Are you happy now?" Peter: "Yes." This brief interview seemed to say it all. Meanwhile, back in the States, the present-day Fleetwood Mac had been spending their usual prolonged spell in the studio to produce the first Mac album in five years. Fleetwood: "The album we've been working on took us fifteen months to finish. Meanwhile, we've done selective road work, and I'm happy to say that, in concert, the band has been extremely successful."

Mick was nevertheless a little nervous. "Now it's the time when we're holding our breath. We're about to see whether people enjoy this latest offering from Fleetwood Mac. We certainly hope so. But it's all in the lap of the gods."

"Time", featuring Mick, John, Christine, Billy Burnette, Dave Mason and Bekka Bramlett was released in October 1995. Unfortunately the gods, in the shape of promotional staff at Warner Brothers, did little to promote the record, and it peaked at number forty seven in the US and failed to make the top hundred in the UK album charts.

But you simply cannot keep a good band down, especially one driven by the likes of McVie and Fleetwood. After the umpteenth collapse of the Mac, Mick nevertheless started work with Lindsey Buckingham on his fourth solo album. Additionally, in late 1996, Nicks, Buckingham and Fleetwood released "Twisted", a song recorded for the soundtrack of the popular film, "Twister". However, the almost unthinkable was about to happen.

In 1997, the classic "Rumours" Fleetwood Mac line up would re-unite. Nicks, aged forty, Christine, fifty four, John, fifty one, and Fleetwood, fifty, would once again enter the recording and TV studios. Thirteen classics, plus four new songs were recorded for an MTV "Unplugged Special".

Twenty years after the release of "Rumours" (sales to date in excess of twenty five million) the Mac were back. "Dance", the album culled from the MTV sessions was an instant success, topping the UK charts in late 1997. The TV special was shown in the States on August the 12th, 16th and 17th, and the CD was released in the States on August 19th. UK viewers saw the programme on New Years Day 1998, and the band was honoured for their "lifetime contribution to popular music" during the "Brit Awards" ceremony in February. In the televised show the night after the award ceremony the "Rumours"-era Mac were seen closing the show with lively renditions of "Go Your Own Way" and "Don't Stop", in which Mick Fleetwood more than made up for his embarrassing appearance on the Brits in 1989.

The lure of the road proved as strong as ever, and 1998 saw the Mac doing what they have always done best, thrilling audiences all over the world with their exciting stage show. The band members could have easily sat at home enjoying their substantial royalty incomes, so, why go back on the road after all the angst?

Mick: "We've been asked many times over the years to reform, but the time was never right. I think we were all still in the process of growing up and discovering that the things that had once pulled us apart didn't seem nearly as important any more. The level of success we had together was, quite simply, overwhelming. We've had the opportunity to step back and get some perspective, to realise that what was important all along was the music."

John: "The 20th anniversary of 'Rumours' gave us a vantage point to look back and forward. We realised that we had created this tremendous body of work and that we wanted to celebrate that accomplishment. 1997 also marks the 30th anniversary of the founding of the original Fleetwood Mac, so the occasion seemed especially auspicious for that reason as well."

Lindsey: "We'd lived through such a musical soap opera and just the fact that we'd survived gave us something in common. The magic, the energy, the pure joy of working together was stronger than ever."

Christine: "It was an odd feeling, being back together, but it was obvious we were having fun. I'd been doing some writing and demos for a new solo album, but had really stepped back from music for the time being, returning to England and restoring a huge, sixteenth century house my husband and I had bought in the country. I was very content with my life, but at the same time, I must admit, I felt the pull."

The Mac were back, but for how long?

Let the bass player have the last word. "Today is wonderful. Tomorrow will take care of itself."

Discography

'Rhiannon'/'Sugar Daddy'
    Reprise K 14430   Apr 1976
'Say You Love Me'/'Monday Morning'
    Reprise K 14447   Sep 1976
'Go Your Own Way'/'Silver Springs'
    Warner Bros K 16872   Jan 1977
'Don't Stop'/'Gold Dust Woman'
    Warner Bros K 16930   Apr 1977
'Dreams'/'Songbird'
    Warner Bros K 16969   Jun 1977
'You Make Lovin' Fun'/'Never Going Back'
    Warner Bros K 17013   Sep 1977
'Tusk'/'Never Me Cry'
    Warner Bros K 17468   Sep 1979
'Sara'/'That's Enough For Me'
    Warner Bros K 17533   Dec 1979
'Not That Funny'/'Save Me a Place'
    Warner Bros K 17577   Feb 1980
'Think About Me'/'Honey Hi'
    Warner Bros K 17614   May 1980
'Farmer's Daughter'/'Dreams'
    Warner Bros K 17746   Feb 1981
'Hold Me'/'Eyes of the World'
    Warner Bros K 17965   Jul 1982
'Gipsy'/'Cool Clean Water'
    Warner Bros K 17997   Sep 1982
'Oh Diane'/'Only Over You'
    Warner Bros FLEET 1   Dec 1982
'Oh Diane'/'Only Over You'/'The Chain'
    Warner Bros FLEET 1T   Dec 1982
'Can't Go Back'/'That's All Right'
    Warner Bros W 9848   Apr 1983
'Big Love'/'You and I' (Pt 1)
    Warner Bros W 8398   Mar 1987
'Seven Wonders'/'Book of Miracles'
    Warner Bros W 8317   Jun 1987
'Little Lies'/'Ricky'
    Warner Bros W 8291   Sep 1987
'Family Man'/'Down Endless Street'
    Warner Bros W 8114   Nov 1987
'Everywhere'/'When I See You Again'
    WEA W 8143   Mar 1988
'Isn't It Midnite'/'Mystified'
    WEA   ?
'As Long As You Follow'/'Oh Well'
    Warners W 7644   Dec 1988

'Hold Me'/'No Questions Asked'
    Warners W 7528   Feb 1989
'Save Me'/'Another Woman'
    Warners W 9866   Apr 1990
'In The Back Of My Mind'/'Lizard People'
    Warners W 9739   Aug 1990
'Skies The Limit'/'Lizard People'
    Warners W 9740   Nov 1990
'Love Shines'/'The Chain'
    Warners W 0145   Jan 1993

Albums 1967-1998

'Peter Green's Fleetwood Mac'
    Peter Green v/h/g; Jeremy Spencer v/g/p
    Bob Brunning b; John McVie b; Mick Fleetwood d
        Blue Horizon 7-63200   Feb 1968
        Epic BN 26402 (US)   (Jun 1968)
'Mr Wonderful'
    Peter Green; Jeremy Spencer; John McVie; Mick Fleetwood + Christine
    Perfect v/k; Steve Gregory (sax); Dave Howard (al sax); Johnny Almond;
    Roland Vaughan (ts)
        Blue Horizon 7-63205   Aug 1968
'English Rose'
    Peter Green; Jeremy Spencer; John McVie; Mick Fleetwood
        Epic BN 26446 (US)   Jan 1969
        CBS 22025 (GB)
'Pious Bird of Good Omen'
    (compilation) Peter Green; Jeremy Spencer
    (Christine Perfect) Danny Kirwan; John McVie; Mick Fleetwood; Bob
    Brunning
        Blue Horizon 7-64315   Aug 1969
        (CBS 32050 in 1981)
'Then Play On'
    Peter Green; Jeremy Spencer; Danny Kirwan (v/g); John McVie; Mick
    Fleetwood
        Reprise RS LP 9000   Sep 1969
        Reprise RS LP 6368 (US)
'Blues Jam at Chess'
    Peter Green; Jeremy Spencer; Danny Kirwan; John McVie; Mick Fleet-
    wood + Otis Spann; Willie Dixon; Shaky Horton; JT Brown; Buddy Guy;
    Honey Boy Edwards; SP Leary
        Blue Horizon 7-66227 (dble)   Dec 1969
'Fleetwood Mac In Chicago'
    same tracks and personnel as 'Blues Jam'
        Blue Horizon BH 380 (US)   Apr 1970
        (also) SIRE 2XS 2009

'Kiln House'
Jeremy Spencer; Danny Kirwan; John McVie; Mick Fleetwood
    Reprise RS LP 9004   Sep 1970
        6408 (US)

'The Original Fleetwood Mac'
Peter Green; Jeremy Spencer; John McVie; Bob Brunning; Mick Fleetwood; Christine Perfect
    UK CBS 63875   Mar 1971
    US SIRE SR 6045   1976

'Future Games'
Bob Welch v/g; Christine McVie Perfect; Danny Kirwan; John McVie; Mick Fleetwood
    UK Reprise K 44153   Sep 1971
    US Reprise 6465

'Bare Trees'
Bob Welch; Christine McVie; Danny Kirwan; John McVie; Mick Fleetwood
    UK Reprise K 44181   Aug 1972
    US Reprise 2080

'Greatest Hits'
various original personnel
    UK CBS 69011   Nov 1971

'Penguin'
Bob Welch; Bob Weston (v/g); Dave Walker (voc); John McVie; Mick Fleetwood; Christine McVie (UK)
    UK Reprise K 44235   May 1973
    US Reprise 2138

'Mystery to Me'
Bob Welch; Bob Weston; Christine McVie; John McVie; Mick Fleetwood
    UK Reprise K 44248   Jan 1974
    US Reprise 2158

'Heroes Are Hard to Find'
Bob Welch; Christine McVie; John McVie; Mick Fleetwood
    US Reprise K 54026   Sep 1974
    US Reprise 2196

'Fleetwood Mac'
Lindsey Buckingham (g/v); Stevie Nicks (v); Christine McVie; John McVie; Mick Fleetwood
    UK Reprise K 54043   Aug 1975
    US Reprise 2225   reissued Dec 1985

'Original Fleetwood Mac'/'English Rose'
various original personnel
    CBS 81308/9   Jun 1975

'Rumours'
    John McVie; Mick Fleetwood; Christine McVie; Lindsey Buckingham;
    Stevie Nicks
            UK Warner Bros K 56344   Feb 1977
            US Warner Bros 3010

'Tusk'
    personnel as 'Rumours'
            UK Warner Bros K 66088   Oct 1979
            US Warner Bros WB 3050

'Live'
    personnel as 'Tusk'
            UK Warner Bros K 66097   Nov 1980
            US Warner Bros WB 3500

'Mirage'
    personnel as 'Live'
            UK Warner Bros K 56952   Jul 1982
            US Warner Bros WB 23607

'Tango in the Night'
    personnel as 'Mirage'
            Warner Bros 925471-2   Apr 1987

'Live in Boston'

'Jumping at Shadows' (US title)
    original band: Peter Green; Jeremy Spencer; Danny Kitwan; John MoVie,
    Mick Fleetwood (recorded 1969)
            Shanghai Hai 107   Feb 1985
            US Varrick VRO 20   May 1985

    'Cerulean'

    (Live in Boston Pt II)
    original line up as above (recorded 1969)
            Shanghai Hai 300 (dble LP)   Mar 1985

    'London Live 1968'
    original line up: Peter Green; Jeremy Spencer; John McVie; Mick Fleet-
    wood
            GB Thunderbolt THBL 1038   Nov 1986

'Greatest Hits'
    original line up
            CBS (US) 480704-1   Feb 1988

'Greatest Hits Live'
    original line up
            Mainline/Commander 2248217   May 1988

'Vintage Years'

History of Fleetwood Mac
    (various original personnel)
            CBS 22122 (UK)   1984

'Rumours'
John McVie; Mick Fleetwood; Christine McVie; Lindsey Buckingham; Stevie Nicks
    UK Warner Bros K 56344   Feb 1977
    US Warner Bros 3010

'Tusk'
personnel as 'Rumours'
    UK Warner Bros K 66088   Oct 1979
    US Warner Bros WB 3050

'Live'
personnel as 'Tusk'
    UK Warner Bros K 66097   Nov 1980
    US Warner Bros WB 3500

'Mirage'
personnel as 'Live'
    UK Warner Bros K 56952   Jul 1982
    US Warner Bros WB 23607

'Tango in the Night'
personnel as 'Mirage'
    Warner Bros 925471-2   Apr 1987

'Live in Boston'

'Jumping at Shadows' (US title)
original band: Peter Green; Jeremy Spencer; Danny Kirwan; John McVie; Mick Fleetwood (recorded 1969)
    Shanghai Hai 107   Feb 1985
    US Varrick VRO 20   May 1985

'Cerulean'
(Live in Boston Pt II)
original line up as above (recorded 1969)
    Shanghai Hai 300 (dble LP)   Mar 1985

'London Live 1968'
original line up: Peter Green; Jeremy Spencer; John McVie; Mick Fleetwood
    GB Thunderbolt THBL 1038   Nov 1986

'Greatest Hits'
original line up
    CBS (US) 480704-1   Feb 1988

'Greatest Hits Live'
original line up
    Mainline/Commander 2248217   May 1988

'Vintage Years'

History of Fleetwood Mac
(various original personnel)
    CBS 22122 (UK)   1984

'White Album' (comp)
   Christine McVie; Lindsey Buckingham; Stevie Nicks; John McVie;
   Mick Fleetwood
         Reprise K2 240243 (US)   1983
'Behind The Mask'
   John McVie; Christine McVie; Mick Fleetwood; Stevie Nicks; Rick
   Vito; Billy Burnette
         Warners 75599-26111-2   1990
'Peter Green's Fleetwood Mac: Live At The Marquee'   [Recorded 1967]
   Peter Green; Bob Brunning; Mick Fleetwood; Jeremy Spencer
         Receiver RR CD 157   1992
'Peter Green's Fleetwood Mac: Live At The BBC'
   Peter Green; John McVie; Jeremy Spencer; Danny Kirwan; Mick
   Fleetwood
         Castle Communications EDF CD 297   1995
'Time'
   John McVie; Mick Fleetwood; Christine McVie; Billy Burnette; Dave
   Mason; Bekka Bramlett
         Warners CD 9362-45920-2   1995
'The Dance'
   John McVie; Mick Fleetwood; Lindsey Buckingham; Christine McVie;
   Stevie Nicks
         Reprise CD 9362-46702-2   1997

Index